Winning the Modern World for Islam

Winning the Modern World for Islam

Abdessalam Yassine

Translated from the French
by Martin Jenni

Justice and Spirituality Publishing, Inc.
Iowa City, Iowa, USA • 2000

Printed in the U.S.A.

Published by
Justice and Spirituality Publishing, Inc.
P.O. Box 2701
Iowa City, IA 52244
U.S.A.

Web site: http://www.JSpublishing.net

ISBN 0-9675795-0-3

Library of Congress Catalog Card Number 99-067216

Printed on acid-free paper.

The interpretation of the Quranic verse on the front cover is *God Is Best and Everlasting* (Qur'an 20:73). For more information about the cover, see page 274.

Cover art: Rohana Filippi, New York City
Cover design: Pivot Design, Ft. Lauderdale, Florida
Book design: Annie Graham Publishing Services, Mt. Pleasant, South Carolina

Contents

Translator's Foreword

IMAM ABDESSALAM YASSINE'S *Islamiser la modernité,* published discreetly in Morocco in March of 1998, proclaimed to the Francophone world at large the heart of the message the inspired Qur'anic scholar and beloved teacher has been enunciating, chiefly in his native Arabic, for nearly thirty years. Its theme is this: what it would mean for the modern world to be radically transformed by total submission to God.

Such "total submission" is the literal meaning of *islam,* and this fact is essential in order to understand the Imam's message—so as to distinguish clearly between this deep and transformative sense of the word and the broader, cultural meaning of "Muslim peoples and their civilization." The distinction is critical even among speakers of Arabic, such as the participants, in nominally Islamic countries like the Imam's own Morocco, in the dialog between Islamists[1] and secularists. It is a distinction in defense of which Imam Yassine has paid dearly, deprived of his liberty under house arrest for a decade (since December of 1989).

The present translation now extends this profoundly powerful message to readers of English. The French title has a degree of shock value—as the singular inversion of the secularist phrase *moderniser l'islam* ("modernizing Islam")—that cannot be reproduced in English. "Islamicizing" is no more at home in English than "Christianizing" or "Hinduizing," and "modernity" is similarly fuzzy. Translating a serious and important argument is not an appropriate occasion for coining novel and ambiguous phrases. The operative sense of *islamiser* is "to convert to, to transform by means of, Islam," "to make something or someone Islamic." The expression "winning *x* for *y*" has, especially for American speakers, precisely this range of meaning and is, moreover, associated with conversion to a better state of existence. It expresses moral persuasion. "Win" is moreover an extremely positive verb. *Modernité* is also problematic: "modernity" merely replicates its form, without bearing its semantic resonance. What Imam Yassine means by the French is a quality of current secular values—and the societies that espouse them and operate by them. In the gospels of the Prophet Jesus, such a secular and essentially benighted society is known as "the world." Modernism—as a secular philosophy—was condemned by both Roman Catholicism and Eastern Orthodoxy as a moral danger already a hundred years ago. Thus, "modern world."

Even as Yassine's title conveys the essence of his vision and message, my translation of it is based on my fundamental understanding of his argument. In a sense, it is a second translation of that argument, since the language of North African colonialism and urbane sophistication, in which the Imam is compelled to write, is already at one remove from his innermost thoughts: these find their source in the deep pools of the language of the Qur'an. It is, as Yassine readily notes in his Foreword, a discipline not without risks: how much of the original will survive in another tongue—how much of the sacred can resonate at all in a *langue profane*? The shift in social, cultural, political, and philosophical contexts affects not only the light in which issues are viewed, but the nature of formulating and resolving problems as well. Translating Yassine's Arabic-born French understandably entails having to deal with both languages in order to arrive at a suitable English equivalent.

A very special case of such twofold translation is that of the Imam's interpretations in French of passages from the Qur'an. Here the sanctity of the original gives the interpreter especial pause. (It is for this reason that no actual translation of the Holy Text is possible; it can merely be interpreted in pale reflection.) Yet the Imam's interpretations represent the very core, not only of his teaching, but of his life: the most intimate and intense encounter with Divine Revelation.[2]

The book's argument proceeds systematically, having been carefully prepared by introductory reflections on communication. Eight major topics follow, each one divided into contributory themes. The first of these topics examines the terms of the relationship—*islam* and the modern world—particularly as these are inextricably yoked in current global affairs. The second takes up the narrower focus of *islam* (and Islam[3]) and the post-colonial environment, with the secularism it inherited from the French Revolution. The third and fourth topics are the crisis cases of Algeria and Palestine, explored and discussed with courageous candor. Algeria's recent political history, and the incumbent horrors for its civilian population, are put in historical perspective and offer a valuable corrective to misperceptions and deliberate falsification; the sham election this summer in Algeria, which all the candidates boycotted except the candidate of the prevailing party, makes the Imam's case all the more urgent. In characterizing the fortunes of the Palestinians as a festering wound, Yassine pleads a cause too rarely championed in the West.

Five multifaceted and closely reasoned essays follow on topics represented in the original by the French infinitives for knowing, being, having, and being able (*savoir*, *être*, *avoir*, *pouvoir*). Knowing, for Imam Yassine, embraces matters beyond the merely intellectual; it is wisdom enlightened by the certainty of faith. The broad topic of Being allows the Imam to consider its multiple modes; to be is also to be defined—as woman, mother, child, sharer in a covenant—and to define one's purpose in a Great Plan. Having introduces questions not only of possession but of patrimony, of birthright. The last topic is the longed-for community of *islam*, freed of the secular nation-state, and enabled to participate in the world at large.

Yassine's reflections on the dignity of woman overturns assumptions about the relative status of Western and Muslim women.

The Imam's assessment of the world of global capitalism is equally trenchant. There is a better way, the way of organized mutual solicitude, the *zakah* (alms tax) as the foundation for the equitable distribution of wealth among members of a prospering society. Even as the Qur'anic path of economic justice differs markedly from the corporate-driven engines of the West, so too the so-called democratic processes, in evident current disarray both in the West and in the post-colonial Third World, stand in stark contrast to the Qur'anic principle of consultative self-government (*shurah*).

In his epilog Imam Yassine invokes the Divine benediction on all those with whom he has entered into dialog—those whom the Great Truths have touched. Here especially Yassine interprets passages at length from the Qur'an, "reading" them to us in the language of the modern world, which for the purposes he is able to transform into a powerful reflection of the original.

The title *imam* connotes a leader: of prayer, of studies—of *islam* (this last is singularly restrictive, especially to some Muslim communities); it is often as well a term of fervent endearment. In this sense particularly Imam Abdessalam Yassine is regarded by his wide network of disciples; may this translation further the circle of his hearers. Yet the title of *imam* is not one he would have bestowed on himself. Yassine prefers to be thought of as *al-morshid,* "teacher, guide, counselor."[4]

Bringing his message to the English-speaking world has been the charge of a pupil of Yassine's, Imad Benjelloun, a doctoral candidate at the University of Iowa. The project was facilitated by the university's Translation Laboratory, whose director, Dr. Gertrud Champe, deftly edited the draft.

D. M. J.

Notes

1 "Islamist" here (and throughout the book) names an observant Muslim, someone whose life source is *islam* in the sense of submission to God. Such persons may well strive for the creation of a society guided by this principle, but it is a grievous (and often intentionally vicious) misuse of the term to represent a religious fanatic or, worse still, terrorist.

2 My translations of Yassine's interpretations should be contrasted to those of a Qur'anic scholar such as Abdullah Yusuf Ali, cf. his *The Meaning of the Glorious Qur'ân* (London: Nadim & Co., 1975).

3 See Chapter I:1, note 1.

4 "Guide, pilot, director" from the verb *rashada* "be on the right path, follow the way, be well guided."

Foreword

> SAY: praise to God who has been given no progeny whatever nor any associate whatever in His kingdom, and who has no need of protection (to screen Him from the assaults of any offender whatever), no powerlessness being imputable to Him. Exalt Him![1]

The interpretation is my own; with regard to the Qur'an, the Word of the Most High God, one cannot speak of translation.

My God, spread forth Your grace upon Muhammad and those close to him, as you have spread it forth upon Abraham and those close to him. Bless Muhammad and those close to him, as You have blessed Abraham and those close to him. Receive my prayer, for You are the Glorious One.

I have written until now in Arabic, addressing myself to a limited Arabic public. I now write in French, that Western language that wages an intense struggle to survive in a linguistic landscape staked out for universality by such powerful languages as dominant English, proud Japanese, and Chinese, rich in its prestigious history and future prospects of limitless ambition.

Arabic, the language of the Qur'an, remains and will remain forever the only fitting vehicle of God's message to humankind. I hope the spiritual emptiness in which the profane languages flounder may not cast its shadow over my unskilled discourse, out of my element as I am in the language I have been obliged to borrow. A change of language entails a change of lighting: the familiar becomes unfamiliar, problems take on different guises, and political, social, economic, and global issues come into the foreground. I can only hope that the tone I am forced to acquire does not veil my prime concern, which is to make known the message of the Qur'an: a message of peace for a violent world, a message of sanity for a directionless world, a spiritual message for an ailing modern humanity.

The second concern of this book is to offer some little contribution to the reflection of the future of *islam,*[2] that is, the future of a world lulled and content with that hectic madness that prevents humankind from living in peace, reconciled to God, open to sympathy and compassion for our fellow humans, anxious to traverse the torment of turbulent modernity, to pass from here below to Ultimate Life in the fullest hope of eternal Goodness.

Thus I shall speak of God and of the Ultimate Life to a modernity deafened by the noise of the new, blinded by the sheen of colored images, dazzled by incessant flashbulbs, seduced by the magic of the "electronic superhighway," dumbfounded by bursts of virtual reality. I shall speak to a modernity at once stunning and stunned, thus risking the ridicule of the modishly irreligious and the jibes of modern disbelievers. I will reckon it worthwhile if but a single soul thirsting for truth finds in this book the means to silence the clamor of doubt that modernity stirs in the mind. I shall consider myself fortunate if a single troubled soul finds in this writing the argument with which to steady his resolve, to set aside that all-too-modern indecisiveness and uncertainty, and thus undertake the journey towards God with sure and determined steps.

To shed light on the path towards a personal spiritual quest is my primary care. To give an account of the historical, political, social, scientific, ecological, and human circumstances that pervade and drive modernity at full tilt is an important goal; yet it is secondary, given the ultimate end of our individual and personal fate after death.

• • •

I believe I was the first, some twenty years ago, to use the phrase "winning the modern world for *islam.*"[3] Since then the expression has been taken up by others. I return to the charge, not to ruminate on a slogan, but to address modernity with questions it has no interest in, and which its citizens haven't the time to ask: Who am I? What am I? Where am I going? What will become of me once I am dead, and my body is embalmed and laid to rest in its oaken casket—or bulldozed into some common pit in the countryside of Algeria or in a Rwandan forest?

Those in search of the truth who are restless for God may, I hope, find something to feed that restlessness and equip their search. As for those who deny, the uncommitted observers, the analysts who have shut their windows to keep out the breeze of a different idea, another thought, I wish them an hour of rest for their souls, a moment of intellectual probity, a flash of candor for themselves, in order to raise once more the question of *islam* and the problems in the world issuing from the Islamic movement. I do so not in terms of divisions among humankind, nor in terms of an insoluble enmity toward the West or a clash among civilizations, but as a gesture of love: a hand of friendship for all humankind, bearing the message of sense and justice for humankind.

To be delivered and received as such—to be fully understood—the message of *islam* requires ample patience and delicacy on the part of both the bringer and the recipient, especially in a climate where disinformation reigns, along with rejection of the other.

God is Expert and Wise: to Him be the praise of a servant!

SALÉ (MOROCCO) SATURDAY, FEBRUARY 28, 1998

Introduction

ON COMMUNICATING

COMMUNICATION between people of the North and people of the South is difficult. It tends to be a one-way operation: dictates pour down from the mighty North in the form of peremptory clauses; the South, covering its shame, calls its submission "friendly cooperation." Communicating with Western modernity—that is, of the North—a modernity "mounted" and "remounted" against *islam,* runs aground when you wear a beard, speak of God, and come from the South. The Islamist speaking of God is routinely taken for a fanatic, an obscurantist, mentally retarded, a terrorist—someone to be condemned out of hand, without further trial.

Of the Muslim who concerns himself with political issues, ceaseless effort and unfailing patience are required to make one's voice heard at all. But he needs still greater diligence and insistence to get himself across, to attract the curiosity, chiefly hostile and suspicious, of a West on the lookout for the sort of "Islamic turbulence" that appears daily on prime time. His least movement is pinpointed, commented on time and again, with citation of examples and proof of the violence of those gallows figures referred to as "God's mad killers."

It takes enormous effort and patient persistence to dispel the smokescreen thrown up more and more each day by the campaign of disparagement waged by those hostile to *islam,* who circulate their images and slogans as the "learned opinions" of authorities and specialists. Communicating with modernity when prejudice, doubt, and suspicion are so stacked against you requires somehow connecting with a listener disposed to hear your voice. How rare this is, when minds are retrenched behind ready-made convictions, resolved to hear and understand nothing.

It seems impossible to make a modern man listen to reason when he himself has little reason to live beyond the fearsome desire to enjoy the "good" things of consumerism. The sway of hostile publicity and its daily hammering have produced a frame of mind that is aimed against all who speak another language than that of "cooperating" submission to the master-culture and politico-economic hegemony of the West. Reaching each other means leaping over a rampart that seems too high to clear.

Two-way communication is beyond reach with a modernity that is comfortably installed in a way of life hardly troubled by the wretchedness of the no-accounts that crowd the screen each day: the horror of genocide in Algeria, the monstrous slaughter in Rwanda. The average citizen—and the answerable politician—wipe their hands of such calamity, such bloodthirsty savagery, and wipe them on the beards of those dreadful Islamic terrorists. Or perhaps they organize humanitarian aid—a ready-made pretext for assuaging tender consciences.

How can you communicate with a world gorged on material goods, a world whose excess disengages itself, as if from some debasing shame, from the dismal backdrop of inhuman massacres perpetrated by the protégés of secular and democratic modernity in Algeria and elsewhere? How can you make yourself heard among the sated, how can you get the well-fed to listen to reason, when you are one of the world's starving peoples? You haven't a say in that smooth-talking, democratic, secular, modern world when what you are driven to cry out, what you must urgently proclaim, is an idea that differs from the received—and receivable—ideas of the West.

What can an idea do? What good is an unarmed idea in the face of a West armed to the teeth?

Aggressive modernity rejects a clear and objective idea when it has no place in the logic of secular discourse, the only sort viable. An idea genuinely peaceable, an open and generous proposal of dialog, is simply *non grata* among the citizens of a culture, of a mentality, of an unapproachably disdainful economic, political, and military force, fiercely alien to a contrary view that might have the temerity to open blind eyes to the light of day.

It is difficult to remind modern man that God is our Creator, not the "almighty dollar," not the god of profit, not the military might of a latter-day Pharaoh, not the economic domination of the Midas of the hour. Crying out with an idea, proclaiming a proposal, to an unreal charade of mad hopes, is but an incongruity before the concreteness of modern reality.

What is the good of the idea, of what worth is the proposition, against the fact of modernity? The fact of scientific technology widens the dizzying gulf between the nameless with their bizarre ideas and a modernity mastering colossal powers.

What is the point of the barefoot idea, the vagabond proposal, against this colossally concrete, concretely colossal, fact?

What is the spiritual and moral value of what an insolvent Islamism has to hawk on the global market over against the market value guaranteed by the greenback?

The arena of modern global politics has no place for an insistent *islam* knocking at its gates, the *islam* here and now that bears the message of God's peace with humankind, the message of justice and kinship among men. Such are the circumstances of *islam* and the modern world that the Islamic voice must for a time remain inaudible, the Islamic idea unreceivable; but the day is coming when a wiser post-modern world will be all ears to hear the Message of *islam,* ready and open to accept what *islam* has to propose, and—if God will—happy to be inspired with the wisdom of *islam.*

A wiser world will understand that *islam* is submission to God. It will learn to gaze outwards to the open sea, and to hoist the sails on its voyage to the land of freedom—the freedom of the servant of God who recognizes no other sovereignty than that of the Sole Creator, who obeys no other law than the Law of the Master of the World, God.

• • •

IT IS MY EARNEST DESIRE in this book to set forth the creed of *islam* and its Law. It is as well my desire to invite a rebellious modern world to God, lest it be shipwrecked like the people to whom Noah foretold the Flood, and who rebelled against God.[4] To do so we must contemplate several examples the Qur'an affords us, and whose lessons modernity ought to draw: for if history changes, the nature of man, the maker of history, remains subject to the same inconstancies. Times change; human psychology does not.

A major lesson should be drawn from the Mission of the Prophet Abraham. He dashed the idols of his people, though they were unable to realize the powerlessness of the gods carved by the hand of man. The flames whipped up by Nimrod to incinerate the Prophet proved harmless, protected as he was by the Almighty.[5] Today's Nimrods no longer burn the teller of truth at the stake, they ignite hecatombs on a monstrous scale. The modern *auto da fé,* though it offers no less horror than the medieval Inquisition, goes about its business ceremoniously and with means even more efficient and "refined."

History's vagaries have raised to power, in the same Iraq (then ancient Babylon) where the stake was prepared for Abraham to be burnt, under Nimrod the Great, a despot equipped with infernal means alongside which the ancient pyre seems child's play. Saddam is aptly named: he is "one who strikes head on,"[6] the paradigm of every sort of equivocation, the hero worshipped and the dreaded tyrant. In the twinkling of an eye he puts the Kurd village of Halabja to the flames, annihilating by phosphoric firebomb whole armies of an Islamic Iran already the target of American vindictiveness.

Nimrod the Babylonian could not, given his primitive means, have imagined that his successors—in Iraq and elsewhere—would one day have command of such infernal machines capable of raining down chemicals on the heads of entire populations, or release nightmarish flying creatures that flash across the sky with lightning speed.

The Bible, that inexhaustible source of gossip petty and otherwise, describes the founder of the Babylonian Empire as "Nimrod, mighty hunter in the sight of the Eternal." However mighty he may have been, however malicious and cruel, he could not begin to conceive of the monstrous armaments that would be forged, thousands of years later, by modern technology. The phantom bomber "hunters" sold by the Powers of Modernity to Nimrod's worthy modern successors—mightier hunters still—will prove capable of diabolic prowess worthy of an age of metal, chemistry, and electronics.

A Nimrod-and-a-half, Saddam overstepped the limits outlined by the World's Policeman when he invaded the emirate of Kuwait, whose oil fields symbolize petroleum wealth. President Bush flushed with anger and marshaled the world powers against the proud Ba'athist rebel of New Babylon. It was not Saddam who went up in flames, but the Iraqi people, and it is the Iraqi people who continue to suffer the consequences of the terrifying deployment of American power.

In his turn, Mister William—alias Bill—Clinton, enmeshed in his closet scandals, has come within a hair's breadth of sparking a grand Mideastern conflagration once again, at the end of February 1998. His tangle with Saddam, christened "Desert Thunder," has had to be aborted, unable to rise to the same level of historic indignation as the Storm of his illustrious predecessor, the gentleman from Texas, Mister George Bush.

Saddam's quixotic policies and brinkmanship tactics laid him open to the consequences of having furnished President Bush with a pretext to vent his surliness against the Arabs in 1991. The same tactics have very nearly allowed President Clinton to strike his own mighty blow against martyred Baghdad.

The inevitable catastrophe dreaded by the entire world—with the exception of the American administration—came within a hair's breadth of happening. Firm opposition from Russia and China, along with the Gaulist position adopted by President Chirac, set the stage for the courageous and artful intervention of the Secretary General of the UN, the African Kofi Annan. Was it a turning point in international diplomacy, a new page in the until-now lusterless history of the UN? Was it the voice of reason, a calculated strategy honed by indignation at the trigger-happy cowboy mentality, one that got the draw on the Policeman of the World, to save the Arabs and the Iraqi people from a second tragedy?

Whatever it was, the Monster of Baghdad is still there, bigger than life in his suit of armor, his eyes peeled on his admirers. The Ba'athist party, with its mad pretensions and monstrously egotistic and violent leader, is still at the helm. Meanwhile the Arab peoples, jolted once more by the imminence of American arms, will, once they are withdrawn, sink again into indifference, spectators amused by the theatrical poses of megalomaniacal presidents who grimace publicly at the enemy, the better to stoop, behind the scenes, before the boot of the stronger.

President Clinton accepts the compromise brokered by the Secretary General of the U.N.—under the condition that the troops and carrier ships remain in place to survey the scene close up, arms at the ready, just waiting to strike back in a flash, unilaterally, at the first sign of the unpredictable Saddam's least twitch of resistance to the imperial will of the United States of America. The US is perfectly willing to destroy Baghdad—martyred Baghdad!—in order to teach stubborn autocrats that she means what she says. Her Arab allies, though docile and liberal, proved insufficiently trustworthy as guardians of America's "national interests." Weren't there distinct signs of unrest and feverishness in Arab streets as the ultimately aborted raid approached the critical stage?

The evidence is bitter: the 51st American state, Israel, remains the one and only pivot around which the strategy of great global power has for years been turning and will continue to turn. No restlessness in the streets, no tactical palliative, is going to deter the American seizure of Arab petroleum—so long as Arabs fail to rediscover themselves as Muslims, fail to recognize themselves as orphans on the world's stage, without the encouragement, support, and efficacious interaction of their brothers in *islam*.

• • •

LIKE TECHNOLOGY IN GENERAL, modern armament technology—far from being an accessory in the service of world peace, a tool in its defense and that of human freedom—is becoming ever more sophisticated in the destruction of more and more human beings and in terrorizing humankind. Its "least inoffensive" products are the land mines, buried everywhere in the earth, that amputate the arms and legs of the child playing along the side of the road, that disembowel the farmer working his field. Sold at bargain prices, these deadly instruments can only be disarmed at great expense, an expense the West refuses to pay.

Murderous mines below the ground and firebirds in the sky: human violence has never had such weapons at its disposal, so obligingly and dearly sold by a worldwide gun-dealing West.

• • •

O MODERN DEMOCRACY of my heart! You are life—and death!

You are that stealthy death humanity thought it saw on its television screens the moment when stealthy (and imaginary, according to the blind and deaf witness of Baghdad radar) airplanes flew over Baghdad. Baghdad the Martyr! Impoverished peoples of Baghdad! The poor rebels of the south of Baghdad, furiously subdued by the tyrant of Baghdad after the burning of Baghdad!

You are life when, not content with words, your sons and daughters of the West and elsewhere form nongovernmental organizations to denounce state terrorism and to defend human rights and the biosphere. We stand under your polyglot banner as your sons and daughters protest, inspired by noble ideals, express their wrath, and mobilize substantial moral and material resources to come to the aid of the victims of implacable modernity.

We are with you, charitable souls, when you rise up against those who perpetrate the base deeds instigated by the powers that be, or whipped up by demoniacal local forces. We the faithful of *islam* are with you, and we will be so ever more and more, disciples resolute in our courage and in the assurance of our father Abraham, smasher of idols. We stretch forth our hand to you, fellow human souls, whatever your convictions, so long as human compassion and love animate your hearts and acts.

Strong and confident in the mercy of God—may His Name be exalted and magnified!—we are and shall ever be prepared to tender our hand to men and women of good will and of noble disposition. We are prepared to conclude a pact of nonaggression towards humankind and human dignity, a pact of universal benevolence towards humankind and our environment, a pact of efficacious, militant, and generous goodness. We are thus prepared to ban discrimination, racial hatred, violence against humankind and our biosphere, and disdain for God's creatures—may God's Name be ever glorified.

This will mean concluding a pact of mutual aid among humankind that crosses the boundaries of state structures and goes above the heads of official institutions. This is our ideal of beneficence strictly bound to our ideal of spiritual perfection. This double ideal, indissolubly united in the Message of *islam,* is explicitly ordained in the Law of *islam,* and it is courageously put into practice in exemplary fashion by God's own Prophets—praised and exalted be the Name of God!

This plan for a worldwide humanitarian coalition responds to the utopian dream and the actuality of the flagrant imbalance that rages between North and South. Yet it seems odd when the sacred cause of human freedom and the loving and generous preservation of human dignity are defended by an Islamist accused of being responsible for the unspeakable butchery perpetrated in Algeria—and if it is not you, it is your brother![7]

The defense of human freedom and dignity is a project for the future and a sacred cause. Transpose the dream, project the utopian dream over the long term and a vast course, and you will jut out over the horizon limned by the Prophets of God, each for his own people and time, and Muhammad (blessed be he!) for all peoples for the rest of the duration of this world. The prophetic message is echoed throughout time so as to call human beings to God, and to remind them that they are creatures of the One God. It recurs throughout space and time so as to address recurrent errors, repeated mistakes, dangerous deviation, moral lapses, and social ills.

To transpose and project the values of *islam* over the long term and the boundless horizon is the ambition of this book. It may well be a foolhardy ambition for one of modest competence, an effort limited and consigned to custody. Nonetheless we intend to clarify the ideas and the ideals that Muslims can share among themselves and with persons of good will, and to indicate the locus and the limits within which concord can grow, and the causes of discord between *islam* and the modern world can be dispelled. Once again it is necessary that modern Westernism consent to lend its ear to a non-Western viewpoint. For too long we have suffered the image of Islam propagated by Western media; it is time, it is urgent at a time when humanity is becoming inhuman, that true words replace invective, and that hate-driven propaganda be brought to a halt. Misunderstanding is all too often the bastard child of an ill-defined word and wicked intentions.

• • •

PERMIT ME a parenthetical explanation here of the need of precise speech as the necessary medium of static-free communication. Discourse is debased whenever the words of one language are forced into the service of the meanings, feelings, and values of another. It could happen that the borrowed language, the Western language used by an Islamist at the end of the 20th century, for example, is utterly inept at expressing spiritual matters, not because of semantic deficiencies of that language per se, but rather that its secularization has rendered such terms banal, bereft of its original apt simplicity.

In order to avoid confusion and misunderstanding, it is fitting to alert the reader to the fact that expressing Islamic thoughts and the meaning of the Islamic message in a secularized language is an uncomfortable intellectual exercise. If in addition the mediator is awkward or insufficiently familiar with the host language, the enterprise is doubly risky. To confide the message of *islam* by means of a language whose semantic and cultural universe is wildly out of tune with *islam*—if not indeed opposed altogether—is to tempt incomprehension and incommunicability. To do so without insisting at the outset on a significant degree of tolerance between the parties involved is surely to expose oneself to a breakdown of lines of communication and to preclusion from one's course of action.[8]

It is thus wholesome by way of introduction to establish a margin of confidence, a certain modicum of tolerance. It is wise to assume that an Islamist, uncertain of Western semantics and culture, has the best at heart when he uses a word that is perhaps too strong or out of place. Just because he distances himself from modernity, why should he necessarily have something against persons, populations, and countries? Harsh words may well conceal an infinite compassion in the face of the wrongs modernity causes humankind.

It is intellectually dishonest not to allow for such a margin of confidence, and not to credit the other with good judgment and integrity. It only proves cultural weakness to attribute to the other the faults our indisposition and prejudices alone cause us to project.

Let us beware the etymological pitfalls that prove fatal in communication. Words misused, poorly written, or ill received are deadly traps!

Thus I will, when naming certain sacred personages such as Noah, Abraham, Moses, Aaron, and Jesus—grace and peace upon the Prophets of God the Most High—I will use their Western forms, knowing full well that these inevitably arouse Biblical connotations, that is, the language of the Bible of the eldest daughter of the Church. I use these forms without retaining the Biblical accounts of these august persons—accounts which have nothing to do with Qur'anic revelation. The Jewish rantings and rabbinical addenda occupy their own space. The spellings are an accommodation meant to facilitate communication. The blasphemies heaped upon the Prophets by the Bible hardly merit attesting. The hand that depicts Nimrod in terms of a valiant hunter before the Eternal is the same as that which spread vile actions of the Prophets of God, slayers of Nimrodian despotism and smashers of idols.

• • •

THE QUR'AN presents the Prophets of God (may His Name be exalted!) as models of virtue, examples to be imitated, the ongoing personification of spiritual perfection, men who have been charged with a noble purpose, and faithful messengers, intermediaries between the Creator and humankind. These messengers are wholly human, but their hearts, minds, and conduct are illuminated by divine rays. They have no relationship with the Christian creed that divinizes Jesus the son of Mary—may Mary and the Prophet of God be honored!

The history of Moses is taken up often in the Sacred Text; it is well worth meditating upon. Moses is one of the five great Prophets, men of decisiveness and valor.[9] The other four are Noah, Abraham, Jesus Christ, and Muhammad—peace and grace be upon these men of decisiveness and valor! Moses, saved from the waters to which his mother confided him, out of fear that Pharaoh would slay him along with all the children of Israel, was taken up by Pharaoh's wife and raised in the very palace of the Pharaoh. Chosen out of all eternity for an extraordinary destiny, Moses received the blessing of revelation and was distinguished among the Prophets by his conversation with God on Mount Sinai.

Moses announced his mission to Pharaoh, who was scandalized by it. The philosophical and cultivated Egypt of Pharaoh was not the rough and militaristic Mesopotamia of Nimrod. Whereas Nimrod, administrative guardian of the rigid tables of the law, was to apply administrative and legal rigor in burning Abraham's intention at the stake, the more subtle Pharaoh appealed to the resourcefulness of his court intellectuals—priests learned in the arts of magic, medicine, and embalming—to confound Moses. But Moses baffled the assembly by producing the miraculous rod, a gift of Providence. The cohort of sorcerers yielded, recognizing the presence of the supernatural in Moses and his miracle, before which their mere artifice was laid bare. It was for Pharaoh to drink to the dregs the chalice of spite. Pharaoh, self-proclaimed god, Master of the Nile, his orders derided, his sorcerers rather facing crucifixion and beheading than deny their allegiance to Moses and to the God of Moses—this is more than he can take!

The Qur'an recounts how the Emissaries of God—may His Name be exalted!—subjected to the sumptuous arrogance of Pharaoh or the murderous conceit of Nimrod, were comforted by the Almighty and inspired with boundless confidence in His protection. So it is over the long trajectory of ancient history related by the Sacred Text with such narrative power that the faithful of post-prophetic times might still be edified.

• • •

LET THE FAINT-HEARTED be capsized by doubt; the faithful remain upright before the threat, when "flexible" men dispense from the treasuries of diplomacy or scrape and bow for the pleasure and delight of the greats of the world.

It is for our example and edification that the word of God (may His Name be magnified!) recounts in detail the character and strength of God's Holy Prophets. The flight of Moses at the head of his people was a compulsory retreat, not mere weakness, not an abandoning of the Mission. The Exodus celebrated by the Bible and the Qur'an was a historical event fraught with consequence for the people of Israel and explosive with meaning through its manifestation of the divine in such miraculous fashion. The Red Sea that was divided before the fleeing Israelites, only to engulf Pharaoh and his troops, was as much an irrefutable historical fact for us as an example and symbol of divine Grace and Solicitude with respect to the Messengers of God (great and all powerful is He!).

The ark was a sheet-anchor for Noah and the handful of the faithful who followed him. Abraham was saved from the flames by a public miracle. Moses and his people crossed the Red Sea on foot. Muhammad, during his Exodus, was saved by a spider who came miraculously to seal with her transparent spinning the entrance of the cave where he hid from his pursuers. I do not know by what exception Jesus the son of Mary should have been the Savior and not the one saved. The truth about him is to be read in the Qur'an. There God informs us that a double was miraculously substituted before the Jewish conspirators who thought they were crucifying Jesus. He was in fact saved, just like his brothers, and the Ascension took place. But polemic aside, the People of the Book have the right to our tolerance, even if tacitly.

Let us recall insistently to mind that the gallery of portraits of the Messengers of God that the Qur'an paints for us is intended to arouse our imagination with symbols of courage and safety. This symbolism so rich in meaning is a moral support such that our human weakness need not buckle before threats, and that our confidence in God be not battered to the breaking point by doubt. The vicissitudes of prophetic history related by the Sacred Book invite us to meditation, to imitation, and to action. We can either find support in its edifying examples—or choose to founder in the trivial things of life and dissolve into meaninglessness. We can either fulfill our duty as free and responsible humans—or sink in our fear to a vegetative existence.

Generations pass, civilizations pass, and with them the history of wars and empires: the modern era—the era of great distress and uncertainty, of great scientific and technological prowess—this too will pass. What will become of me, poor mortal that I am? What will happen to me after death? What is the point of my ephemeral life? Will I find my stay in the edifying models of the Servants of God whom the Most High God perfected—or shall I be a mere passerby in the daily bustle, my days dropping like grapes from the stalk?

Winning the Modern World for *islam* begins with a warning cry addressed to modern man, whose life is feverishly blinkered by the here and now. I intend to jolt him out of his torpor and prevent him from stumbling and reeling, waylaid as he is by nonsense at every turn. Indeed the poor victim stumbles, reels—plunges in!

To his rescue comes the helping hand of the perfected models of the Servants of God, His Messengers. The symbol of the helping hand is to be imitated in our behavior, in both our personal and collective lives, in our moral stand, as in our political involvement, the sole point of contact capable of serving as a mooring for boats in distress.

• • •

Let us then banish verbal booby-traps and distorted meanings, adulterated words such as "religion," which reeks of secular universality. The advice, rightly or wrongly attributed to Jesus, to "render unto Cæsar that which is Cæsar's" collides with the slogan of the French Revolution, "let the last nobleman be hanged from the guts of the last priest" to do in the word "religion" for good. Such words, emptied of meaning by European secularism or French anticlericalism, can only be met with firm distrust.

Introduction

Islam is not a "religion" in the debased and cheapened sense of the word; it is submission to God our Creator. *Islam* is obedience to revealed Law, a full and determined participation in the human adventure, in the history and the fact of humankind. Having submitted to the Divine Sovereign and obedient to God our Master, the Prophets—as supports, models, symbols—participate in the history of humankind, trusting in the protection of God (may His Name be exalted!).

These Prophets were fully and eminently historical. To confirm this for ourselves, let us read the Qur'an not only on rare occasion but whenever we find a moment's respite in the midst of modernity's noise. Let us read the Qur'an whenever we can steal a moment's solitude from the promiscuity of modern multimedia. Let us read it whenever informational bottlenecks on the Internet allow us to turn away for a breath of fresh air, to interact with one another as our true selves and not in the guise of modern madness that programs us like robots.

Let us read the Qur'an to put a rest to the secularizing insanity which teaches that *islam* has nothing to do with politics. The Holy Book teaches us precisely the opposite when it shows us Noah, Abraham, Moses, and Muhammad taking on the concerns of their times. It shows them in the grip of the political issues of their times, in hand-to-hand combat with the despotism and injustice of their times. They are *islam: islam* is their allegiance with the One God; *islam* is the sum of their intentions and their acts, it is the action they take. *Islam* is their faithfulness and their respect for revealed Law.

The perfect model, the Seal of the Prophets, Muhammad (grace and benediction be upon him!) transmits to us the message that bears the final and definitive Law that Almighty God affixes upon the account-book of creation like an authenticating stamp, safe-conduct for the well-being of humankind, personally and socially, during our passage aboard the vessel of our worldly lives, full of the allure of the world, of our country, our duration, our civilization.

The Qur'an—this document of incomparable authenticity—was sent and written during the lifetime of the Prophet and through his dictation. It was later collected and submitted to a critically studious authentication. And here it is, the living Word of God, Message and Law, history and participation, justice and spirituality, tenet and battle cry.[10]

Fashions change, human models come and go—but the Qur'an remains intact.

Human sentiments shift, along with the passing of human cultures and societies—but the Qur'an bears witness of the Absolute.

Languages disappear, and with them modes of expression—but the Qur'an communicates forever to the human heart and mind.

Human foibles are forgotten, the good and the ill—but the Qur'an engraves the indelible history of the sacred in the memory of the faithful: the men God sends to witness on earth, during their lifetime and beyond His oneness; their obedience to God, their partaking in the trying adventure of human life on earth.

Human notions follow upon one another, ideas cancel one another, concepts are annulled—but the Qur'an holds true answers to the intimate and primordial questions of human existence: Who am I? Where am I going? What is life? What is death?

The scene changes and changes again, a hundred flowers fade in the cultural garden of arts and letters, a thousand philosophical systems are erected and pulled down one after the next—but none of this responds to the primordial question, whose meaning modernity seeks distractedly and uselessly, and which the Qur'an alone affords.

The sciences progress by leaps and bounds, technology their offspring encroaches upon our lives and directs the mad song-and-dance of world markets—but humankind sinks further into ignorance, from which only the Qur'an can draw it to a knowledge of why we are here.

The prolific tools of technology, though fearsome devices in men's hands, do not allow everyone to lead a decent and proper material life, nor help us to find the way to meaningfulness in our earthly lives. The Qur'an alone, so neglected a treasure, can serve as guide on the way of well-being.

• • •

TECHNOLOGY reels from revolution to revolution. The internet, though a precious instrument of communication and transmission of scientific information, is also a channel for every kind of harmful matter. More and more the network of multimedia reduces essential questions to a subsistence allowance that litters our lives with pointlessness, burying us under a mass of idle information, drowning us in a torrent of secondhand ideas. Increasingly more accessible and sophisticated, that network trivializes knowledge by making it the wherewithal for people to fool each other with the loud ready-to-wear miscellany backed by the stock market—or, worse, the citizen of the internet-world, madly surfing along, drops anchor in some pornographic mud-puddle or hornet's nest of mafiosi.

Modern man, to his own risk and peril, must function in the service of what occupies his goods and his time—indeed, his life's substance—which steadily decreases even as the demands increase. He lives constantly bombarded by "revolutionary processes" that "allow" him to dismantle his life as his days and nights crumble away before the keyboard of the magical "timesaving" tool that wantonly devours everyone's time. His cellular phone will soon be able to function as a computer, it would seem, and, who knows, the internet will be hooked up on every subscriber's electric line.

The wealthy of the North have everything they need to sacrifice their lives on the altar of desire as clients addicted to a consumers' market—or to something still more poisonous. Modernity's victims—those of the South, that is—also have such of these means as modernity graciously deigns to dispense, so as to exhaust their life-capital in dire misery. Opiated on the cheap, or reckoning their disgrace in terms of the wealth they must pawn, the casualties of the South waste away in rancor and hatred.

The life of modern man is squandered and wretched. His misery is palpable and quantifiable, even if at times it is camouflaged and unconscious. The greatest misery of the victims of modernity is their misinformed state. The divine Word of the Qur'an is truth offered to all who can and, in this time of spiritual aridity, who dare to open the Holy Book and endeavor to read. *Islam* is the antidote of ignorance.

But that, my brother, my sister, will certainly prove difficult for you, whatever your ideological formation, your religion, or your political inclination, because you are scattered by a thousand preoccupations, forever distracted, often depressed, and rarely in the proper state of mind. Still, I tender my suggestion that you open the Qur'an; perhaps it will find you in a privileged moment when the inquietude that inhabits us all, and which we suppress in order to affect unconcernedness, comes once again to the surface. Perhaps then you will be disposed to listen to the Message. Read a page—just one! Perhaps you will find there an answer to the question regularly posed by an interior voice?!

• • •

THIS BOOK will discuss—and rightly so—those questions that arise from the depths of everyone. It will question as well the modernist notions of knowledge, possession, and power. But let us first attune ourselves to what we have in common, the better to communicate. Before communicating, then, let us commune by listening solemnly to our interior voice, to our innate openness to receive the heavenly Message that allows us to partake of the Great Information.

Let us uncover the evidence of that being in the Sûrah called *Ar-Rûm.* It is a Sûrah that, like so many others, situates humankind in the theatre of life, a theatre where scene succeeds scene with the rhythm of our days and nights, where each is free to extemporize, to realize his loss—or his salvation. The Qur'an calls us, as actors, to center stage, endowing us with the freedom to choose between two roles, suggesting one possibility, offering gratification, making a summary of our personal history: life, and, after life, death, and, when the curtain of death is drawn aside, another world, another life, true life.

Thus the Creator speaks:

Sanctified be God when evening enfolds you and mornings awaken you. Glorified be the Name of God in the heavens and on earth, at the drawing nigh of night and midday.

From the dead He draws the living and from the living he draws the dead. He revives the dead earth just as He requickens you.

To have created you from clay, to have breathed in you a soul, is one of the signs of His power.

To create for you of yourselves your spouses, so that you might alleviate one another, binding yourselves to each other with bonds of tenderness and love, is one of the signs of His power perceived by thoughtful minds.

Among the signs of His power stand the creating of the earth and of the heavens, and of the variety of your languages and colors; signs clear to those most wise.

Your sleepiness at night as well as during the day is one of His signs, as is your quest for His gifts; signs self-evident to all who are trained to hear.

He shows you a light that awakens in you both hope and fear, and sends from heaven the water that will once again restore life to the dead earth. This is a sign most sure to all who ponder it.

Among the signs of His power are heaven and earth when they submit to His order. When His call awaits you (after death), lo from the earth you will rise.

All who are to be found in the heavens and on earth belong to Him; all have need of Him.

He it is Who brings forth creatures from nothing; He it is who will as easily refashion Creation once again. The Incomparable is He, the Almighty, the All-knowing.[11]

• • •

HAVING sketched the points of contact with the culture of the interlocutor of modernity, we pause for a moment of serenity to listen to our own innermost being, so as to remind ourselves of a deeper level of communication. We shall continue our search towards mutual communication throughout this book; may it help to establish a dialog between two worlds, that of modernity and that of *islam*. We shall thus have to answer the questions we deem fundamental in this context.

How to win the modern world for *islam*? What does it mean to do so?

Notes

1 Sûrah 17 [*Al Isrâ'*] verses 111.

2 TN: See Chapter I:1, note 1.

3 TN: *Islamiser la modernité* (to Islamicize modernity), in *La Révolution à l'heure de l'islam* (1980).

4 TN: Sûrah 7 [*Al-A'râf*] verses 59–64.

5 TN: Like many ancients whose tales are recorded in both the Hebrew Scriptures and the Qur'an, the latter often provides independent details. This Nimrod (or *Nemrûd*) may bear the name of the descendant of Noah in Gen. 10:8–9; he is as well the Assyrian king to whom the subjection of Abraham to fiery flames (S. 21: 68–69) is traditionally credited. The incident bears some resemblance to the Lot stories of both Scriptures.

6 TN: From the verb *ṣadama,* "strike, knock, handle roughly, rouse, scandalize, jam, shock."

7 Even if this would-be brother is merely a mercenary in the pay of a militaristic partisan clique, even if he is not simply a horrible butcher disguised in battle dress, with a stick-on mustache.

8 An example of the danger that waylays dialog between Islamists and secular Muslims with respect to transcultural communication is the accusation of intent the secular hurls against the Islamist when the latter seeks, in choosing his words, to establish a link. The secular—whether by illiteracy in his mother tongue, or deliberate resolve and political feuding—attributes all manner of dark purposes. I have, it is true, rather too openly challenged my country's democratic intellectuals by referring to them as *fudala'*. The Arabic word has always meant "learned, educated, cultivated"; why then have I been reviled by those who tell me, "You insult me, you drag me through the mud, you sully my honor, you make an attempt on my worthiness as a militant, on my patriotism, when you include me among the *fudala'*!" Yassine is referring to his *Dialogue with Honorable Democrats* of 1994, and the hostile reception it has found in some quarters.

9 TN: *ûlu al 'azm.*

10 TN: *Politique et combat.* AY: Maurice Bucaille's book, *La Bible, le Coran et la science* (Ed. Seghers, 1976) provides fruitful considerations in this regard.

11 Sûrah 30 [*Ar-Rûm*], verses 17–27.

I. Islam and Modernity

1 Proposing and Opposing

Is it a sign of weakness not to be able to propose without opposing, or is this something in human nature that characterizes individual behavior and motivates history itself? Does the West's intransigent campaign against Islam[1] represent the strategic positioning of a frightened West that will find itself in the near future confronting an islamo-confucian coalition? Or is it the infamy of colonialism still ringing in the European consciousness, keeping keen its bitter memory, honing it anew with atrocities?

Such a laboriously cultivated lack of understanding between the modern West and Islam can only be the manifestation of ancient rancor toward emancipated peoples or the ideological preparation of a future contact desired in order to have a "Green Peril"[2] take the part once played by the "Absolute Evil" of the now dead and buried Soviet Union. The latter would appear to be the argument of the eminent Samuel P. Huntington, who prophesies an "inevitable clash" between the two blocs—one of which being Islam in the larger sense. This is ideological machination, exasperation in scholarly language.

The eminent ideologue of the clash between civilizations takes his givens from reality—an Islam in ferment, Southeast Asia on its way to dominating the world market, China in a phenomenal state of development—but he fabricates his arguments largely by basing them on the illusions engendered by Western anxieties, either justified or to be justified at all costs.

Anticipating and announcing catastrophes like some modern Cassandra naturally requires academic training and an established reputation. It also takes the ability to exacerbate the paranoia his side is prone to, to give body and consistency to its ill-checked fury. It offers an outlet for ancient Western frustration, both that of former colonialists and the kind more recently triggered by the American fiasco in Vietnam and the pitiful and clumsy response to the Iranian Revolution.

Prophesying an islamo-confucian menace that must be forestalled is now an ideological disinformation industry intended to prepare grounds for future offensives against Islam while ignoring the doings of the great power of the Middle East, the land of Islam rebaptized as a "geographic zone."

The American expression "self-fulfilling prophecy" perfectly illustrates the ingenious spawning of the clash argument: I predict an event, I huff and I puff until it occurs as predicted, and there you have it. Short on memory for want of historical depth, the American illusion howls its fears, not only in theories like Huntington's, but also in concrete facts: the Gulf wars—the one against Iran as well as the latest one—give vent to intense vindictiveness against a renascent Islam. They are preventive actions born of the fear of powerful armament falling into Muslim Arab hands, even if these were yesterday's allies happily enough armed by the West to counter the Iranian Revolution.

As set forth, the theory denounces the hidden motives of the Western malevolence that ignores its democratic principles in order to overturn elections in Algeria won by an impetuous Islamism. The cultural and civilizational differences between Islam and the West are explained by two separate histories, two states of mind, two conceptions of humanity and the universe. But the dangerous ideological myth-making simply feeds into the daily sensationalism of Western media, so eagerly consumed and amply profitable: something to "turn on" a public bored and gorged with trivia.

It is pointless to cry out against scandal or to rant against preconceived ideas; we must reason calmly and patiently. To glimpse what such hostile purpose and ill-intentioned theorizing is concealing, it is necessary to lift the veil so as, having discovered the cause, to put a stop to the scheming that strives to discredit *islam* and misinform the world. Professionals artfully dubbed "specialists" have raised the art of swaying public opinion to the rank of a highly profitable science.

These chattering commentators on Islam and Islamism focus their attention (and all their attentions) on the "oddness" of the way these curious simpletons dress—those jallabias and kaftans, those veils that are so scandalous to the French and that so disturb the public order. If occasionally one or another of them deigns to quote an Islamist, he will look for some phrase taken out of context, some angry remark from a folkloric leader, that just fits the image the reporter or analyst wishes to convey. Serious and responsible thinking about Islamism is meticulously passed over in silence in order to lend credence to the prejudices that sell so well.

Setting oneself up in opposition passes into mere finger-wagging and gross caricaturing of the otherness of the other, the oddness of the foreigner, the effrontery of the former native who has the temerity to affirm his identity. Cultural and social distinctions are worked up into monstrous relief. Political ends are then served by applying sanctions to cultural and social differences which will reduce the rebellious recalcitrant to "politically correct" conduct and force him to "take his place."

2 What Is Modernity?

Let us try to escape the bitter polemic that provocative display against *islam* can legitimately arouse. Let us try to rid ourselves of the hasty surmises that polemical retort raises and fosters. Let us listen first of all to what modernity has to say for itself, how it defines itself. (We will, however, tolerate a few small remarks from the outside.)

"Modernity"[3] came into use with the literary quarrel between the Ancients and the Moderns in seventeenth-century France. Since that triumphant era, and as a prolonging of the Renaissance that awakened Europe from its medieval slumber, modernity has become for Europeans a way of being, of thinking, of living, of governing oneself, of taking one's bearings in the world. It is a socio-cultural and political manner of being, in contrast to the autochthonous Middle Ages, to an outer world given over to barbarity, and, ultimately, to colonization, predation and underdevelopment, and to public contempt. Central to the notion of modernity is a reference to a historical memory, and the perception of having progressed from medieval Europe.

The overtaking and underestimation of an outer world, indeed the contempt and desolating aggression, are the sentiments that have driven—and will continue to drive—modernity in its encounter with a fallen world unfit for modernity dignity. Scientific and technical attainments have constituted—and increasingly constitute—the crushing argument of the superiority of the modern over the archaic other: the crushing argument and the very cudgel for justifying and proving the cultural insignificance of the other. This is the pretext invented for the military and economic colonization of the world of the South, that world as the market and depot of the products of modernity, where material, cultural, and residual waste—all of it harmful and polluting—has been thrown around willy-nilly.

I cite from the analysis of modernity of the renowned French sociologist Alain Toraine, in his *Critique de la modernité*.[4] According to him, modernity is enlightened humanity's revolt against tradition. Modernity sacralizes society, submitting it to natural law and reason. In its Western manifestation, modernity is "reason's work itself, and hence above all of science, technology and education; the social politics of modernization should have no other goal than to disencumber reason's path by suppressing the rules, corporatist defenses, or customs barriers."

We are thus face-to-face with a modernity that eradicates, a modernist ideology which calls for "disencumbering the way" so that "enlightened humanity" might dispel the darkness of "tradition"—a tradition which, in the eyes of the West, is currently incarnate in the "illuminati" of an obscurantist *islam*. When Touraine speaks of the archaic in connection with the modern, absolutist (and proselytizing) sectarians of the new religion of Modernism think of *islam* as something to be rejected, something to be set aside like some unworthy and shameful archaism.

Modernity is thus a "sacralization" of the natural law of reason, and a submission to all that this entails. To be modern, it is supposed, means one must rebel against the sacred, against the divine. Ideological modernism owes it to itself to have as its goal "disencumbering the way." This is rationalism's violent indictment of the irrational, it is the crushing argument against the tatters of tradition by armed and wealthy scientific technology. Disencumber! Smash to bits! Native modernists, ever colonizable—and ever yet colonized, hide their faces from their warrant officer lest he find them in flagrant disobedience, insubordination, and nonconformity with the standing orders.

Islam is submission[5] to God. It is a peaceful submission, nonviolent toward others, not puffed up, not out to exterminate others' sense of identity just to tidy up and clear the way for its majestic and exclusive progression. Amalgamation is quickly achieved: once you submit, you yield to reason's latest flowering, democracy. In a democracy I submit to a law in whose deliberation I took part—not to some despotic cleric or some divine-right despot.

Bent over the tormented history of a decadent era during which Muslim peoples have suffered—and still suffer—the oppression of feudal regimes, you are easily tempted to subscribe to this view. This encroaching oppression has seized on the message of *islam*—the law of justice and submission to God—and diverted it for its own ambitions of domination. Still, faced with the single-mindedly propelled advance of modernity on the world's stage—so sure of itself, so ready to label anyone who thinks otherwise a reactionary in the way of the path of progress—one might be tempted to buy in. "Disencumbering"—history's wrongheaded foot soldiers on the march! Wipe the slate clean of traditional archaisms! O beauteous logic, o triumph of sovereign logic: *Cogito ergo sum*, I think, thus I am—which all too often means: I am the only thinker, my thought alone counts!

The West has conceived and lived its modernity essentially as a revolution against its past, that hateful past of conspiracy between the Church and the ruling princes under its yoke, keen on the privileges of a feudal system under which the populace is reduced to the condition of serfs and peasants, to be taxed and expended at whim. The revolution of a middle class inundated by luminaries of the 18th century—the age of the *Encyclopédie* of Diderot and d'Alembert, rational, naturalistic—ended up erasing the slate of the attainments of clerical feudalism so as to maintain only those values modeled on scientific demonstration.

Touraine concludes: "[Modernity] wipes the slate clean of beliefs and forms of socio-political organization."[6]

A novel political concept is born, replacing God by society as the principle of moral judgment:

> Essential to the ideology of modernity is the idea that society is the source of values, that goodness is defined by whatever is socially useful, and evil by whatever is harmful to its uniformity and effectiveness.[7]

Reinforced in its revolutionary role by its latest scientific and technical exploits, modernist thinking settles into its maturity, having come to terms with its nineteenth-century exploratory scientism, declares itself naturalistic and evolutionistic by definition, recognizing no divinity other than reason and owing allegiance to nature alone.

"Modernist thinking," writes Touraine, "affirms that human beings have the right to live in a world governed by the natural laws discovered by reason and to which reason itself is subjected. It identifies people with a nation, and social body that also functions under natural laws, and which owes it to itself to discard the forms of organization and irrational domination that fraudulently attempt to legitimize themselves by recourse to superhuman revelation or divine will."[8]

3 Armed Capitalist Modernity

Anything that did not conform to what had become the world's only answer had to be a fraud, contrary to "natural" law; it had to be discarded in order to make way for the truth. Let the new pass unimpeded, get rid of the old—by force if necessary. Modernity was not some simple philosophy aflutter in the abstract, the salon topic of debate. Soon after its birth it became an engine of evolution and revolution that overturned the concrete realities of life and bid farewell to the timeworn, slashing and slaying.

Slowly at first, at the dawn of the Renaissance, then more and more rapidly, science and technology, Enlightenment philosophy, and the social movement took flight, nourished by a trenchant and violent ideology. The French Revolution, followed by its fearful and murderous undoing by the Emperor Napoleon Bonaparte, would spread the flames of change throughout all of Europe.

Yet another revolution played its role: the Industrial Revolution permitted Europe to enrich and arm itself so that European nation-states could now enter into conflicts far more modern—that is, murderous—than the amateur butchering of the Napoleonic wars. Manufacturing capitalism, more industrial and mechanized, needed space to live and prosper—hence the necessity again of disencumbering and pruning.

In Alain Touraine's critical analysis we read that "the social politics of modernization should have no other goal than to disencumber reason's path by suppressing regulation, corporate defenses, and customs barriers." To do so, it must pursue its goal "by creating the security and foreseeability the entrepreneur requires, and by forming a management class and competent and conscientious operators."[9]

The desire to serve enterprise and open its markets by striking down all barriers developed early on in the history of modernity—as much the child of philosophy as of merchandizing and trafficking. The colonial expansion of Europe's nation-states, like the wars among them, always have strategic motives of mutual defense. In the feverish competition that jolts the world and sets it aflame, the stakes have always been a share in economic resources and the opening of outlets for industrial production. The situation only grows with time.

Atrocious as they were, Europe's wars and colonial onslaught were merely a foretaste of current and future economic wars. Ideological modernism, modern mass-production, and pulverizing mechanism have not yet had their last say when it comes to aggressiveness. Now that postmodernism is no longer exclusively Western, the new world order has shifted into high gear in pursuit of a policy of expansionist capitalism. Such capitalism, savage-born in the bosom of modernity, grows utterly mad in its worldwide manifestation.

The feudal structures that modernity has come to clear away used to shelter productive professional guilds, that is, occupational families that developed a sense of solidarity in the shadow of a pompous aristocracy, a network of human relationships that united the apprentice with the master and the artisan with the patron. While the rule of capitalism has survived along the lines in which it was conceived, aimed toward efficiency, productivity, and increasing profit, the solidarity once enjoyed among free craftsmen, and associations directed by the unwritten law of sanctioned usage, have disappeared—erased from the registries of the modern era.

Sociologists are all too willing to admit modernity's role as a steamroller clearing the path of progress. The Industrial Revolution swept the social landscape of guild solidarity and peaceable rustic conviviality. The populations of farming villages who led a life of subsistence—poor, to be sure, but warm with human sympathy—were forced to leave the welcoming bosom of their soil to become the fodder of a cold manufacturing industry greedy for labor. The lives of millions of persons were turned upside down and plunged into anonymous suburban misery so that capitalism, whose sole allegiance was to profit, could prosper. Little by little the religion of profit replaced that of the deity of the Revolution (Robespierre's Supreme Being) which had driven out the Church.

The cult of money launched a dynamic that first carved up European societies so as then to take on the world, carving it up into colonial empires. Conquering strategists, driven by the glory of their nation-states, took their place at the table along with shrewd geometrists in the service of science, with whom they carved up the world at pleasure, for the benefit of the imperialist powers. Two world wars in this century have demonstrated the dreadful dimension and the destructive force modernity is capable of engendering. Unable to share among themselves the spoils of the colonized, modern European nations have come to sacrifice whole generations on the altar of savage competition between quarrelsome imperialisms; the winner is the one who invents the most efficient mechanisms of death.

Hitler's war, which brought fire and blood to the whole world in order to conquer *Lebensraum,* is nothing but the decisive manifestation of a modern notion of progress founded on reason and committed entirely to efficiency. His tanks, in their day the epitome of technology, were used in the service of the mad fury of an enraged ideology with modern means at its disposal. Since then, Hitlerism and the apocalypse of World War II head the list of calamities suffered by humankind.

The rational means of organization, invention, fabrication, and military strategy distinguish the modern war of the middle of this century from the exploits of the Napoleonic era, where prehistoric homemade bombs brought death on short notice. Hitler's war is but the legitimate heir of the savage war of 1914: the heinous affiliation and hellish process of modern capitalist imperialist violence, devoted entirely to the modern cult of efficiency and profit. These wars are but momentary eruptions of a volcano that "labors" in the bowels of modern society, and that discharges its boiling lava over the natural environment and living things alike.

The arsenal of modernism-modernity consists of three weapons: the critical weapon of modernist ideology, the capitalist weapon that worships the god of profit, and, for good measure, the rather limited weapon for beating a path for capitalism and the ideas that establish it.

Critical ideology, by far the most dangerous weapon of the lot, fires at everything that is ancient, decreeing it archaic, supported merely by the irrational, to be rejected as fraudulent because it claims its basis in some "revelation" or "superhuman" volition. *Islam* thus provides a direct target for modernism: it rests upon a sacred revealing, and its authority is that of the Messengers of God (God be praised!).

To qualify the divine as "superhuman" is an anthropomorphic assault on the sacred, debasing it to the human level and conceding to it merely a degree of superiority. "Superhuman" is not just a linguistic construct; it is the expression of an entire ideology that arises from disgusting pagan origins, going back to a belief in an Olympus populated by "divinities" and "superhumans" who rub up against humans and share their passions, customs, and carrying-on.

The critical weapon of modernist ideology taps and bores into the minds of those of our compatriots whom systematic secularization, by cultural assault, has alienated, in part or completely. Current propaganda against Islam the civilization and against *islam* the conviction and faith, would, in our eyes, never make historical sense to us unless the defamation were underlain and fed by the doubt, bickering, and mistrust that modernism has sown in some minds.

Ideas cannot be killed by pillorying them, nor can that pluck the faith from hearts, or conviction from minds. But reeducating people and plundering their souls by instilling and fomenting doubt in them, and by describing the revealed as fraud and lies: this is to undermine the very basis of a personality, to lay waste and ravage much more treacherously than any economic pillaging or military invasion could ever do. To raise generations to beg their meager cultural and intellectual allowance from their thinking-master, the one anointed by the power of modernity, is to prepare and promote allies who are willing and able to be mobilized at a moment's notice to execute the master's commands, and it thrusts obedient underlings into power, however patriotic the overtones of their slogans.

These agents, trusty resident proxies wearing local masks, are worse than the capitalist invader with a house of his own, comfortably positioned to bag your economy. Military weaponry and the armaments of capitalism play merely an instrumental role in the invasion of a civilization: this is total war.

4 Post-modernism

The colonial gunboat and colonialist capital both serve the same triumphant ideology that awakened and armed expansionist intentions: thus we became subjected to modernity. We are always subjected to its most advanced form; that is now something called post-modernism, an even more aggressive continuation of the modernist offensive than ever before. This form of acute domination is stimulated by international competition and a free and easy access to world markets.

We are consumers of modernity, modernity's consenting or coerced objects, cheap dumping grounds for modernity's polluting trash, guinea-pigs for use in modernity's experimenting. Haven't they discovered clandestine channels, criminal branches of European laboratories that experiment with their pharmaceutical products on Africans and on other peoples of the South, as a follow-up to experimentation with mice and rats? And all so that the white man can be sheltered from health hazards.

Attempts on the lives of poor and "insignificant" populations are not limited to the ways of old-fashioned slaughter; the Southern guinea-pig—very often Muslim—is supposed to ransom the European's life with his own; he is, without even knowing it, to sacrifice himself for his master's good health. We are hostages of post-modernism caught in its criminal tentacles. Our blood, having already been poured out, is now sucked white, contaminated, exploited.

This must cease! In order for this state of affairs to stop we must take back our destiny and interact with modernity as an equal. We should appropriate to ourselves whatever positive aspects of modernity are useful to us, without letting ourselves be fooled by the glitter of post-modernity, without letting ourselves be overshadowed by modern advertising that tries to fob off what is false at an exorbitant price.

Thus we will buy into modernity, but on our terms. We will need to conduct ourselves as canny purchasers of modernity. A shrewd buyer examines the merchandise, in order to uncover damages and spot the cheat. It is along such lines that we ask such questions of modernity and insist that the past be taken in account. And it is with the intention of requiring justice and equity from modernity that our plan of making modernity Islamic must begin, by posing such questions and exploring the terrain so as to ascertain meeting sites.

Sanctimoniously holding hands in order to pass for understanding and amicable clients is pointless if, in the dark, each side makes annoying questions disappear. Only by mutual frankness, solicitude, and a rare degree of "transparency" can we even hope that *islam* and modernity may one day cease to be the terms of an irreducible paradox, rancorous debate, and no-win conflict.

One day, when the convulsions of Western rejection are long since past, *islam* the conviction, and Islam, 40% of humanity (on the horizon, according to those who study the future, by the middle of the next century—tomorrow!), will be the salient fact in the world and its undistortable Message. The Islamic world of tomorrow will be, we hope, a vast horizon open to peaceful coexistence, to respect for diverse cultures and for nature—which industrial and post-industrial modernity pollute ever increasingly.

One day, the "post-post-period" will be Islamic, because *islam* is the Message of God (God be praised!). The permanent crisis of post-modernism will end in bringing the inhabitants of this sick planet to the foot of the wall, to be smashed there against the injustice insufferable to four-fifths of humanity; where commercial competition will have advanced to a stage of market wars complete with nuclear threats, the final argument of enraged titans.

What world order, what international discipline, what legal system, what UN, what "world policeman" will stop economic wars, played today with mutes on, from exploding into an uncontrollable conflagration?

Meanwhile, this giant of a post-modern universe is still on its feet for some time. Signs of moral decadence announce the end of a cycle of civilization, though the expiration date seems far enough off: God alone is Master, God alone governs, God alone knows—exalted be His Name!

Meanwhile, no one still listens to the Spenglers and Toynbees of history: now the fashion is that of Huntington, where no one can see past the end of his nose for analytical bias and shallowness. Meanwhile, it serves no purpose to expound on any probable Islamic takeover of power in the immediate future. The prospect of a reflective maturity comes tomorrow—a tomorrow of several years, or two to three decades. God alone knows and disposes, God be praised!

In the meantime, it is useless to speak of an economy governed by the law of justice, of development which is not predatory, and of growth which is friendly to man and the environment, without applied study of all that post-modernity represents in the way of knowhow.

Meanwhile we must humbly apply ourselves to the task. The project of an overtaking, "post-post," turns inevitably to acquiring the mastery of what is. We will slowly have to adapt social practices of the jungle by softening them, progressively humanizing them, taming the savage brutality of globalization intent on destroying the biosphere and keeping four-fifths of humanity destitute so that a minority might wallow in luxury and strut in their joyless opulence and bovine consuming.

Post-modernism is here for some time to come; global neocolonialism is going to resist any expansion of a new Islamic civilization. In the frantic race for profit, in the heightened need of the energy in the hands of Muslims, it will not hesitate to shackle and counter anything of the kind. Western politicians, refusing to recognize where their permanent interest lies, have no other criterion than whatever is of immediate interest. Difficult times are in store for us, but God alone is mighty—may the Name of our Lord and Protector be exalted!

The advent of a new Islamic civilization, of a unified Muslim world rich in material resources to back its worth, rich in a young and dynamic human potential, has historical logic on its side. As an aging Western demography falls inexorably into decrepitude, Islamic youth flowers arborescently: the statistics announce a rotation in the history of civilization.

Nothing will save the West—too rich and too comfortable—from disappearing, pure and simple, if marriage and family life continue to be in jeopardy. A slight and (demographically speaking) rickety population will not be able to sustain the dominant role that the West claims to play on the world stage. Flaunted homosexuality, wedded to diseases once thought to be shameful and now frankly acknowledged, will wind up razing a proud and smugly self-satisfied civilization to the ground. The coming of a new and unified Islamic civilization is logically in the cyclical order of things; above all, it is a calling announced by our Prophet Muhammad (blessed be he!) who speaks to us of a second caliphate.

But now I would mark a pause. Let us give rest to speculation and turn our attention from forecasting to what has been revealed. Otherwise our prose would be mere babbling.

5 Modernity and Identity

It is the duty of all previsional human forecasting to yield before prophetic promise. It is another, equally important duty to prepare oneself for it, to make a sure-footed dash to the summit. Our goal is not to overtake modernity on its slippery slope, nor to attain the hedonist dream that accompanies ante- as well as post-modernism; it is, rather, to acquire the scientific and technical means that the world of advanced technology continues to develop and to adapt them to our final social state, which is justice, and our final personal state, which is spirituality.

It is a rule of the game we cannot escape, nor afford to overlook, that the West will stop short of nothing to sow obstacles in our way and abort our plans. But what sort of scientific potential and technological mastery is the West going to represent in the foreseeable future—indeed, what does it represent already in high-tech terms, compared to the accomplishments and legitimate ambitions astir around the Pacific Rim?

The West, the cradle of modernity, has lost the lead and seeks to fall back on defensive positions to confront the Yellow Competitor, the distinctive color of an authentic culture, unyielding in its identity and proud of its difference. The West is reduced to craning its neck, mounting its observation posts, its industrial espionage, to see what's happening on the other side of the Pacific, and copy what is being developed under other skies. The West can only spy on the technological jewel cases in the strongboxes of Japanese laboratories, and copy the Japanese method of organizing work and the nonadversarial, familial relationship between patron and workforce. The post-modern period is already Asiatic; and tomorrow, when China is finally revealed. . . .

China frightens the world's Huntingtons because of its enormous size and potential. Its rapid and sustained growth rate, in the two-digit neighborhood, is the object of envy and covetousness for a West whose most optimistic chances do not exceed 3%. The "little dragons" of Southern Asia, studiously modeled on the Japanese system, are astonishing, both for their flexibility and efficiency and for the speed with which they bear forward and even make California's prestigious Silicon Valley sit up and take notice.

The financial and monetary crises arising from corruption and a loss of confidence that is crisscrossing the economies of Southern Asia in no way diminish the importance of those economies. They are youthful growing pains the West spurs on to dam up fears that the global economy might feed altogether in the backwaters of those little dragons that have become incontrovertible players on the court of the grown-ups.

The culture of distrust and rejection—indeed of haughty scorn—that Western modernism nourishes with regard to former colonialized peoples—good-for-nothing natives—is gradually becoming all-too evident. Aspirants to the rank of "dragon," such as Malaysia, with its Muslim majority, and Indonesia, 90% Muslim, benefit little by little from, if not the sympathy of their former masters, at least the respect due to nations capable of catching up with all the scientific, technological, and organizational aspects of modernity while remaining culturally themselves.

The emergence on the scene of the economic development of India and Vietnam, both of them participants in the competitive race, has the effect of rebuffing the West and beating its proud culture into more conciliatory and less disdainful positions. Pakistan, still in training but resolute, worries the West, which wavers between the panic of seeing an Islamic state in possession of nuclear weapons and the desire to maintain balance in a strategic zone. The assassination of General Ziaulhaq, a man of integrity and unfeigned Islamic convictions, precedes and prepares the entrance on the scene of the photogenic Benazir Bhutto, a volatile and corrupt woman, but one of a "Westernized elite" and an ever-faithful ally, notwithstanding the half-veil perched on her coiffured hair and her well made-up face.

America's pathological fixation is focused on Islamic Iran. The object of all its worries beyond the Atlantic, Iran is for Europe a rich client that needs to be treated with "critical diplomacy," a brief and embarrassed phrase that says much about the uneasiness of a divided West. The phrase describes diplomacy with a strong and wealthy state whose constancy and permanence belies Western prognoses that had given it up for lost, stopped in its tracks by men in turbans. The mullahs offend Western taste; in the opinion of the West, they are incapable, in their comic outfits, of thinking or of running a modern entity the way the beloved adopted children of the West do.

The Islamic state of Iran is here to stay. Those who try to sow discord between Shiites and Sunnites will pay for it dearly. Among us Muslims this family quarrel will be settled; it will find the grounds of understanding and mutual aid that those faithful to *islam* are expected to cultivate. God willing, this will happen sooner or later.

That leaves us with the Arabic countries, the cradle of *islam* and the geographic center of its history. The glorious past of our civilization (called, abusively, "Arab") weighs dreadfully on our present. We Arabs are more weighted down with our heritage than the other Muslim peoples who have also participated in the centuries of Islam's edification. We are too burdened with history: our memory, intellect, and imagination form a kind of obstacle that prevents us, on the one hand, from returning for refreshment to our origins, and, on the other, from steering the tide of modernity toward a future where we can find ourselves once again, and not some bastardized being. The cry of a lost identity, the demand for identity amid the whirling rapids of modernity, the quest of an identity that revives us: these are obsessions and the topics of bitter dispute between Islamists, who constitute a substantial presence, and the "Westernized elites" that cling to their privileged status.

Aging Europe has pursued a long road to get from its Middle Ages to modernity. There should be no reason for apology if we embark on a different road to shake off our torpor and remedy our situation. Europe's greatest mistake would be to ignore the deep stirring that animates the Muslim world—and not just Mediterranean Arabs, but Turks, Iranians, Turkmeni, Azeri, and so on, as well. The greatest disservice Southern Europe—Latin Europe—could render the cause of uniting with the rest of Europe would be to upset European progress in coming to terms with an aging and politically agonizing political class along the African littoral, biding its time while crying for help and appealing for a European guardian. Their safety is risky indeed.

European thinkers, as politically minded persons with long experience and a just point of view, alert Europe's managers to the drift toward a rupture with the future on the pretext of a shortsighted pragmatism. The downfall and overthrow of the Shah of Iran is a lesson that has been too quickly forgotten or not noted at all. The same mistakes keep being made. The European politician, enmeshed in his preoccupation with election, goes along complaisantly with the interpretation of a sensationalist press whose sole concern is increasing sales.

Politicians and media personnel fabricate the hideous image of an "Islamist" killer who exists only in their heads. The military-partisan mafia who officiate and direct unnameable operations in Algeria are unjustly compared to an Islamic movement, turbulent, surely, and thunderous enough during the elections six years ago—but popular, competent, responsible, and above all utterly at odds with the blood baths for which it has been made to bear responsibility. By what aberration, by what hocus-pocus, has the noble and respected figure of Abbasi Madani been changed into one of a mad hired murderer? Is this some sort of sleight-of-hand, some cynical surrealism, some tale spun of whole cloth?

No! It is nothing but malevolence and gross political stupidity!

It is an insult to the future and a misreading of the present to buy into such xenophobia as "Arab terrorists," "Arab extremists," "Arab fundamentalists." It is also an insult to human intelligence to attribute the atrocities of masked bandits to an organization that has proved itself, that has performed with competence and responsibility in tens of mayoralties, before the mafia put an end to an experiment at once too promising and too threatening for comfort.

The founders of the FLN [*Front de Libération Nationale*], such as Ben Bella and Hoceine Aït Ahmed, politicians of stature, have not ceased to argue that it is impossible to identify the criminals responsible for the daily genocide in Algeria. How could a foreign press, preoccupied with its own circulation, and operating in the dark, pretend to longer-standing expertise on what is going on in Algeria than the Algerians themselves, with local antennas, and well-known to one another? Who other than Ben Bella, the first president of the Algerian Republic and one of the principal leaders in Algeria's resurrection, could give clearer knowledge of what is happening in Algeria? On 16 November 1997 he stated in the Spanish newspaper *El País:*

> There is a time for war and a time for peace; everything has its limit, and we are there . . . but at some time or other the military must return to their barracks and let the people speak. Algeria is a country rich in phosphates, petroleum, gas, mercury, and gold, and it is the military that control everything and fight among themselves to do so . . . We have come to the point where no one knows any longer who is doing the killing and who isn't. Algeria has many parapolitical organisms that were created during the liberation. These groups have been turned into infernal killing machines aimed at the people. . . . There is a market in crime where not only the GIA [*Groupe Islamique Armée*] take part—who kill among themselves—but also the police, the army, and still others engaged in the service of the regime who commit similar if not even worse atrocities. What all these killers have in common is that they are not alone: there is always some general covering for them. The war and its executions have been privatized; tribal warfare and warfare among mafias for whom the stakes are fantastic economic interests.

The accusations of the former Algerian minister, Abdelhamid Ibrahimi, are more crushing and more detailed than the declarations of president Ben Bella and the testimony of Aït Ahmed, cofounder or the FLN and current head of the FFS [*Front des Forces Socialistes*].

Ibrahimi, who has spent ten years in the Algerian government since before 1992, of which four were as prime minister, denounces the "heavy industry of slaughter" of civil killings; he singles out three Algerian army generals by name and lists their offenses. Like Aït Ahmed and numerous other members of the opposition, he insists that he can back up his charges with proof. Brought up in the seraglio of Algeria's only party, the FLN, and conversant with its ins and outs, he affirms that militia recruits, armed and directed by the three generals in question, number more than 200,000, and that the atrocities committed by police agents and the military-partisan nomenklatura are blamed on the Islamists in order to discredit them.[10]

Ibrahimi has been prosecuted by the Algerian government and the military junta for defamation. The same have demanded the extradition of this rebel who divulges state secrets. Granted refuge in Great Britain, this "Mr. Truth" has been invited about a little bit in Europe to places where minds that are not roped in are disposed to listen to his important witness. Only France and Spain declare their unconditional alignment with the government case issuing from the very democratic regime of General-President Liamine Zeroual.

The elections bossed by the three generals courageously fingered by Ibrahimi unfurl on the backdrop of the daily tragedy. Today as I write,[11] a former Algerian minister named Mrani announces that the government in which he takes part has freed criminal prisoners by common law and that they have been given every possibility of devoting themselves to the massacre of the people. The treason of corrupt personages has subjected Algeria to fire and blood.

Next door in Morocco, the tragedy, although not as daily nor as savage and horrible as that in its neighboring country, is no less flagrant. Actors in the comedy called "consensual rotation"[12] have stepped onto our stage. (It is to be noted how the vocabulary of democracy has grown.)

One of our most responsible personalities declared publicly that the former parliament, while it was in session, was nothing but a circus. Since the installation of the government of "consensual rotation" and the two subordinate chambers, it's a veritable Punch-and-Judy show. The show has taken on more extras, the music is new, but it's the same comedy.

The socio-consensual government of Makhzenian-formula rotation had hardly been inaugurated before it definitely adopted, as a program of reforming the university, the treatment applied by the Israeli Itzhak Rabin to Palestinian children. Students wearing beards or veils are the object of systematic slaughter. Their heads are staved in, their shins broken, their ribs cracked, their shoulders put out of joint, their femurs fractured, their knees smashed: the students, in short, are given a masterly course in democracy replete with practical studies.

The reputation of our consensual democracy is ruined when too many Islamist students are brought to trial on charges of political activity. So, it is more discrete to reduce the group to putty by breaking the bones of the leaders. The whole crowd of Islamist students is fit, pure and simple, to be shut out of the university.

What kind of present is this after forty years of the country's independence? What future for the country is prepared by the politics of violence against vital elements of the nation?

Does the violence come from the peaceful students defending their rights, or from the authorities who transform the campuses into barracks—and the amphitheaters into slaughterhouses?

In the European parliament, it is France and Spain that spearhead a policy of unconditional support for Algeria's bloody regime. In their Moroccan confrères' access to government, the socialist International sees a large step toward democracy—even when they know that the elections here continue to be subject to tinkering and shameless frauds, and that the famous "consensual rotation" is merely an episode in a two-bit tragicomedy.

So?

Well, for one thing, let aging Europe, our neighbor forever, stop forging hypotheses from fantasies. The region's tormented stability, which it props up by betting on the losing horse in the short- or midterm, will never find its footing until the truth is discovered and accepted. Only the building founded on solid rock can last; castles constructed on shifting sands inevitably collapse.

Our cousin Europe's secular protégés are fully aware of the error on which their constructions are based; they have constantly refused to allow a neutral inquiry commission to shed light on what is happening. These ill-chosen protégés do not want their past predations to be exposed to the world—nor their present crimes. The killers who now wear masks were the same who came forward with uncovered faces the day they interrupted the electoral process.

When will the talents for fencing stolen goods developed by a press devoted to disinformation yield to fairness and honesty? Our cousin Europe owes it to us to see us as we are, and not as a certain out-of-date Eurocentrism would have us appear. The electoral triumph of the FIS [*Front Islamique de Salut*] demonstrates that the Algerian people, bullied for so long by an implacable colonialism and by an alienated and corrupt political class, can only be confident of those with whom it identifies itself: Muslims faithful to God (exalted be His Name!) and those who announce a program of justice and moral probity.

Let aging Europe put up with accepting us for who we are, and let us make our entrance on the stage of cooperation, on our terms, without imposing conditions. Fairly and uprightly, reciprocal recognition and mutual respect will iron out the difficulties and permit a fruitful exchange, with dignity and with the interests of each guaranteed. The European Union cannot fly unless the wing of this side of the Mediterranean is healthy and in working order.

As for us, it is inconceivable that we should seek to satisfy our need of modernization and development from far-away regions so long as Europe, united, renewed, and strong, is within calling distance.

Notes

1 I write Islam with an uppercase initial when I mean the Muslim peoples, their civilization, their presence, both globally and, particularly, as immigrant minorities in the West. I write *islam* (italicized) when I mean submission to God—avoiding as much as possible the word "religion" (with its ambiguous connotations).

2 TN: The color green is emblematic of Islam.

3 TN: *modernité;* "modernity," inspired by the French, is, according to the *OED*, first found published in 1627.

4 Published by Fayard (Paris) and cited by D. Wolton in his *Penser la communication* (Paris: Flammarion, 1997), p. 384.

5 TN: "Submission" is the meaning of the word *islam.*

6 Op. cit., ibid.

7 Ibid.

8 Ibid.

9 Op. cit., ibid.

10 See, for example, *Le Monde* of 11 Feb 1998.

11 TN: 26 February 1998.

12 TN: *Alternance consensuelle;* critics of the policy point out that no "rotation" has been forthcoming.

II. Islam and Secular Society

1 Secularism: The Divorce of State and Church

Secularism[1] is the principle of separation of civil and religious society, the state exercising no religious power, nor the Church political power. It is the heart of French modernity. Its somewhat attenuated and more conciliatory form is the modern way of being democratic and tolerant with other Europeans. In France it is a militant religious indifference; elsewhere it is a facile secularization of life. This is because the violent rejection of the Catholic Church took place two hundred years ago in Paris, not in Berlin or London.

France's relationship with its former colonies—Algeria especially—is grounded, in the realm of the passions, with such typical anticlerical virulence. Add to this the bellows with which the media fan the flames of discord, and there's a chart of the political and psychological troubles of Algeria's conflagration. Booted beyond the borders, antireligious France cannot stop ruminating on the memory of a forever lost "French Algeria."

She cannot stop nourishing hopes that these bearded youths and veiled women disappoint when they burst suddenly onto a political scene forbidden by definition to the religious. Such confusion is hard to excuse from a France that occupied Algeria for a hundred and thirty years. Surely this was long enough for them to have realized that *islam* has no clerical structure, and that the separation of religion and politics is impossible, for the simple reason that allegiance to God among us cannot abide interference with one's person. The affair has always been personal, the relation to God direct: notions of secularity and religious indifference are foreign to *islam*.

Simple and good, that is reason enough. The other reason that can be invoked—and it is bad and historically complicated—is that the jurisconsults among us, those who pronounce judgments according to our law, have always been either reduced to silence altogether, or ranked willy-nilly alongside the sovereign as temporal and spiritual leader.

Thirty years after the death of the Prophet (grace and peace be upon him!), during which his chosen successors, the four caliphs, exercised power, this authority was usurped, and the word "caliph" came to have nothing more than vestigial meaning, a high-sounding title the dictator of the moment assumed in order to clothe his actual authority with the fiction of legitimacy. But never was this usurped political authority declared overtly hostile to *islam*.

Even the religiously indifferent who now govern us earnestly inscribe in their constitutions (if such exist) that their regime is Islamic. The Francophones among us, like Anglophones elsewhere, practice a religious indifference that is both a cultural given and a modern "religion," though they never do so blatantly before a people deeply attached to its identity—whatever its collective or individual shortcomings. Such is not the case in Europe, where a long process of dechristianizing has resulted in a veritable detachment from all religions—except the ones called modernity and post-modernity that we shall soon be examining.

The process of revolution in France, prepared by Enlightenment philosophy and, in 1789, broached with the general support raised and directed by an "intellectual" middle class, led in 1801 to laicization by the concordat signed by Napoleon Bonaparte and Pope Pius VII. After a good deal of violence and convulsion, the anti-feudal and anticlerical French Revolution settled for the compromise negotiated between a general promised an imperial destiny and a pope on the defensive. According to the concordat, the French majority is recognized as Catholic—not the state, but the Church's honor is safeguarded—and it is the head of state who is to designate bishops: the pope is to content himself with imparting his canonical benediction on them afterwards. The triumph of "Holy Secularity"[2] is consummated.

The process of laicization, so abrupt and brutal in France, took much longer and was more nuanced elsewhere. The sixteenth-century Lutheran Reformation in the Germanic principalities subsided into a "religious peace" that guaranteed to each his choice of cult. The tolerance expressed in the concept of *cuius regio religio* is affirmed even in our days by the fact that the German federal state still assesses a religion tax that it redistributes to the various Churches.

England's Henry VIII concluded a treaty with the pope of Rome that wrests his kingdom from the authority of the Catholic Church so as to reunite spiritual and temporal power in the hands of the king. Anglicanism is a state religion, and Elizabeth, for example, is both the queen and the head of the Church of England. It is true that, nowadays, public opinion in England, so worked up over—and moved by—the spectacle of the carryings-on of its princes and princesses royal, is slowly heading toward secularization, toward the gentle separation, perhaps definite divorce, between the ancient institution and the British throne.

The case of the Americas is special. The president of the United States swears the oath of office on the Bible; in Latin America, a militant Catholicism dedicated to the rights of the poor is regaining popularity.[3]

In our days, the secularized states of Europe gently register in their constitutions the religion by which their country is recognized. Certain constitutions go so far as to forbid access to presidential function to anyone who is neither Catholic nor Protestant. The British constitution (unwritten, though in effect) is an example of this, as is that of Sweden, the U.S.A., Switzerland, Spain, and Ireland.[4]

2 "Holy Secularity"

The phrase was coined by François Burgat,[5] a fine observer of the evolution of Islam, and one whose contribution to the debate about this burning issue merits particular attention. While the subject's "specialists" remain in the shadows of their study, Burgat deserves praise for having sought information where it is to be found. While sociologists lecture at length from their armchairs about Muslim societies and the Islamist phenomenon, he is the one who surprises the actors on the spot.

Rare indeed are those Europeans who avoid the prejudices of their time concerning the fact of *islam.* With very few exceptions, French journalists are particularly handicapped in this regard, ever harping on the nation's still lively acrimony over the emancipation of Algeria. Even the learned French, whom Burgat takes on with especial verve, remain cooped up in the sanctuary of their "holy secularity" that obscures their horizons and prevents them from being objective.

Burgat also deserves merit for attacking the idolatrous environment and briskly disabusing the secularist with iconoclastic methodology. An artful exegete as well, he presses the art of detection to the point where he holds the trumps. With direct access to the Arabic text—he speaks the language perfectly—he interprets accurately; he hides his knowledge of your language from you so as better to "nab" you by making you struggle to respond in your belabored, rough-and-ready French. By the turn of a single phrase he will be able to detect your cultural shortcomings; he spots your problems in expressing yourself when perhaps you flounder without recourse to your everyday vocabulary, when a lapse betrays your political intentions.

What indeed can this so atypical researcher and writer have to tell us about *islam* and the problem of religious indifference?

Noting the difference in the way Muslims and Frenchmen understand secularism, he poses this question:

> For some years now, from Cairo to Algiers, in Amman or Sanaa, "secularist" has become a term used to describe political enemies. How can one of the most cherished values of French culture come to be taken as a connotation of infamy by our closest neighbors? By what historical alchemy has our "good" become their "ill"? How are we to understand "secularism" as used by those who curse it and renounce its present spread?[6]

Burgat's concern from the onset is to inquire about the other's point of view, and he takes the laudable methodological precaution of not falling into the fleeting impressionism and doctrinal aberration of those who, to the detriment of objectivity, observe reality through the wrong end of their binoculars.

> In order to understand how a value so central to us could elsewhere have acquired so negative a sense, we must retrace the logic of how it burst in upon those who reject it today so passionately.[7]

I should add that a cultural grid that does not take into account the evolution through time of the concepts and dispositions of a society cannot situate the present state of others without relating it to its own past. The exact bearings of history escape the superficial observer, especially one who is driven by malicious inclinations. The result is thus blind defiance and a refusal to see.

> For the North, secularization is the capacity of the French revolutionary society to put a well-regarded end to clerical tutelage, the emergence of a political order finally freed from "arbitrary religious law," and a guarantee of the rights and novel liberties of individuals and minorities alike. For others, however, the same word has a very different taste, the marked moldiness of retreat.[8]

To put it in other words, the secularization so positively acquired in France's history is, in the experience of Muslims, the weapon with which France came to North Africa and destroyed its liberty. The same distancing from religion which shored up the French occupier then is now brandished by Algerian secularists as an instrument of liberation, an ideological argument, and a weapon of war furbished and refurbished in the struggle against *islam* and against those who would reclaim it as the sole truth. Islamists, aware of the wolf ever prowling about the sheepfold, combat the wolf and its progeny by struggling against this concept-become-ideology despite its historical contradiction. In so doing they merely put a name to the oppression Muslims have undergone during the hundred and thirty years of occupation and more than three decades of independence.

> Secularization, for the Islamists who combat it, has never existed as a guarantee of rights or further liberties. This is because its arrival coincided with the triumph of the armies of the West. Beyond this, however, within their sometimes reductivist but never unfounded logic, it has rather served to guarantee the rights of the foreigners who imported it, or the non-Muslim minorities, Christian or Jewish, those foreigners often empowered in establishing their domination.[9]

It is clear that the secularism imported into Algeria in the luggage of an invading army was part and parcel of the colonial arsenal with which the armed forces raped a territory and prepared the ground for the expropriation of lands and the violation of the culture and sacred tradition of Muslims. Muslim law, by which life was regulated, either effectively or symbolically according to particular regimes and eras, was dethroned in favor of secular laws framed to institutionalize juridically the fact of colonialization. The brutal intrusions of a foreign body, secular laws, and ideology, resented today as aggression and denounced in all conscience by Islamists, existed during the colonial era as sad proof of how the living flesh of Muslims was torn away.

> This secular stance, intriguing as a Trojan horse, is thus perceived above all as the most pernicious of the West's ideological weapons: it was the one that gave juridical assent and respectability to killing off the normative system of Islam during the heyday of the colonial adventure. It has thus come to lend credence to the idea that the inherited normative capital of nearly fourteen centuries of Islamic civilization is suddenly no longer fitting to guide an entire society.[10]

Secularization—and what it meant to the Muslims of the colonial era—is analyzed today in terms of an "overturned juridical regulation," a "detested cultural alienation," and the disturbance of civilized order. But it was rejected by first the resisters of colonial occupation—as it is by contemporary Islamists—above all as a threat to their reason for existing, their Islamity, their allegiance to God, their faith. Unfortunately, Burgat's analysis hardly speaks of this primary aspect of the rejection of *islam*, then as now, of the conquest of colonialism and its neocolonial prolongation. Religion being a forgotten, misunderstood, or unknown issue in the sphere of Western intellectuals, however whole and intelligent they might be, it would be an epistemological incongruity for them to speak of God, the Qur'an, and the resurrection after death in the same way Islamists speak of these matters—certain Islamists, at least: those whom Burgat hasn't the time to address, or who conceal their intention, judging the debate too intimate or putting it between parentheses.

3 The Secular Crusade

If in dealing critically with history your conceptual categories are disengaged from the sacred, if you express yourself with words that have been "disinfected," words that are allergic to the sacred, you can only achieve a mechanical analysis of violent passions. Profound inspirations are beyond the reach of political perception. That is why the secular outsider's research never get farther than socio-political and economic phenomena.

Burgat, more sensitive to cultural motivations, sees in Islamist effervescence and its success a movement comparable to a "cultural revolution." He speaks of the ultimate phase in a process of liberation of Muslim societies: political emancipation, followed by economic independence—both illusory—have brought Muslims disappointment as they await the restoration of their cultural identity.

While most commentators on Islam see the Islamist phenomenon as merely the onrush of striking, unemployed, and despairing youth, responding to a promise of jobs and well-being, our author rejects this summary point of view as being an analytical dead end. More judicious, he alludes to the rich Islamists of the Gulf Emirates, neither desperate nor marginal, giving the lie to the usual thesis, and lending favor to the idea of powerful cultural determination.

That is about as discerning as the best authors get.

Elsewhere one encounters all too often, even among the ranks of Islamists, people indignant at the blows to their cultural identity struck by the West, denouncing the crusade and the offensive aimed against their symbolic patrimony, without going deeper to criticize the nefarious effect of the total aggression that victimizes us: the spiritual dispossession, the flattening of one's being, the disfiguring of the soul.

To denounce the crusade and the total war is a fitting repartee to the modern assault of a West nourished, ever yet and evermore, by ancient sentiments of animosity and hostility. It is impossible to extirpate the memory implanted in people by secular history. There were crusades and religious wars between Catholic Christians and Muslims, and there are still crusades today, undertaken by a dechristianized and secularized West against a Muslim world still faithful in its obedience, and whose spokesmen at the front of the action and in sight of the future are Islamists.

In calling up the past, it behooves us to exorcise the demons of hatred and violence. Nothing can grow in the spiteful silence but the darkest plots of revenge. That is why the frank and honest recalling of certain historical facts can initiate a salutary catharsis. An honorable improvement in the general interest is conditional on disabusing our minds of mistrust and leading them once again to knowledge. It is the condition for the peace of a better future that we await for the propitious propagation of the Message of human brotherhood that is *islam.*

Whatever our quarrel with the divorce of state from the Church, and its liberal and liberating corollary, democracy, the rights of man, fortunately, open wide to us the spacious pathways leading to the individual consciences of Westerners cut off from spirituality and deprived of direction. Our sincere and dearest vow is to make known the Message of *islam*, not one of making war and igniting hatred among people. The secular democracy from which we shall keep our distance throughout this development is our ally the moment it allows people to embrace the truth of their choice, and the choice of their truth.

This course may well surprise the militants of political causes—on either shore: for us, the preeminence of bringing the appeal of *islam* to individual consciences conditions the rest. Political and economic combat, the development of our straggling countries, plundered by global neocapitalism—these are very important aims, but humanity's right to know the truth concerning its being remains the ultimate goal.

When speaking of God, of the supreme right of mankind, and of the means of gaining eternal happiness after death, it is indispensable to show as well the historical course of another strategy, one that consists of obstructing and thwarting, of outfitting humans with blinkers and ear-plugs so as to prevent them from seeing and hearing. The preventive information crusade and the current repression of everything that is not pro-Western—and thus modern—acquit themselves of such a charge in the name of perfection and "civilized" ways, with no cunning or hypocrisy intended of course.

Let us take a look at the crude and brutal way the religion first of the Church and, later, of "Holy Secularity" launched their hostile plots against *islam*. In all candor, their intents and actions have an advantage over modern ferociousness at least in being transparent; modernity hides its crimes behind blustering and lying slogans.

Secularism took up the banner under which the entire Holy Church waged war against the Muslim. Which was the fiercer battle? Not the one you may think: secularism is more hateful and more determined in other ways.

With spontaneous frankness, Pope Urban II harangued his flock at Clermont in 1095, exhorting them against "a cursed race, a race utterly turned away from God." This race so slandered by Christian vindictiveness was Muslim, those who "invaded Christian land." The supreme pontiff's preaching inflamed his listeners:

> "Be not a degenerate generation, let all hatred between you dissipate, let all quarrels end, let all war cease! Take to the road! Go to the Sacred Sepulcher to snatch this ground from the cursed race and subdue them! It is God's will!"[11]

With such vehement imprecations the man of the Church unleashed no less than two hundred years of wars between the Christians of an allied Europe and Muslims, principally of the East. Eight savage expeditions were organized by the Europeans under the sign of the cross, under the ægis and with the direct and frightfully snarling inspiration of the Church. Eight Crusades with their varied outcomes: the first crusades opened the gates of Jerusalem after a slaughter in which 70,000 Muslims were massacred. The blood of the victims flooded the streets (so wrote the horrified Arabic chroniclers of the time), and horses floundered in the scarlet flow: this was war!

Two centuries later, when our Salah ad-Din (Saladin) chased the Franks from Jerusalem, it was the European chroniclers who marveled at the magnanimity with which the grand chief treated the vanquished. History's revenge, the reverse of fortune: the taking of Jerusalem, then its liberation, and the contrast between the liberator's knightly tolerance and the conquerors' frightful bloodbath, give solemn lie to the prejudice that insists it is the Muslim who by definition is the bloodthirsty fanatic.

The Frankish kingdom in Jerusalem, as well as three other principalities and earldoms, had lasted two centuries, time enough for five or six generations of Europeans to become acquainted with Muslim civilization and bear witness to Europe of the more refined mores than those of feudal chivalry, heavily accoutered, haughty, mired in illiteracy, and reveling behind the walls of their medieval fortresses.

The influence on Europe of Muslim Spain was all the more a benefit for Europe, cut off as it was from the flow of civilization. The arts and sciences, crafts and trades, mathematics, astronomy, chemistry, and medicine brought about an extraordinary outburst of knowledge from Granada and Córdoba—the Gharnata and Qortoba of Islam. The Spanish *Reconquista* put an end to the fruitful exchange between two worlds, and Islam withdrew to its side of the Mediterranean.

The Inquisition of ecclesiastical police that chopped back European society to size from the 12th to the 18th centuries, fell implacably on the Muslims of Toledo, Córdoba, Seville, Grenada, and all the cities that had formerly been refuges and centers from which a brilliant civilization radiated. With Muslim and Jewish victims, the Spanish Inquisition was even more barbarous than with Christians.

The Church has a horror of spilling blood. For this reason it contented itself to interrogate its victims, breaking their bones and splitting their organs without spilling a single drop of the sacred liquid. Christian charity obliging, other affabilities of this sort were invented, causing no more than inoffensive bruising—such as extinguishing an eye by fire, or piercing an ear with a stiletto—quite within the rules: not a drop of blood. Albigensians and Jews were burned alive; suspected of being in league with the residual Muslim presence in the south of France, they passed through the hands of a most pious canonical executioner.

The incursion of Muslims into the south of France at the beginning of the 8th century was a mere lightning flash, but their establishment at Toulouse and environs lasted only long enough for the Franks to regroup and deal them a crushing defeat under Charles Martel. Such was the luck of arms, but the extermination of the vanquished and the inquisitorial persecution of every heretic charged with conniving with the Moor served only to promote a permanent crusade.

4 Secular Republics at Work

Here I mean to speak of two republics: the French Republic, which has been at it for close to two centuries, and the Algerian Republic that continues the work of its absent—but oh how present—parent. By "work" I mean the continuation of the Crusades over which both parent and child competently preside. Eight centuries have passed since the pope's exhortation at Clermont, and here is the same speech, secular now, more virulent still, even more violent, plainly racist, abject, inhuman.

The speech we are about to cite is even more incendiary than Urban's frank words. It dates from the end of the 19th century, but it serves as both a program for future work and a summary of past Western action against Muslims. The shockwave of the first armed Crusade, raised and incited by the Church, continued to figure century after century in Western discourse and thought, a message of rumbling rancor passed on and amplified generation after generation.

A rare externalizing of this groundswell, basely infamous but singularly outspoken, is offered by the renowned historian Ernest Renan. Renan, the priest *manqué* who reveals to us in his writings how he lost the faith and abandoned his clerical vocation, portrays himself as very firm and certain in his resolution to cry shame on the Muslim. The plucky defrocked priest decrees in 1862:

> At this very hour the essential condition for European civilization to expand is the destruction of Islamism.[12] That is the eternal war, the war that will not cease until the last son of Ishmael has died of misery or has been relegated to some remote desert. *Islam* is the most complete negation of Europe. . . . Europe will conquer the world and bestow on it its religion of law, liberty, and human respect, the belief that there is something divine in the human heart.[13]

Son of Ishmael, the Muslim of Renan's day was merely a distant outline of an absolute stranger. Now that Muslims populate the suburban catastrophes of French cities, the Renanian plan is more than ever the order of the day for pillorying the immigrant, doubly hated and exposed to contempt if he is found to be an Algerian. Le Pen's *Front National* is the embodiment of hatred for the Son of Ishmael.

What is going on is hardly less than a religious war—and one, moreover, of extermination. The "cursed race," that absolute negation of Europe, must be driven back to the desert; the sons of Ishmael have to be destroyed to the very last one. Eight years after Renan's murderously provocative speech, France suffered a crushing defeat in the war with Germany, united under Bismarck. France lost Alsace-Lorraine and swept all of Europe into the process that resulted in two world wars, one of whose aims was the dividing up of the countries of the children of Ishmael.

Algeria was a colonized and annexed country a generation before Renan's inciting speech. For him and those of the France of his day and for a century after, Algeria's identity was crystal-clear: a French land forever. The sons of Ishmael, along with their Berber cousins, were flattened, driven out of the fertile lands and reduced to the state of slaves drudging for their European lords. One hundred years before the political independence of Algeria, Renan announced from his lofty magisterial stance the extension of colonialism to all Muslim countries, now destined to suffer the fate of Algeria. The French defeat of 1871 was to tumble the Second Empire only to put the republic in the saddle and to radicalize laicization and secularism, and to reinforce the religion preached by the passionate ex-cleric.

Jules Ferry, another passionate contemporary of Renan's, lost no time in acquiring the portfolio of national education and then that of prime minister, in order to put into execution his methodic reform of laicization, which was to endow every Frenchman with the priesthood of "Holy Secularity." From now on primary school would be free, compulsory—and secular. Schoolmasters and -mistresses, resolute missionaries of modern religion, were sent to preach the gospel to the four corners of the French colonies, to shape native youth in the values of secularism and in total contempt of their identity. The "civilizing" work of secularist education was to complete the "pacification" begun by the armies of occupation.

Physical occupation has passed from view in our day, but the psychological and intellectual traumas still gnaw at the guts of people in the former playing-fields of colonialism. The Algerian abscess today is the monstrous eruption, the sequel, to the crime against humanity which was and is the outrage of the "eternal war" laid out by Renan and instrumented by Ferry's education reforms. A fiery continuation of the medieval assaults under the sign of the cross, the military onslaught of colonialism, however ferocious, could not destroy a people. But, opening the way, it allowed a cultural and moral destruction still perpetrated by the educational infantry. One can scarcely describe how profound the blow of colonial secularism has been to the moral being of Muslim peoples.

To jog the memory, as if to perform a therapeutic cauterization to heal the grudges between ourselves and our secular "eternal neighbors," here is the testimony of but one act of arms of colonial soldiery. A commission from the French parliament came to Algeria in 1833, some twenty-nine years before Renan's manifesto. As though to declare the effect of military order in the field and assure administrative compliance with regulations, the commission reports to those concerned:

> We have desecrated temples, tombs, and house interiors, sanctuaries among the Muslims. We have slaughtered entire populations later proved innocent. We have cast judgment on men reputed to be saints of their countries, venerated men.[14]

But this is not some administrative account filed to inform the leaders that its authors have acquitted themselves of a horrible mission. This is a commission of inquiry, doubtless conducted by a vigilant opposition. It is the voice of a democratic opposition that is driving the nail into the wall by decrying the treason of the government troops who have covered France's face with opprobrium with their barbaric crimes. It is to the conscience of a nation that the appeal is made with shock-phrases such as "we have slaughtered,"[15] "we have desecrated the temples and tombs."

It is one of the enviable aspects of modern Western democracies to be able to denounce the inadmissible. The torturing of FLN resisters during the Algerian revolution has finally been denounced, if not officially by a worthy son of France like General de Gaulle, at least by a free and outraged press. For want of leaders in Paris of the caliber of the general, who had foiled the schemes of the OAS of unhappy memory, the free press is there again, luckily, to reveal the hypocritical conspiracy between an Algerian "Republic" at bay and an official France little aware of its interests and even less disposed to consult the weather map of history to know which way the wind is blowing and whether a storm is impending.

This morning again, 23 October 1997, French newspapers—the independents, not the merchants of sensationalism—have published the testimony of a soldier who deserted from the Algerian army. According to him, the army trains soldiers to wear stick-on beards and butcher women and children in order to terrorize the population and heap discredit on the Islamist movement. Claims like his have been published continuously in France throughout the six years the drama has lasted.

Notes

1 TN: *Laïcité;* the definition, as Yassine acknowledges, is that of the *Dictionnaire Robert.* The concept reflects historical developments in France; there is thus no exact parallel in English. The distinctly anticlerical origins of the French secular state contrast with the nominally Christian secularism of the rest of Europe and (North) America. In the U.S., the debate over "separation of Church and State," though singular in its particulars, has certain parallels to the situation of secular government and religious fundamentalist organizations in Yassine's North African framework.

2 TN: See II:2 below.

3 TN: "Liberation theology" is, however, often in conflict with the institutional hierarchy.

4 See Tariq Ramadan's excellent book, *L'Islam, le face à face des civilisations* (Editions Tawhid, 1995), p. 129.

5 "Sainte Laïcité," in *L'islamisme en face* (Paris: Editions La Découverte, 1995).

6 Burgat op. cit., p. 70.

7 Ibid.

8 Ibid.

9 Ibid.

10 Ibid.

11 Antoine Sfeir, in *Atlas des religions* (Paris: Hachette-Jeunesse, 1990) [from the French].

12 A curious linguistic anticipation! These passion-charged words will rise up again like vengeful ghosts.

13 Cited by Vincent Monteil in *La pensée arabe* (Seghers, 1987), p. 191.

14 Cited in the prospectivist journal *Futuribles* (October 1995, no. 202), p. 23.

15 TN: *Nous avons égorgé* awakens the echo of the French national anthem, in which it is the forces of tyranny that butcher (*égorger*) "our children and companions."

III. Resistance: The Case of Algeria [1]

1 Resistance

When your country is laid waste and your kinsmen slaughtered, you suffer physical wounds and human loss. Your losses are material when you are dispossessed of your land and despoiled of your goods. So you resist to the death and ransom your honor by standing up to the enemy, even if his armament and organization heavily outweigh your flimsy equipment.

That is what the Algerians did for seventeen years under the leadership of their saintly chief Amir 'Abd al Qadir.[2] Individual and collective heroism set the example time and again over several generations—in vain. The people wind up drained, without further resource, just as the troops of that holy man, armed with their pop-guns and meager munitions, were met by heavy cannon well fed by colonial aggression.

But what is to be done when someone profanes your sanctuary, violates the tombs of your ancestors, and inflicts you with a moral wound much more serious than any other injury? What is to be done when, after occupation and "pacification" by fire and blood, someone attacks your soul? How do you oppose a normalizing strategy that kills your identity through constant vexation over the long haul? How do you respond to the secular schooling (both before and after the reform imposed by Jules Ferry) that cunningly and methodically robs you of what is essential to your future, having already overtaken and ruined your present?

Secular schooling ousted traditional schools even as the colonists were confiscating the lands. What the fact of colonialization meant for Muslim Algeria is in many ways an example for us, and Muslim resistance in Algeria, both past and present, illustrates the historical potential of the irreducible resistance that resides in the soul submitted to God, forever recalcitrant and rebellious under the yoke of tyranny.

To speak of Algeria—yet again, always Algeria, the Algerian drama—is thus not the symptom of a morbid fixation, but a soberingly concrete counter-lesson that has much to teach an Islam ever ready to sacrifice in order to preserve its dignity—and a modernity that seems not yet to have taken into account the urgency of a peaceful and negotiated solution to the contentious struggle between them.

The cyclical bouts of remorse that sweep the conscience of Europe, France in particular, are dwarfed by the detestable indifference that constitutes the daily bread of Western politics. It was not until the slaughter and genocide in Algeria became a daily affair and reached monstrous proportions until the official West, states and international institutions alike, began to take due notice of the scandalized protests of (chiefly Western) NGOs [nongovernmental organizations].

At the United Nations there is bashful talk of the Algerian problem, with allusions to possible interference. Then, offended and outraged by human rights allegations, the Algerian government rumbles at having its affairs snooped into—it is perfectly capable of mastering the situation quite by itself, like a grown-up—and the U.N. falls in behind it.

One keeps waiting for external intervention that will not come—or, as in Bosnia, will come only after half the people have been wiped out. Testimony denouncing and incriminating the military authorities continues to come from deserting soldiers. While Algeria's citizens wait for intervention that seems ever less likely, they witness assassins daily plying their macabre and horrible trade under the uncaring eye of the troops who are encamped a few hundred feet away, or who leave so as not to get in the way. How could it be otherwise? Aren't they in the same boat, under the same orders?

The Muslim people of Algeria and elsewhere wait for the periodic conscience of the West to flip between somnolence and those twinges that result in the odd diplomatic visit. Meanwhile, however, their resistance—in all its forms and strategies (like the feelings that inspire it)—will never belie the glorious legacy of their forebears.

The armed uprising led by Amir 'Abd al Qadir took its power and spontaneity from the ardor of the unbroken faith of a pious people assembled behind a revered man of God: 'Abd al Qadir's father, Muhi ad-Din, descended from a long and saintly line that enjoyed the unanimous respect of the armed tribes.

The lineage of Ben Badis is completely different.[3] The great man's contemporaries were differently disposed than the resisters of the emir's day. Seventy years of French occupation and repressive pedagogical "work" have attempted to distance Algerians from their source of inspiration and to cut off their traditional channels by repressing Qur'anic instruction in the *zawiyas*[4] which were desecrated and subjected willy-nilly to the colonial military administration.

Ben Badis went to the East to renew his roots, in Arabia, cradle of Wahabiism.[5] From there he came back laden with attainments, and he struggled courageously before being recognized, albeit conditionally and with ill will, by the authorities for the Association of the *'Ulama*[6]—the "literate natives," as the French disdainfully nicknamed them.

From the Sufi school of the *zawiyas* came 'Abd al Qadir and Muqrani and so many other saintly men and leaders of resistance; when this began to decline, other channels of a literalist *islam* prevailed, arising from the free Badisian schools or joined up with neo-Wahabiism. Ibn Taymiya remains the favorite author of the current imams of Algeria, as he is to some extent elsewhere.

Abbassi Madani,[7] a man with an open mind and solid upbringing, finds himself straddling several currents of thought. Wise and patient, he succeeded in reconciling the fiery tribunes of poised intellectuals more acquainted with what happens in the world. The intellectual tendency called *jaz'ara*—of deep Algerian origins[8]—identifying solely with Algeria, however doctrinally independent, is one of the important components of the FIS.

These more overt Islamists need not look outside their milieu for their authority: it is Malik ben Nabi, a highly ranked Algerian thinker whose renown extends widely beyond his country's borders. If a large segment of the Islamist movement, in North Africa and elsewhere, know neither the politics nor the doctrinal bases of the principal contemporary Sufi school, the Muslim Brotherhood, the abundant and beneficial production of this school is widely read by Islamists everywhere. The instruction of Sayyed Qoth, the Brotherhoods' great writer, nourishes their ideas along with the rigorous thinking of an Ibn Taymiya.

The literature of both of these rigorous *fatwas*[9] and their current productions determine each group's capacity for embracing both modern reality and classical teaching. The diversity of the literature is reflected in the organizing plan, and the form of resistance to hostile reality is graduated by political participation (so far disappointing though always reclaimed) in armed activism.

But the activism of a Bouyali[10] or that of the *Armée du Salut* has nothing to do with the inhuman proceedings of baby-killers. In fighting state terrorism, hand weapons are a legitimate defense, whereas attacking innocent civilians in as abject and dishonorable a manner is an unspeakable crime that no circumstance or contingency excuses.

No one, moreover, is able to prove any Islamist identity whatever of the killers. To imagine that after the interruption of the 1991 elections in Algeria the earthquake felt by a diverted formation would have disoriented elements driven mad with anger and spite, even Satan in a fiery foam would have been able to recruit if he could have put explosives and automatic weapons in your hands. The crime rests with the devils, not with *islam*.

Satan—that Satan, to be sure—is quite ready to invent both the existence of a rabble and the satanic stratagem of enlisting false-bearded types armed with hatchets to sow terror among the people and discredit the frustrated opponent. Cold steel replaces the automatic pistol, to have it believed that the criminal comes from the wretched and abominable fringe that all but won the elections, and to seize the power to run the country with an uncertainty and bloodletting illustrated by infant genocide. To make any human being shake with horror at the very idea of such creatures possibly seizing power, the image is presented to the world of monsters who chop children into pieces.

2 "We Are Muslims"

Let us pursue the topic of resistance to follow the course of the degradation of feelings that can have caused men to skid from the verdant summit of saintly nobility, Amir 'Abd al Qadir, to the disgusting Satanic scum clasping its threatened privileges, driven by the vilest of motives.

France arrived in Algeria as a conquering avenger. The spirit of the Crusades emboldened political leaders and military commanders. Marshal Bugeaud,[11] direct descendant of Europe's Napoleonic army, and sent to "pacify" the conquered land, did as he was expected. His friend Poujoulat, congratulating him in 1844 on his accomplishments, wrote: "You continue the work of Godefroy, of Louis VII, of Saint Louis. . . . Our Algerian war is indeed a continuation of the Crusades."[12]

In 1844 the Berber Kabyles formed, like the Arabs, behind an elected emir, reply to the crusade marshall's ultimatum: "We are Muslims . . . and God comes to our aid. Do not reckon us among the number of your subjects."

Today, more than a century and a half since that message from Berbers certain in their allegiance to God, the efforts of secular schooling have yielded the anticipated results: a handful of barbarous Kabyles call themselves simply Berber. The banners of an ethnicity embraced like a religion, and in sly partnership with Francophone interests, float over the headquarters of little parties converted to Amazighism, as they utter hypocritically—or, surely, complacently—the sincere and courageous cry of their ancestors, "We are Muslims!" Except that today's Amazighs[13] are engaged in a very different sort of combat than the one the ancient Kabyles gave, faithful to *islam,* counting on God's help, and entrusting their fate to a man of God.

Let us remind these amnesiacs that in 1871, one generation after the surrender of Amir 'Abd al Qadir, another holy man, Muqrani by name, declared *jihad* and gave combat to the crusading invaders. Muqrani, a Berber name, is the saintly champion of Berber *islam* who raised the banner of *jihad* and did battle with the colonial troops. He was defeated, crushed by the incommensurable imbalance between horsemen armed with primitive rifles and armed colonials equipped with cannon—the very cannon defeated that year by the Germans and turned now against the bare-chested peasants sacrificing themselves so that *islam* could live.

Is it surprising that the Amazigh congresses, financed by an all-too-well-known patronage, took place in France? Is it surprising that it was

France that collected North African Berber-speakers so that the ideologues of African racism from both shores could organize and indoctrinate a youth athirst for identity and uninformed of the nature of the plot against *islam*?

The sudden support of Amazighism we have witnessed is merely the reactivation of a front against Islamism that the colonial administration of Morocco opened in 1930 when it promulgated the villainous law, the Berber Dahir, by which the Muslim juridical system in vigor was to be replaced by a system of tribal custom. It was the Berbers themselves, like the Kabyle victims of Bugeaud, who were the first to protest this infamous law: "We are Muslims, we are Muslims!"

In response to Islamist claims, a lay coalition of Arabs and Amazighs sets aside its quarrels over other matters long enough to unite—since it is a matter of "bashing the bearded." But this is hardly the least of the obstacles that face Islamist plans. Ethnic dissension has taken its toll in Afghanistan, where Pashtos and Azeris tear at each other with the wild abandon of tribal totem worship, oblivious to their allegiance to God. To sow discord among the tribes has always been the favorite Trojan horse of schemers against *islam*.

Dividing peoples and making them doubt themselves is one way of martyrizing them; humiliating and dragging them down is another. In 1871, the year of double defeat, the year of illustrious resistance in Algeria in the face of imperialist troops—and of the imperial armies of Napoleon II in Paris—the code of the native population was promulgated at Algiers. Algerians by heritage were now citizens of an official second zone, some sort of peasantry to serve the aristocracy of white men.

Eighteen years later, in 1889, any European living in Algeria was honored by French nationality and could claim the privileges that afforded. Later, the Muslim was promoted from the status of native French subject to the conspicuously discriminatory category of French Muslim, to be carefully distinguished from French Frenchman.

Algerians wore their skin color as a sign of inferiority like the yellow star the Nazis were to force the Jews to wear. They had to produce, at every request, identity documentation duly attesting their racial blemish.

Jean-Marie Le Pen, at least, exercises his racial hatred and his mistrust of the other on his own turf—a sad distinction!

A little before World War I, when the authorities were in need of native cannon fodder, they dropped the ballast. Algerian natives, Muslim notwithstanding, were to acquit themselves of their "citizen's duty" by sacrificing tens of thousands of their youth, regimented and bombarded in the trenches of France and Navarre alongside their "fellow citizen" masters. Out of generous and condescending gratitude after the war, they were allowed the right to organize themselves in "nationalist" political parties.

It was at this moment, about 1920, that Ben Badis and his Association of *'Ulama,* men of knowledge and quality (though simple literate natives as far as their occupiers were concerned), came upon the scene to oppose the nationalist parties for their ambiguous identity, though daring enough to reclaim independence in 1919. In the matter of political reclaiming, Ben Badis's association would yield nothing to the nationalist parties.

Beyond the nationalist awakening the *'ulama* had in common with the better nationalists, the spearhead of their struggle focused on the essential: the Islamic nature of the Algerians. I speak of "better nationalists" since there were worse ones as well who, until the eve of independence in 1962, sought nothing further than obtaining full French nationality. Naturalization, after being bestowed on Europeans and Jews, was offered to those Algerians who could defy the public opinion of an Algeria that remained Muslim to the core.

Knowing this, the association of Islamic sages lay in wait. Ben Badis's password was simple indeed: Algerians are Muslims, and their bond with Arabhood is solid. The conviction was beautifully expressed in a famous poem by the Master.

In 1938, a manifesto from this organization aroused the indignation of the Algerian people against the colonial attempt to naturalize Algerians by luring them with the prerogatives that had up to then benefited Europe alone. The virtuous sages were formal: whoever accepted the offer of naturalization would immediately abandon *islam*, and when they died could not be buried in the Muslim cemetery.

However secularized or unbelieving an Algerian, no one could bear being buried in unhallowed ground. The great majority—everyone, in fact, except a tiny wavering element—had always kept the faith of their fathers and mothers buried in their hearts; they would not expose themselves to God's wrath and incur eternal damnation by denying that faith. Others whose faith was wavering or absent nonetheless feared to attract the opprobrium of their own people, since it was a badge of shame to have a family member buried among the infidels.

3 Changing People

It was the German poet and playwright Bertold Brecht who said, "Power no longer trusts the people; we must change the people!" The witty saying exactly expresses the answer the military partisans tried to put into practice during the "hold-up" of the 1991 elections—and the one French colonialism had tried to apply for a hundred and thirty years. Even as the French achieved no lasting result, the current government's response has no future.

Thank God, despite political gangsterism, brutal repression, a taming and secularizing education, the interdenominational squabbles of European missionaries to Algeria, and the naturalizing—and denaturing—seduction of Algerians practiced by the colonial administration—(that miscarried, thanks to the indignant insurrection of a people united behind their imams)—the essential nature of the Muslim people cannot be changed.

"Taking on a non-Muslim nationality," according to the manifesto of Ibn Badis, "means abandoning one's Muslim status. The renunciation of a single Qur'anic precept is synonymous with apostasy. One who has been naturalized is thus a renegade."[14]

Addressed "to the Muslim people of Algeria, to the French government, and to the French," Badis's 1938 manifesto had its effect. The colonial administration, unable to bribe the people with the crude ruse of naturalization, attempted to finesse its position in vain—or nearly so—through political and cultural means. The sages of *islam* kept watch and waged their combat of resistance.

In 1950 they cast off colonial politics, which "had lost no occasion to scoff at *islam* in a country where it has been in full bloom for some thirteen centuries."[15] Ibn Badis's rallying cry—"*Islam* is my faith, Arabic my language, and Algeria my homeland"—came to be heard from more and more lips.

But a hybrid slogan, brandished by nationalists, hesitated between an *islam* necessary to win the Muslim masses and a modernity without which political action would be no more effective than the traditional peasant resistance. The situation was as depicted by 'Abdelhamid Shorfa, an Algerian intellectual, in his judicious and well-documented analysis (if perhaps pessimistic with regard to future prospects) published in the journal *Futuribles* I have several times cited above:

> It will be recalled that the colonial period in Algeria, as throughout the rest of the Arabic-Islamic world, was to have decisively engendered, from the outset, a shriveling up of *islam* on the part of the large mass of disinherited populations from the towns and countryside, illiterate or with very little Arabic, but very pious, that were soul of the resistance. The checking of uprisings led under the banner of *islam,* and the discovery meanwhile of the rules of a political game of French society, gave rise to an *aggiornamento* of resistance that has had recourse to the political opposition thanks to the biases of the legal parties. The functioning logic of these parties, requiring the refuge of a discourse whose reference point is a Western value system, has been resented by the Arabic intelligentsia as suspect and potentially liable to create a drifting in the organization of Islamic resistance.
>
> The birth of the Association of *'Ulama* denotes this preoccupation with political watchfulness, and it constitutes, by virtue of this fact, the first step of *islam* in the direction of statesmanship. From that time on, fundamentalism began its incubation, and the demarcation between Nationalist

> Secularist francophones and Authentic Algerian Arabist Muslims was squarely placed on the tracks of history.[16]

I should say that the split between secular francophones and authentic Islamists is justifiable not only by the manner in which the political parties function; the cunning and pernicious action of secularizing pedagogy and the daily shoulder rubbing with the European population resulted in an erosion of the profound sense of belonging to *islam* in certain French-speaking Algerians. The sense of identity had been more or less eroded in certain cases, but obliterated completely in a tiny and politically insignificant minority, who were treated by the populace as degenerate pariahs.

As for Algerianness, the francophones stake an even greater claim than the Arabists, by making it their platform for ideological resistance. When the sages teach the people that they are first and foremost Muslims and that their allegiance to God links them with an Arabic universe and the much broader universalism of the world of Islamic events, the secularists in contrast insist on the Algerianness of Algeria, without however renouncing the facile slogan (with its certain political payoff), "We are all Muslims."

In the countries of North Africa and elsewhere here and there among the formerly colonized Muslim countries, the political class that governs was formed (and deformed) by modern, more or less secularized, schooling—more perhaps since independence than before. To be modern is to be secular. But secularism expresses itself politically by an attachment to a territory, geography, or nation-state, not to the history of the Muslim community, the *Ummah*.

The West's sickness of enclosure within bitterly defended borders at the cost of atrocious wars, is picked up by former natives imbued with secular modernity as a sign of sanity. To create local color and attest to its nationality and nationalism, fidelity to the national language is proclaimed far and wide, even by francophones unlettered in Arabic. The Arabic-speaker head of state Boumediene is the exception that proves the rule.[17]

On the eve of independence, francophone nationalists of the North African countries were co-opted by their European counterparts in leading the negotiations and concluding the treaties. It was the ultimate attempt to "change the people" and to institute "valid spokespersons" suited to one's purpose, hold them out at arm's length so as to keep them in power, and thus guarantee the project's result. Wondrous how "our people" ran the show!

In independent Algeria, after several settlings of accounts and a coup d'état, French-schooled francophones took hold of the administration and monopolized influential posts, marginalizing or blacklisting altogether the Arabist component trained in Badisian Qur'anic schools.

Resistance: The Case of Algeria

Jacques Berque, former civil controller in the colonial administration, "friend of the Arabs" and himself an Arabist of renown, never ceased to depict in his finely honed literary prose the deeds, accomplishments, and spiritual state of the numerous friends this professor at the Collège de France made throughout his brilliant career. Here, casting the glance of an outsider on the Algerian intelligentsia, he offers another facet of the portrait sketched for us by Shorfa:

> Was it necessary, at the beginnings of independence in Algeria, for traditionalist *al-qiâm* values[18] to be opposed to socialism? What metaphysical values would stand in the way of evolution, and what becomes of historical values if they abandon the unchangeable truths the people cling to?[19]

The problem is precisely as our keen observer has posed it, writing long before the arrival on the political scene of an opposition between the Islamists, in whom the people recover a "metaphysical" truth, and the self-recommended secularists, self-proclaimed as the sole guarantors of a democratic evolution.

Here precisely a portrait of "democracy's champions" who, a decade after Berque's book appeared, are smothering democracy for fear those designated as its "metaphysical" enemies touch its spotless robe. Since Berque's examination of the secular intelligentsia, it has only grown more treacherous and ruinous.

> For a long time now the intelligentsia has been harping on its themes. Any entire romantic literature bespeaks frustration and loss. What the intellectual is actually debating is between the influence of power, parochial sectarianism, confessional networks and solidarity, on the one hand, and, on the other, the requirements of his status as an intellectual which, alone, allows him to interpret the will of the people after his fashion.[20]

The author speaks of intellectuals torn between a borrowed culture and the traditional values to which the popular masses are attached. The intelligentsia is not entirely constituted of engaged intellectuals, and those who are engaged are not all politically militant, nor are all militants in positions of power. But the whole of this little francophone world breathes the same air of frustration. Sectarianism and solidarity along factional and familial lines are everyone's lot. The common stamp is the concern of the intellectual type to honor his elitist position by interpreting the will of the masses "after his fashion."

Some thirty years after Algerian independence, another elite rises with new strength and an active will, having long remained in the shadows so as to cultivate its values and gather its forces: the Islamists. The traditional values of *al-qiyâm* manifested itself at the university, where confrontation between secularists and Islamists could not be long in coming. The FIS of Abbassi Madani and the passionate Ali Belhadj[21] burst upon the political scene, forcing the everyday drift of the Algerian drama to turn to serious matters.

4 The Leprosy of Humankind

Torture. Sow the wind and reap the storm, as the adage has it. But what will be the harvest when the seed is storm from the outset? In the first part of this chapter we read part of the report of the parliamentary commission of an inquiry that branded the profanation of Muslim sacred space and the systematic slaughter of Algerian Muslims.

Tens of thousands of Algerian Muslims were mown down by machine-gun fire during the upheaval at Sétif in 1945 by an army that had survived a historic defeat in World War II and were now avenging their honor by dealing with unarmed civilians. The torture of an entire people by the French army during the Algerian Revolution remains an indelible stain in the military and civilian annals of colonialism.

We share the indignation and disgust of the NGOs over what takes place in Algeria. But indignation is not enough: one must see to its being changed, and to do that requires understanding. For mercy's sake let us look upstream to see how the disorder took shape, and what kind of contagious epidemic flogs the innards of a martyred society.

Humanity's leprosy is torture; it is an illness latent in the nature of low, mean-spirited souls. Like a virus that thrives in the broth of a nourishing culture, the torturer is in his element in today's political chaos.

We have reviewed the actors of this drama, the Islamists that came out of the political vacuum to spoil the party for the ruling elite, immured in its privileges and self-contained in its sectarianism. The victim, now made to bear the blame for the daily genocide in the streets, is henceforth to be the agent of the crimes. The origin of the situation has been forgotten, the motive of the crime no longer known. How has this come about? What set of circumstances have led the blows and counterblows to the catastrophe we have now?

A record of more than 800 pages, titled *Livre blanc sur la répression en Algérie* [*White Paper on Repression in Algeria*], has recently been published in Switzerland.[22] These pages, red with the blood of Islamist victims, are poignant testimony, with names of persons, dates, and the dreary locations of torture. Here are recorded in detail the methods of the hooded—and sometimes barefaced—torturers. It is a catalog of the last word on the subject of cruelty: ripped out teeth and eyes, broken shins, cracked ribs, and other indulgences of this sort. Electrodes and chemical products complement the macabre punishment.

O horror and curse!

In their cultural genes the torturers bear the heritage of the gentleman, educated at the Collège de France, whose administration was instituted at the time when he officiated in Algeria and Morocco as a civil controller. He knows his milieu inside-out; having grown up under guardianship, later, after independence, given authority, he knows what he is talking about when he reckons the distance between the former pupils of colonialism and the Muslim population clinging to their "unchangeables."

Schizophrenics newly come to power defend at all costs their prerogatives and the prebendary State, their *raison d'être* and the singular source of the comfort and prestige they enjoy. Let the people come in their gowns and veils to threaten the present and future of the masters of the house and let the beast go at it tooth and nail. The chief of the brigade, of military rank or agent of the lofty works of the republic, wears the boots of the French adjutant who, not long ago, filled the same offices now fallen to national frustration.

Whether or not subjected to colonial torture himself, he has become an expert in the field. A member of the intelligentsia in power knows how to hang on.

Given the upper hand, the lay clerk of a democracy, having become the assassin of democracy, clings to his instruction and his justification of classical Machiavelianism by which any prince is lost who does not make use of violence and more violence. Paired with pitiless Florentine cruelty, the school of wily craft still holds forth.

A socialist, perhaps, nourished on Leninist theory, he holds true to the expeditious methods of Stalinism, whether undercover or in the open. For him the methods of changing people amounts to an industry copied from the land of the gulag. For it is a gulag these shameless fundamentalists want who come to usurp power by means of a democratic middle-class ballot!

I will spare my reader the dreadful scenes of torture, collective or individual, and let my Islamist brothers speak. I do not know whether the founding president of the Algerian league for the defense of human rights, Professor Abdenour Ali-Yahya, takes upon himself the qualification of Islamist—so discredited throughout the world; but he has with exemplary courage taken up the duties of a man of law and a man of honor. In his preface to the book titled *Algérie en murmure,*[23] the valiant jurist writes:

> Algeria has yet to strike a balance between her past and her future, between her history and her modernity. Met with crises of society and power, Algeria incurs two dangers—taking economic insolvency as a measure of political failure: (1) an already rotting political life will grow worse, with a high price in human life, and significant economic, financial, and social cost; (2) civil war is inevitable, unless the power in place takes into consideration a platform of a social contract that delivers an overall peaceful solution as a way out of the crisis.

The Social Contract mentioned here is the pact signed in Italy by the members of a coalition of Algerian opposition parties and the military-partisan regime of Algiers comprising particularly the Islamists of the FIS and the Berber socialists of the FFS. Sponsored by the Catholic association of San Egidio, the act is denounced by the power in place and dismissed as a scandalous interference in the internal affairs of a sovereign state.

The Social Contract has remained a dead letter on a scrap of paper, even as the words hang in the air like so many objurgations and appeals for the commission of inquiry to clear up the situation and determine those responsible for the massacres and torture.

The pact was motivated on the one hand by the desire to turn the page, limit the damages, and put an end to the hellish process, and on the other by the hope that light might be brought to bear on the rot and complicity.

The stubbornness of the executioners could not stand for that: they happily continued the butchery. Their cynical procedures are those of a determined and implacable mafia. Did they not icily rebuff Boudiaf when an appeal was made to him to come to the rescue and procure a bit of dignity and respectability after he had uncovered the intrigue? The poor man, one of the founders of the resistance and of the FLN,[24] was assassinated by "his own guards" and in full session.

If it takes wisdom, moral force, and simple human decency to recognize one's mistake and seek an escape from horizonless situations, one cannot ask an organization blinded by power, without faith or law, to face the task. The sitting power likes neither the people nor their legitimate representatives: change the people and get rid of the managers.

Let us return to Professor Ali-Yahya's preface:

> A power that is neither legal, legitimate, nor democratic presumes to save Algeria from itself each morning for having made an evil thing of freedom of the vote.[25]

To lay claim to changing the government is an unpardonable attack on the law. It is proof of political immaturity to make an ill use of democracy by voting for newcomers and disavowing the masters. The corrective chastisement will serve the rebels right!

If those in power no longer trust the people, is it the people who must change? Ali-Yahyia describes the Algerian people as follows:

> For their part the people are neither immature, backward, nor irrational; they are a lighthouse that has led the way to liberation in many third-world countries, reduced for the present by the power to a lantern that can no longer light its own house, let alone ratify the confiscation of power. They no longer trust the political regime and want a change *of* regime, not in it.

> It is a very serious error of judgment to take Algerians for minors who cannot vote and who need tutors, when in fact they are responsible adults.[26]

Another jurist, a Frenchman this time, demonstrates how the people of a million plus martyrs, during the war of independence, was put under guard and its elected members conducted under military presence to the gridiron of the Sahara under conditions of terrible torture and lack of hygiene.

> More than ten thousand persons, a hundred and fifty of whom newly elected, eight hundred mayors, four thousand members of municipal counsels or wilaya, were arrested without charges or sentencing and led to seven internment camps in the desert, a thousand, two thousand, sometimes even three thousand kilometers from their homes. . . . Officially, the coup d'état was perpetrated to save democracy.[27]

The lawman, preoccupied with reports and formal errors, tried to take into account the fullness of the injustice at another camp, not that of the "friends" to whom the open letter is addressed. His testimony deserves our respect, but no report can fully sound the insanity of assassins and the murderous madness which has possessed them to bring tens of thousands of persons to the desert hell and the slaughterhouse of a nation.

• • •

On the subject of torture, we must not pass over in silence the tragedy of the Tunisian Nahda. Murderous madness does not belong only to the elite who hold the Algerian people hostage. The Islamists of the Tunisian Nahda, of whom no one speaks, suffer in silence for having committed the unforgivable crime of being too popular and having taken a significant percentage of the elections.

Six thousand men and women have been dumped into infected cells after having been tortured; this has moreover been a daily occurrence, before, during, and after trials—or without trial altogether. The families of the imprisoned have been made to suffer a thousand torments while their loved ones agonize in jails of foul repute. No one mourns the martyrs of Tunisian torture.

No one mourns the martyrs of the Nahda: it is a forgotten incident in the hurly-burly of the international campaign against Islamists; neither the media nor the NGOs much care about the lot of millions of people.

Notes

1 TN: A certain general familiarity with the (recent) history of the neighboring North African state is assumed. For a concise and impartial account, see John Ruedy's *Modern Algeria: The Origins and Development of a Nation,* Indiana University Press, Bloomington, IN, 1992. The transliteration of Arabic names in the present discussion is Ruedy's.

2 TN: 1807?–83; according to Ruedy, "the greatest Algerian national hero." *The Spiritual Writings of Amir 'Abd al-Kader* (ed. Michel Chodkiewicz, Albany, N.Y.: SUNY Press, 1995) contains a biographical sketch pertinent to the argument here.

3 TN: 'Abd al Hamid Ben Badis (1889–1940), leader of the Islamic Reform movement.

4 TN: Mosque schools.

5 TN: Reform movement in Islam founded by Muhammad b. 'Abd al-Wahab (d. 1787) resuscitated by the Saud family at the turn of the 20th century.

6 TN: in 1931, under Ben Badis.

7 TN: Founder, in 1989, of the *Front islamique du salut* (FIS).

8 TN: The word is derived from the root of *jaz'iriy,* "Algeria."

9 TN: Juridical opinion.

10 TN: Moustapha Bouyali, founder (early 1980s) of the Group for Defense against the Illicit.

11 TN: Thomas Robert Bugeaud (1784–1849), French governor general of Algeria 1840–47.

12 *Futuribles,* p. 23. TN: Godefroy IV of Boulogne (1061–1100), leader of the First Crusade, proclaimed king of Jerusalem; King Louis VII of France (1120–80) took part in the Second Crusade; Saint Louis (Louis IX, 1214–70), fought the Sultan of Egypt, was held for ransom in Palestine, and at the end of his life took part in the Eighth and last Crusade.

13 TN: The Algerian Berber term for themselves, especially used by the Kabyles, "the largest and most politically active community of Algerian Berbers" (Ruedy, p. 9).

14 *Futuribles,* p. 25.

15 Ibid., same page.

16 Op cit., p. 25.

17 TN: Houari Boumediene, second president of Algeria, d. 1978.

18 TN: The Arabic means "values, worth, what is priceless."

19 *Les Arabes* (Paris: Sindibad, 1979), p. 143.

20 Ibid.

21 TN: Imam in Algiers and highly popular preacher during the 1980s.

22 Editions Hoggar, Plan-les-Ouattes CH.

23 Editions Hoggar (cf. n. 14), 1996.

24 TN: *Front de libération nationale,* created in 1954 by the *Comité révolutionnaire d'unité et d'action* (CRUA).

25 Ibid.

26 Ibid.

27 Vergès, *Lettre ouverte à des amis algériens devenus tortionnaires* [*Open Letter to Algerian Friends Who Have Become Torturers*] (Paris: Albin Michel, 1993), p. 20.

IV. The Wound of Palestine

1 The Palestine Project

For centuries, Jews lived side by side with Muslims under the protective wing of the Caliphate of Spain. Jewish historians themselves recognize and demonstrate that the golden age of their people was situated geographically and historically in Muslim Spain. At a time when the race which, according to Christian belief, betrayed and crucified Christ, was disgraced and persecuted as a deicide enemy in Europe, Jews in Muslim Spain enjoyed the status that *islam* guaranteed minorities, particularly the People of the Book, Jews and Christians.

Longtime brothers in the bounty of a prosperous and tolerant civilization, the Muslims and Jews of Spain together fell under the repressive yoke of the Reconquista and the pitiless Inquisition that tortured and burned alive without regard to confession. Dispersed after the Spanish reconquest, the Jews once again found refuge and a viable lot in North Africa and the Muslim Mashreq.[1]

Compared to the life—or rather, to the fight for survival—that had been the Jews' in Europe, regularly abused and massacred during periodic pogroms, that of the Jews in North Africa and the East seemed a good life, for they enjoyed at least absolute security.

The Jewish "historical theme" awakened in Europe in the course of the 19th century. It is represented by the Zionist movement motivated by a secularist ideology that turned its back on the Talmudic tradition and divorced itself from the image of the wandering Jew in long curls in order to present him with the modern features of a rich German banker or an Oxford-educated gentleman.

The Rotschilds and Hertzls were modern secularists in their frock-coats and butterfly cravats; Jews in soul and conscience, however, of a sort that was abominable to their brethren who led miserable lives in the ghettos of Warsaw and Russia. The Hungarian Hertzl founded the Zionist movement, the Jewish facet of secular modernity, and conceived the ambitious scheme of a Jewish state to be built somewhere in the world.

Europe needed a reservoir where it could dispose of its overflow of Jewry: the Jew is too shrewd, too active, too able a businessman—and so, too annoying. Now organized, the Jews pursued their claim, clamoring to the nation-states of Europe—on their way to becoming democratic—for their rights and a place in the sun.

The Dreyfus Affair in France well illustrates the emergence of the Jew; the era offered him possibilities for defending himself against injustice, and for rousing a segment of public opinion with the help of a free press already infiltrated by pro-Jewish finances and a Semitic intelligentsia.

The racist notion of "overflow" found the occasion to rise to the surface; historic opportunism, in the pragmatic interests of British and imperialist politics, accommodated Zionist ambitions with a home in Palestine.

After World War I, Jewish immigration into Palestine accelerated. Encouraged—indeed, openly impelled by the English government's promise—the massive exodus of Jewry, especially Eastern European, lost no time in establishing a state within a state in the territories under British mandate. The ideological and motivational Israelite Alliance, of cosmopolitan character, was quickly supplanted by politico-terrorist activism of second-generation Zionists.

During World War II the Jews who survived the massacre took refuge in Palestine. The myth of the Exodus, perpetuated by a technicolor film, presents the sympathetic world with the image of the Jewish survivor, the victim of inhuman injustice for which Nazi Europe—and European accomplices—are responsible.

The tattered conscience, weighted with remorse, of Europe coming out of World War II, was a windfall for the Zionist movement. The lode has been much exploited elsewhere as well. Zionist leaders, whose administrations have proved their hitlerian parallel, change their act to attack the conquerors and accuse them of tacit or active complicity in the massacre of the Jews; they hold them responsible for it.

Taking the tortured conscience hostage was conducted by the hand of a master. For Europe, seating a Jewish state in Palestine solved two problems: getting rid of Jewish noisemakers, and paying a debt of honor.

The U.S.A. has three reasons, different from those of Europe, and more important, for supporting the Zionist state, both initially and ever after:

The first is on confessional grounds: the advent of the Kingdom of Zion is a dogma common to both Jews and Protestants, great readers as they are of the Jewish Bible.

The second is that Arabic countries harbor the most important petroleum sites in the world, and that they need a steady guardian to watch over the treasure at close hand—in the event of a "desert storm."

Both economic and dogmatic considerations merge and develop as a third reason, which is political and in direct control of the events: the existence of a Jewish lobby in Washington, sustained and financed by six million American Jews, rich, very powerful, active, and influential.

The European and American aid that the Jewish state receives is diverse, without counting the contributions of a rich and ardently solicitous diaspora; the American-Israeli pact of mutual defense, along with

European reparation, translates into an uninterrupted pipeline of military, financial, technological, diplomatic, and security assistance—and whatever else may be desired.

2 The Ordeal of Palestine

The affair of Palestine is a series of painful ordeals, a path of suffering strewn with landscapes of desolation: disaster in 1948, scourge in 1956, catastrophe in 1967, calamity in 1973, and many other reverses of fortune along the way.

The Arab defeats at the hands of the tiny state of Israel have laid bare the deadly dislocation of Arabic societies and the ineptness of their governments. They have revealed very sad truths: what kind of nameless treachery was it when those in power armed their soldiers in 1948 with defective ammunition and rifles that did not fire, or when in 1967 there were no Egyptian generals—they were too busy with their debauchery to respond—during the Israeli blitz attack.

The lack of response from a depraved general staff was perhaps Egypt's last chance to fight as equal to equal against the Zionist state, since Uncle Sam would soon settle that score. In 1973, while the penitent Egyptian army took to the field under its rallying cry, "Allahu akbar" (God is great), America, Zion's unconditional protector, unleashed an airlift worthy of its might to flood the field with warplanes and tanks.

Uncle Sam's protection was called into play once again when it flung its veto at the heart of the U.N. to decisions running counter to the Zionist state. Sure of its rear, the U.S. dismissed the resolutions of a world of law like so many useless scraps of paper.

Spoiled child of Protestant America so fervent in its Biblical mythologies, the state of Israel and its formidable propaganda apparatus in the U.S.—press, radio, and television channels in particular—inflated the number of Hitler's victims at will and drew from common Biblical sources such motivational themes as Exodus and Shoah.

The slogan "a land without people for a people without land" made of Palestine a no man's land, a waste ground and lost heritage found again by the chosen people.

A recovered "promised land," Palestine is only the beach-head for the expansion of a "greater Israel" depicted on published Zionist maps, embracing a large part of the Arab East: Jordan, Syria, Iraq, Egypt. Israel acts, confident and certain of its allies. Its principal ally is the profound sense of guilt developed after the so-called Holocaust.

During World War II, the Vichy government was steeped in Jewish persecution; afterwards, France was persuaded that it owed the Jewish people a historic debt. This debt had to be repaid clean at the cost of squandering the democratic principles by which human rights are upheld.

To redeem Europe, this debt would have to be paid by Arabs. Not only would Arab lands be occupied and split up to receive Jews called to the land of their ancestors, but the same myth that lies at the base of the Jewish claim is preserved at any cost. The Gayssot-Fabius law, enacted in France and promulgated in 1990, severely sanctions all criticism of the Zionist political creed; casting doubt on the existence or extent of the "Holocaust" is a crime, and the doubter is prosecuted at law.

Thanks once again to Jewish propaganda, Hitler, the enemy of the human race and the instigator of a war that had fifty million victims—twenty million of whom were people of the Soviet Union—passed into history merely as a slaughterer of Jews. At Tel Aviv and Jerusalem, the numbers are gently reduced so as to be believable; the six millions long sung and lamented have become four million, and this is pared back to a million and a half. This is the official tally engraved on the commemorative steles.

Inflating the number of victims adds nothing to the horror of Hitler's carnage; a single innocent victim, Jew or not, is already one too many according to our deeply held Islamic convictions.

The favored child of America is also cherished by Hollywood. Jewish production funds and Jewish cinematic talents have combined to honor a mythical Schindler, casting a deaf ear to the protests of his widow who denounced the falsification of the facts.

Serviced by such prestigious advocates, the Jewish cause is omnipresent in the world's conscience while other causes are erased forever. Neither side erects plaques to mourn the sixty million Native Americans exterminated by the white Protestant American pioneer. No stele commemorates the hundred million dead black Africans packed in the compartment of the slave ships. America's cotton fields never received more than one out of ten of these human cattle, nine having passed beyond the realm of the living at the time of their capture, or chained and crammed for the crossing. Who thinks any more of them? Only the Jewish state lays claim to attention and memory!

Let us not allow the martyr image, maintained by the Jews to promote and exploit, turn us from the Zionist scheme or prevent us from discerning certain character traits and precedents of the protectors of the Zionist state.

Both the protected and the protectors demand the impossible. They have had the audacity and historical mindlessness to work toward the goal—projected sometime in the future—of having seven million Jews occupy the lands and the economy of 300 million Arabs, already there and backed by a billion and a half Muslims who are surely mindful of the Palestinian stakes and are always capable of responding to the appeal of their brothers!

When the impossible is demanded, when it is known to be out of reach—and when one possesses a nuclear arsenal—the temptation to use it will one day prove irresistible. Will humanity wake up one day to hear the news of a new Hiroshima in some Arab capital?

The menace no longer seems uncertain, judging by the arrogance, irresponsibility, and want of maturity on the part of the current head of the Zionist government, Netanyahu. When we consider the Jewish dogma by which "gentiles" (non-Jews) are ripe for exploiting, whether it be financially (through usury) or any other manner, nuclear aggression can no longer to be excluded. According to the Jewish Bible, "gentiles" can and ought to be exterminated if they stand in the way of the plans of the chosen people. What better means of exterminating than nuclear weapons?

The nightmare cannot be excluded when you think that the head of the Jewish state, at the end of October, 1997, provoked a popular storm when he cast into doubt certain Bible verses threatening the enemies of Israel with extermination, and that the extremist right-wing in power, whose justification rests on such passages as justification for Israel's insatiable expansion, cried scandal.

The very existence of this artificial and menacing Jewish state is itself menaced with self-destruction by being constituted of a rabble of heterogeneous peoples.[2] The heavy burden of a nuclear arsenal that a fit of temper of a paranoid head or the self-arousal of a military general staff might compel the government to activate, contributes to internal malaise as well as to our worries.

The state that has maintained itself for fifty years, supported by its Western friends, is internally driven by a centrifugal dynamic. The façade of democracy that has operated thus far cannot hold the building together indefinitely: the edifice will crumble sooner or later.

Still, we must not dream that our aggressor will fall of his own accord, brought down by some invisible magic. We must not dream! We must understand and act! We must understand history and prepare ourselves for the conditioned promise God makes to us in the Qur'an. It is written thus:

> Afflict not others (O Muslims) nor let yourselves be beaten down. You are most high so long as you have faith. If a wound enfeebles you, the same wound enfeebles your enemy. We make the days (of rising and falling) alternate among the peoples so that God may recognize the faithful (by their conduct) and that He may choose you among the martyrs. God loves not the unjust.[3]

These verses were revealed after the defeat of the Muslims at Uhud, but the Qur'an is not a record of events limited in time, it is the living Word of God, invaluable instruction for all "days," the promise of a rotation, of a rise after a fall.

Thus the kingdom of Jerusalem founded by the Crusaders lasted two centuries. The Franks were chased out after that. The feudal regime of the ancient kingdom of Jerusalem, though iniquitous and inhuman, seemed stable. Even though under this cruel and enslaving regime the land was sold or inherited along with serfs under the whip, it seemed to exist as if it would last forever.

Modern democracy in Israel has proved to be a system not for liberating the people but for subjugating them. It will not last forever; it is here for only a certain time. It is there as our ordeal, an ordeal for Arabs and Muslims. The ancient crusader regime was overthrown by a Muslim society united around a sultan. Saladin the Kurd gathered Arabs and non-Arabs behind him.

Today, when the ethnic wars between Muslims are a gaping wound, tearing us apart in fratricidal fury, all of this seems distant. Today, conquered Muslims are divided into little entities: they are no more than Afghans or Turks or Arabs or Berbers. . . .

The Ordeal of Israel will remain for some time until those scattered billion and a half Muslims become aware of their true identity. The Ordeal—by which God recognizes the faithful and distinguishes them from those who are not—is a central notion in *islam*. God willing, we shall return to it.

God's explicit promise in the Holy Book is bound up with certain conditions: faith, political and social readiness, resistance, and martyrdom. Let us take a long breath in preparation for the "day" of rotation. Victory is earned!

On the theme of historical challenge and the psychology of a people, the phenomenon of the rotation of civilizations has been attentively observed by the British historian Toynbee.

It is difficult for Western civilization to admit its decadence and downfall, however, since it is beclouded by so much force, so much wealth, and such great capacity to exploit and tame (and so, destroy) nature. But the student of the psychology of modern man—that of the Zionist Jew, for example—discovers irrefutable signs of a certain and inevitable downfall.

That may be, but the Muslim is not in the ideal position. To his moral depression is added material misery, underdevelopment, social injustice, political dismemberment—the list is long.

Observation of historical contingency and the psychology of peoples makes Muslims highly improbable candidates for playing an honorable role on the world stage, and casts doubt on Toynbee's cyclical theory.

But let us leave the historians to their cold examination of conjunctures; let us bring to mind the history of the Prophets of God recorded in the Qur'an. Whenever an unjust city attained the zenith of power and rebelled against God, it was cursed and struck down, to leave its place for others more just and less corrupt. That was the fate of 'Ad, the people of the Prophet Hud, of Thamud of the people of Salih,[4] of Pharaoh the enemy of Moses, and of many others.

The scorned and sorely tried of yesterday are the very ones to whom victory is promised tomorrow, of course, but it would be false to think that our faith is compatible with contemplative waiting and confident quietism. Victory, God's gift, is to be earned—we can never repeat that enough!

3 Islamicizing the History of Palestine

It would be pointless and nonsensical to read history through a non-Islamic grid when we are proposing to seek the means of winning the modern world for *islam.* Modernity is the current face of the Ordeal.

The history of the Prophets is recorded for us in the Qur'an not for our entertainment, but as an example. The Zionist challenge is altogether operative in lived reality and in the psychology of Arabs, Muslim and non-Muslim. Taken on its own and magnified by our preoccupations and suffering, it seems insurmountable; but considered on the scale of the history of Islam, it is only a passing squall. A Qur'anic reading of history brings the pain of the moment and the disappointments and defeats of the hour into relative proportion.

Seen across this grid, historical "questions" and "problems" become inscribed in the broader circumstance, in the complexity post-modern thinkers love to talk about. They are also inscribed in the long term. That is why the snapshots and flash pictures of impressionism tapped by political crises cannot bring us into a true relationship with history.

Mankind's acts and words and the necessity of responding and reacting should not sever our connection with the Absolute, the divine Plan. There is absolutely no way we can flee the current fight except by calling once again on the divine and a suprahistoric continuity. The unconquerable vivacity and audacity of Islamic organizations in Palestine and southern Lebanon demonstrate that men of faith are not inevitably nonchalant fatalists. Hamas sends its best elements into martyrdom; so do the Jihad and the Hezbollah.

In the struggle waged by oppressed peoples, their courage and resistance distinguish these groups in no aspect more than their motivation, at once highly spiritual, patriotic, and ideological. The human bombs in occupied Palestine yield in no degree in terms of self-denial and sacrifice to the Buddhist monks and Tibetan patriots who set themselves ablaze. Only the elevated nature of their goal hoists the former to the plane of

History, while patriotism and revolt against injustice place the others on an ordinary human plane.

Called by a spiritual aspiration, the Islamists resisting Israeli occupation cannot however permit themselves contemplative ecstasy at the moment of the ultimate decision, the moment of losing or winning the fight. They cannot escape the earthly rule of combat, nor the scourge of defamatory propaganda: like all other Islamists, the Palestinian combatants are pilloried vulgar terrorists.

It is humanly irresistible to besmirch one's enemy with lying propaganda. It is also the rule of the divine Plan to suffer the assaults of the enemy: Did we not read above about the wound in both camps as a condition preceding the "rotation of days"?

Islamicizing history means bringing about a reading that is just and concurrent with the reality of the Qur'an; the Word of God illuminates reality. To submit to the rule of God's Plan is the contrary of the sanctimonious nihilism of wait-and-see.

To Islamicize history is to accept the conditions of the fight just as the Prophets of God did (grace and peace be upon them!), by accomplishing, like them, the duty of the hour with firmness and constancy, without becoming distracted by scrimmages and wounds. The prize is the "rotation of the days." Like the Prophets, we must attack piece by piece, on the ground, step by step, resisting the aggressor and responding to hostile fury with the tenacity of those who know they are in the right.

To Islamicize history is not to fly in the clouds or collapse on the soft couch of fatalism. Pretending it to be God's Plan when it is my fault that catastrophe arrives is to place myself outside of history.

One of the great faults among conquered peoples is to seek refuge and compensation in the consoling dream of grandiose schemes, without the least concrete effort. That is the worst way of being beaten, since the inertness of the dead is added to intellectual ineptitude.

For a long time, modern Arabs have cherished the dream of a unity that never materializes, the utopia of a world role that is more than ever out of reach, the dream of independence and power that dissipates as soon as it is formulated. Now that Islamic dynamism has been launched, it is no longer the time to build sand castles, it is the hour to act surely, without haste, without violence, without needless words, but with determination and confidence in God (may His Name be magnified and exalted!).

It is time to act, knowing that action will be met by the enemy's blows. It is in the spirit of the verses cited above, enjoining us never to let ourselves be afflicted and thrown down—that those blows should be received. The history of the Prophets, our models forever, is full of examples: their peoples, rebelling against God—before the "rotation of the days" removed them from history—offended and humiliated them, hunted and tortured their disciples, and confiscated their possessions.

The Qur'an assures us as well that resistance to injustice and tenacious combat will always bring an end to the haughty, closing one chapter of history and opening another. Those who today look down on the lowly will be cast down tomorrow. We have God's promise for it.

4 The Ungrateful Children of Israel

Let us read the Qur'an to enlighten ourselves regarding the rule which directs the "rotation of the days" by lingering over the example of the ungrateful children of Israel, rebelling against God in modern times, and afloat in illusion. Let us read the Qur'an to find God's testimony concerning His Jewish creatures. It is a reading that will lift a corner of the veil that envelops the divine Plan.

Verses 78–82 of Sûrah Al-Mâ'idah describe the children of Israel in vigorous terms. The renegades among the children of Israel (which allows us to understand that some were not) are reproached.

Nine times in the Qur'an the Jews are mentioned by the generic noun *yahud*. Forty-three times, the "children of Israel" are cited or summoned as such. Christians are on the agenda a mere fifteen times. The historical circumstances of the era of the Prophet during lawsuits and battles between Jews and Muslims, you say? It is, rather, a history in which Jews participated significantly.

The numerous Prophets sent by God to the Jews are cited by name, as well as the treason of the renegades among the children of Israel, whence the summoning of the children of the Prophet Jacob, the Israel of the Bible and the Qur'an. The first betrayal by the renegades is their invention of blasphemous and stupid farce: God (exalted be His Name!) is measured against Jacob and the latter bests Him in single-handed combat. Playing on the sense of the two Hebrew words (close to the Arabic), *isr* and *El,* they interpreted them as "conqueror of God" instead of "servant of God." The renegades do not intend it as a blasphemy, but they come to the very edge! The verses of Sûrah Al-Mâ'idah read:

> The renegades from among the children of Israel were cursed by the voice of David and by Jesus, son of Mary, because they rebelled (against their Prophets) and transgressed (the Law). They did not forbid themselves any crime. Reprehensible conduct! You see a great number of them going with the infidels. What a sinister inspiration which has merited the wrath of God and eternal punishment! If they truly believed in God and in His Prophet, they would not have gone with the infidels. But most of them were scoundrels. You will surely admit that those who are most fiercely hostile to the faithful are the Jews and nonbelievers. As you will note, those with the closest affinity of friendship with the faithful are found among

those who call themselves Christians. It is among these latter that you find priests and monks and those who are not arrogant.

At the time of the Prophet Muhammad (grace and peace upon him!) relations between Muslims and Jews were extremely strained: knavery and scheming of a rich and cunning minority, Jewish alliances with the Muslims' enemies, betrayal of the pact of solidarity that the Prophet had concluded with the Jewish tribes upon arriving in Medina. After years of evasions and offences, above all after the Jewish betrayal of their Muslim allies at the "battle of the trench" (*al khandaq*), the Jews were definitively driven from Medina.

Elsewhere they did not forget this trench in the history of their people, and today, Zionist pretensions do not stop at the Biblical territories of Palestine, Syria, Iraq, and Egypt; they stretch toward Medina, which they consider to be part of their patrimony. Talk about the covetousness and rapacity of the tiny Israeli state!

Whether declared or concealed, the Zionist aims of our time are served by an insolent temerity. Their insolence surpasses all measure when, in the annexed territories, they bulldoze the homes of their powerless owners and before the eyes of an entire world that has become indifferent and blasé from daily repetition of the same images.

It is true that Muslim (and Christian) youths of the intifada have moved, for a while, the spectators of Jewish soldiers attacking stone throwers with machine guns, wounding or killing them. Still, the protests of human rights organizations are raised less and less often. What good is it, when the American veto has rejected more than thirty Security Council decisions in order to protect Israel, and when it has determined to reject them again and forever? The White House's services to the Zionist state are so generous and unconditional now that the Jewish counselors of the democratic administration are no longer countable.

The Qur'an verses we have just reviewed end in the affirmation that "those who call themselves Christians" are a category of people capable of nourishing feelings of friendship for Muslims. The president of the United States does not seem to be among them when he announces during a speech before the Jewish parliament that he feels fraternal affinities with his hosts. Does such a remark arise from sincere convictions or from electoral expediency? It is true that in general, politicians are not persons of principles, whatever they say, whatever they call themselves, and however they are spoken of.

There remain the men of the Church who, always calling themselves Christians, seek dialog with Muslims and have, since Vatican II, been declaring that it is time to turn the page and inaugurate a new era of understanding and cooperation with Islam. With exception of theology, where no progress is possible, cooperation with them is welcome.

If, as the Qur'an counsels us, we avoid the apple of discord, theological controversy, we could, as persons of good will, cooperate in view of a better future for humanity. If our heavens are not of the same color, our earth is the same, and on it we contend with the same urgent problems: material and moral misery, the destruction of the biosphere, the lot of children and minorities, wars and many other human ills.

Perhaps we may arrive together at establishing in every corner, for every people, for each human being, for each living creature, universal charity, peace in the world, and love for our neighbor; all of these are virtues that our Law and our Book teach and enjoin on us. Did not the holy Prophet Muhammad (grace and peace upon him) welcome the disciples of Jesus (peace and grace upon him) who came from Najran? He sheltered them in his mosque, most holy place that it is, and he conversed with them.

In our sacred Book we read—and shall read until the end of our days—those verses that suggest that we be well disposed toward those who call themselves Christians. In what the Holy Book records for us of renegades of whatever stripe, and especially renegade Jews, everything should inspire us with absolute suspicion.

5 Arrogance and Cruelty

The arrogance of the latter knows no limits, encouraged and supported as they are by other renegades who call themselves Christians but who are atheist and iniquitous.

As to Jewish arrogance, God revealed these verses of the Qur'an:

> We have established this with the children of Israel in the book (of Destiny): twice you shall commit great disorders on earth and will exhibit great arrogance.[5]

The founding Jewish dogma is arrogance itself: the Jews are supposedly God's chosen people. Such a dogma is shot through with the principle of racism. The first time, spoken of by the verse above, where Jewish racism demonstrates a haughty arrogance, is perhaps that of which we find an echo in the Biblical account:

> On that day, Joshua took possession of Makkedah and put it and its king to the sword: he vowed them to destruction, along with every person found there. He let no one survive, and he treated the king of Makkedah just as he had treated the king of Jericho.[6]

The account continues, "putting to the sword" and exterminating the kings and inhabitants of Libnah, Lachish, Gezer, Eglon, and Hebron.[7]

We can well believe the Bible when we read of the cruelty of the Jews, since we are eye witnesses of the same today; but, that aside, what credibility can these bloody recitals have that present a Prophet, Joshua, as a bloodthirsty tyrant? In contrast to the Qur'an which was committed to writing during the lifetime of the Prophet Muhammad (grace and peace upon him!) as dictated by him, the Bible is merely a collection of oral traditions accumulated and reported during the centuries after Moses (grace and peace upon him!) before having been notated in writing. The Prophets of God, Messengers of mercy, cannot be butchers of humanity; these epic recitals of extermination cannot therefore be anything other than the fantasies of sick souls.

This first instance in history of the children of Israel appearing as a united people, rather than nomadic tribes wandering in the desert, was under the leadership of Joshua, who led them into the land of Canaan. But if they laid waste, killed, and exterminated, it could not have been until after his death. Does not the Qur'an inform us that the Jews had the habit of killing the Prophets themselves? The Prophets were not the initiators of the violence of the children of Israel, though they were its victims.

The Bible account, a fabulation and medley of popular confections, is in itself a falsification based on epic models that reveals the intentions—still lively in our time—of putting the "gentile" to the sword whenever an occasion for "ethnic cleansing" presents itself. It is instructive to consult a book by Maurice Bucaille and be edified by the confabulating genius of the authors of the Bible:

> Before it became a collection of books, it was a popular tradition that rested entirely on human memory. . . . Enlivened by the function of story-telling, the narrative is never at a loss in dealing with subjects and epochs whose history is little known.[8]

The Biblical accounts of bloody exploits, historically little known, are awash in confusion. This first time that the children of Israel showed themselves to be arrogant devastators in the land is, in any case, the object of several interpretations among the commentators on the Qur'an also.

On the other hand, the second time about which the Qur'an verse cited above informs us seems to be the current establishment of the state of Israel. The haughty arrogance of Jewish racism this time is well known. No ambiguity is possible here, since "ethnic cleansing," an entirely modern phrase, is carried out in front of the camera and broadcast direct on the television screens of the entire world.

Before the trivializing effect of television—and before its omnipresence—the descendents of the exterminators of the nations showed what they were capable of. On 9 April 1948 Menachem Begin, the future prime minister of the future Zionist state, invaded the village of Dir Yasin with his gang of terrorists, massacring its 254 inhabitants, women, children, and men. This was the terrorist tactic of the terrorist organization, Irgun, to make the Palestinians flee by sowing terror among their populations.

Thirty years later, the arrogant state of Israel having been established and its justice guaranteeing the peace, a Jewish assassin attacked the village of Bir Kassem and wiped out its population; he was arrested so as to be "severely condemned"—and then released after paying a symbolic fine.

Two years ago Doctor Baruch Goldstein, a settler of American origin and gallant knight of terror, entered as conqueror the mosque of Al Khalil and machine-gunned the Muslims bowed down in prayer, killing twenty-seven and wounding more than fifty others. His tomb has become an object of a veritable cult, a site of pilgrimage and a place of worship.

But if a Muslim, seeing his house reduced to rubble by a bulldozer, his fields confiscated, and his children gunned down in the street, should attack a single Jew, international protest is immediately unleashed, leading to a media lynching: Islamist terrorist! Extremist! Barbarian!

No one imputes the savage massacres perpetrated by the Serbs in Bosnia to the Orthodox religion, nor the bombs of Ulster to the Catholic Church; yet this is the image that a certain sort of modernism seeks to give Islam, at the cost of truth, objectivity, and fairness.

It is objectivity that Europe needs in its effort to unite and in its quest for a new communitarian identity. Perhaps it is to be found in a ready and open spirit of cooperation with the Other, the strongly isolated identity of the Arab and the Muslim, and in mutual respect. Perhaps it is to be found if Europe refuses to succumb to the siren's song from across the Atlantic that spouts the theory of a "clash of civilizations" like a battle cry for a new Crusade.

• • •

I do not wish to close this chapter on a note of resentment and bitterness, the petty ideas and sentiments that are destined to vegetate in sick minds like great untruths, barren and harmful.

Let us instead speak of a great common project, useful to humanity and beneficial to individuals, that should attract the good will of those who have goodness to impart and love of neighbor to dispense. When generous souls lend good graces to the call of wisdom, the embittered will see the procession of a reconciled humanity, a procession where the means of modernity will serve the final goal of *islam,* which is justice on earth and hearts filled with spirituality.

Everything will pass, the ephemeral sojourn of individuals and civilizations, each following its determined cycle and age, following the "rotation of the days" and the predestination of each.

Everything will pass; what remains is the human person who dies and is raised up by God to give an account of his acts in this world below.

Everything will pass; what remains is the human person forever, a welcome guest in the presence of the Eternal, or racked forever by the flames of Gehenna.

We have begun, in the preceding pages, to lay out the contentious record of *islam* and modernity. This careful exposition is necessary in order to overcome mutual recriminations and to escape the perpetual torments that make us each other's opponents; for this merely distracts us from the final purpose of humankind on earth, and it beclouds our horizons.

To see clearly into the past and into the present is the condition for conceiving the future and being guided toward it without going astray. If we have recalled the historical and ideological genesis of modernity and its corollary—which we have called "Holy Secularity" (the expression of a European)—it is in order to inquire of secular modernity about the bases of its knowledge and its concept of humankind, to question its foundations so as then to draft the general outline of our economic and politically communitarian scheme.

I cite from memory the Roman philosopher Seneca: "the boat that knows not where it is going cannot profit from favorable winds." God's promise is both the lighthouse that signals danger by showing the banks of salvation, and the favorable wind of sure sailing. It is for us to get under way, keeping our eyes on the horizon—without failing to note the treacherous undertow.

Notes

1 TN: Mideast.

2 Sephardic Jews, immigrated from Arab countries, are, like Israel's Arab citizens, treated with distrust. Begrudged of their rights, they ruminate bitterly against the Ashkenazi minority of European origin who are the sole masters of the Zionist state. There is much to be said about the dissensions between master-citizens and slave-citizens of dubious status.

3 Sûrah [*Al-'Imran*]: verses 139–40.

4 TN: About the 'Ad people, see in particular Sûrah 26 [*Ash-Shu'arâ*]: verses 123–40; the Thamud were their successors (cf. Sûrah 7 [*Al-'A'râf*]: verses 73–79).

5 Sûrah 17 [*Al-Isrâ'*]: verse 4.

6 Joshua 10:28.

7 Cf. Joshua 10:29–37. TN: The place names have been cited as they appear in the *New Jerusalem Bible.*

8 Maurice Bucaille, op. cit., pp. 17–18.

V. Knowing

1 What Is Life For?

What is life for? This is the central and vital question, the question no one can suppress or muffle, the question no one dares consider foolish.

But it is a question that is not to be asked publicly in an age deprived of sense and occupied with other problems that have more to do with "how" than "what for." Curious about everything, open to the universe of space as well as the universe of molecules, meddlesome, punctilious, inquisitive into the least detail about every subject, our technical and scientific era remains, for all that, tragically irrelevant to this question.

The meaning of life, the purpose of life, these are issues no longer taken up except within the closed circle of philosophers infatuated by metaphysical speculations, or by those who are marginal to modernity, such as Muslims and a few other outmoded types.

The manner of thinking that has become anchored in modern society is positivism: nothing exists except what the senses perceive. Nothing exists apart from the palpable, the concrete, the material. Anything that is not scientifically verifiable and measurable is merely conjecture.

The anthropocentric questions that seek a meaning of life are indubitable proof of mental backwardness! The field of scientific research is concerned with the functional utility of things and the efficiency of their organization, not with futile ramblings about the unknowable. Modern man seems resigned to a life without value, to the tragic state of an inescapable death putting an end to a life without an end purpose.

All the while a tiny hope clings to the ledge of a window that opens on a wall: that science will one day give us the means to prolong our lives. In the developed countries, life expectancy is in the neighborhood of eighty years; tomorrow it will exceed a century and may perhaps attain a century and a half. Is this not a reasonably plausible dream, given the unprecedented progress science is making in the field of genetics?

Modern man clings to the desire of prolonging his life and enjoying a better life thanks to material progress and better health, but he takes great pains to elude the essential question. He escapes his anxiety by amusing himself, so as to forget the inevitable and to avoid facing the fact of his own death. Why live at all if life is nothing but an absurd coincidence, and if after life there is nothing but death and the foulness of the grave? Might as well commit suicide now!

In post-modern societies, comforts may repress the essential question, even as misery can make us forget it; but nothing can manage to suppress it altogether, since it lives in the very heart of every human, whether he can formulate it or not. It always returns, like a shooting pain, urgently, demanding an answer.

At the base of each conscience, in some intimate corner, there resides the hope of a call, a helpful voice that will come to announce that our existence has a significance beyond our simple vegetative presence in the world.

Even if the noise of modern culture is terribly invasive and agitating, nature—our primary nature—the conscience that lies at the base of our innermost being, will never be totally convinced that we are here for no reason.

At the base of human conscience there is also a straining toward what is above, toward the spirit. This tension may swoon and faint, but it can never die. It may be deafened during childhood and disabled from hearing the external call, or it may be blinded to the light of day by a certain kind of education and an uncertain culture, but it does not die. It retires to some dungeon of modern man's conscience, duped by the hope that science may one day be able to revive the dead. A victim of his illusions, modern man may have himself frozen in some cryogenic morgue for millionaires. Science may one day offer everyone the elixir of an extended youth that ancient alchemists dreamed of—but will it answer the question that dwells in us?

Will modernity ever answer, having detached itself little by little from its judeo-christian values so as to acknowledge nothing but its greco-roman origins? The utterly modern attitude of suspicion and indifference, if not outright hostility, to the irrational now rejects any notion of the metaphysical. The eccentric harum-scarum who occupies himself with parapsychology or some such whim is at best tolerated and always suspect.

Modernity is relentless in driving out the spiritual; yet the latter is so much a part of human nature, that it cannot be banished. Instead it returns in fatal forms: the industry of charlatanism flourishes in the nooks and crannies of modern societies that combat the true nature of humankind.

The outlet of sectarian spiritualism runs counter to true spirituality. How many are those who fall into its macabre clutches: the sects that devour live human flesh, the collective suicide cults, are always lurking around the edges of modern societies, along with the practice of sorcery and old-fashioned spiritism that raises tables and makes dead children speak.

Stage left: Greco-roman culture blazes with all its lights, having now become the sole official reference point of a civilization at odds with its spiritual roots. The body, the beautiful figure of the athlete and the beauty queen are, along with the exploits of the Olympic champion, the certain values of our time. The values most appreciated are the aesthetic and the well-heeled: the football hero, the opera diva, and the movie star make much more than a prime minister—and sometimes much less than the champion boxer who in just a few moments in the ring can amass a fortune.

Stage right: Repressed and muffled, the natural question of the meaning of life seeks an answer in private booths and in the bosom of clandestine sects where Satan is pleased to recoup his losses.

2 Nihilist Tenets

The peaceable stage right of modernity is precariously built on a nihilist tenet. A tenet is an undemonstrated or undemonstrable principle. Nihilism is a philosophical doctrine whose fundamental principle or tenet is that there is no foundation to morality and that life has no meaning.

Let us go further in our research and ask the engineers of this grandiose edifice of modernity about the foundations of their structure.

Torn between two histories, between two minds, secular modernity has chosen to repudiate the principles and the thinking of its Christian religion while preserving politically a nostalgic tenderness for its judaic basis. The triumphant science of the last two centuries is wedded to the positivist materialistic philosophy whereby greco-roman polytheism is finally reborn under the form of two hypotheses which are mutually corollary.

The first tenet: Man is an animal, the product of life's slow evolving, and he is created entirely with respect to nature's challenges of survival.

The second tenet: There is no creator, no God, and thus nothing after death.

Thus the two villainous principles on which modern thought is founded concerning the reason of life lead to a gratuitous and counternatural certitude.

Nihilist philosophy, sure of its advances, is coupled with experimental science based on methodological doubt and the meticulous verification of results. Together the two give birth to a monstrous hybrid that makes man out to be a beast without significance, struggling for survival, and life a blind phenomenon of chemical action-reaction *in vivo* susceptible of being reproduced *in vitro.*

Darwinism—for that is the name of modern nihilism—has the effrontery of presenting itself as a science, and neo-Darwinists articulate untiringly the skeletons of primates in order to shore up their doctrine.

This book is not a treatise for specialists, and in any case it is useless to do battle with the pseudo-science of evolution on its own ground. It is nonetheless fitting to shake off this construct of lies and invite reason and innate humanness to open wide the eyes of both the head and the heart. The complicity of complaisant or pusillanimous silence about the central question—not reason, not science—is what stupefies men and perpetuates their ignorance of the meaning of life.

The consumerist mentality that rules modern destiny prevents human nature and reason from devoting the time necessary for each of us to consider his own account and to reflect on his own meaning. The human personality is hostage to the criminal complicity and ignorance cultivated by the education system and by the network of paths leading to existential nothingness.

Blunted by his own creations, his time occupied and colonized, modern man is hyper-informed about everything but miserably ignorant about himself. The medical, biological, and genetic sciences instruct him superbly about how his bodily mechanisms function, but they tell him nothing about the destination of his journey through life. Digital technologies offer him the key to a wonderland where he can now navigate, but they leave him neither the time to see nor the time to reflect. Everything is said, everything is thought, everything is recorded on the keyboard! All he needs for existence is to surf!

We are born equipped with a sensorial constitution and, later, with sufficient reason to see, reflect, and receive the Message that answers the question of our primordial nature buried in our hearts. These innate dispositions are strengthened or debased by the influence of our family structure and cultural education.

Debased man becomes deaf and dumb, blind and bestial. Not that he is deprived of hearing sounds or seeing forms and colors, but these senses do not serve to astonish him with the perfection of the perceivable world; they do not allow him to transcend immediate reality to deduce the existence of the work of a Worker.

To the eyes of the blinded, the astonishingly harmonious universe is nothing but an accident without an artisan. Duped by a socio-cultural environment that says nothing about the central question of life, or victim of the active teaching of atheism, debased man lives and dies without ever knowing the secret of his life, without ever asking why.

Grieved, we witness the spiritual murder committed by society on its members. We are present at the spiritual suicide of those who insist on their atheist positions, denying the evidence and professing their faith in bestial tenets.

3 The Bestial Tenet

By "bestial," I mean the Darwinian hypothesis. I take the term from the Qur'an, where it is used twice in this sense in the same Sûrah. The first occurrence is more general, the second more explicit:

> The vilest beasts in God's sight are indeed those deaf-mutes who are incapable of reason.
>
> The worst beasts in God's sight are unbelievers who have no faith.[1]

In ten other passages in the Qur'an the reference is to the deaf, dumb, and blind who wish to hear neither the question within them nor the answer that Revelation brings to these questions through the mouth of the Prophets (grace and peace be upon them!).

In 1859, the English naturalist Charles Darwin published his major book, *On the Origin of Species,* in which he advanced the working hypothesis that man is an evolved animal and not the *ex nihilo* creation of any god.[2]

This "scientific" hypothesis, finding a propitious wake in the scientific progress of a century smitten by science, has known a vogue for nearly a century and a half and has proved more and more tenacious. Man is thus self-made, the result of his own action, and owes his existence to no one.

Absurd as it is, the hypothesis can be seen in the framework of a settling of accounts with the Church—and the god that instructs the Church. In 1517, more than three centuries before Darwin's book, a sincere German monk named Martin Luther, scandalized by the corruption of churchmen, published his ninety-five theses against the Catholic Church.

In this internal revolt among Christians, Luther took the position of denouncing the traffic in "indulgences," warrants by means of which a priest would "remit" the sins of a believer over against resonant and well weighed-out "repentance." Luther then made other demands, among which was the abolition of even the principle of indulgences. The fervent monk's struggle led ultimately to separation from the papacy: the protestant Church was born.

Three centuries after that event, and seventy years after the French Revolution that had taken its toll in the blood of both monarchy and church, the antipathy of a cultivated European élite toward clericalism grew and took expression, among other forms, in the voice of Darwin. A return to nature was preached which was in fact a return to greco-roman paganism. The idea of the god-man taught by the Church was rejected in favor of clinging to variations on a mythical Areopagus rich with gods, demigods, and the bastards of goddesses and humans or vice versa.

As a revolt against God, Darwinism completes the work of Prometheus, who stole fire from the gods of Olympus and is the very symbol of man's emancipation from the tutelage of the gods. Man is his own god, having created himself: that is the dignity Darwin wished to have believed. Why not? Does not the Church worship a man? Do not the historical roots of Europe and its civilization swarm with divinities? Man, god—it's all one.

Darwin the naturalist presents nature as an absolute; science has discovered nothing whatever of a creator god. By the same token he establishes man as the craftsman of his own existence. The notion that things came to be by chance is buoyed by "scientific" conclusions, the results of observations that the British precursor came upon during his voyages chiefly to the Galápagos Islands, a living museum of exotic animals and a site where the imagination is easily inflamed.

He condensed his observations in order to arrive at a stupid conclusion, that man is a naked ape. Darwin's successors obstinately continue their research to find scientific data to support this bestial tenet that has no skeleton.

The bony battle-horse of neo-Darwinists is that those animals alone survive that are best adapted to their natural environment and the most able to overcome the difficulties of competition in the jungle. Thus, the ape ancestor of man, clever little devil, developed its cranium and the volume of its brain before leaving the trees and walking joyously on its two hind paws toward progress, in order to become the master of the animal kingdom from which he descended.

As an intelligent biped he was able to rule on earth, coming a long way in his evolution toward a cosmic destiny. His distant ancestor, a superfish, left the blue-green sea to become civilized, tame the atom, conquer space, invent robots, and make genetic discoveries like cloning, that will be applied to humankind tomorrow. With cloning, the loop will be looped and the theory verified: man makes himself, directly and rapidly, without having to wait millions of years, since, when he wants something, he gets it, so there!

Darwin's idiotic tenet is breached by paleontologists who demand that neo-Darwinists demonstrate the "missing link" that remains unfound. Darwin himself admitted that the number of (imaginary) intermediates between animal and man is "incommensurable." Geologists, putting words in the mouths of their fossils, and discovering tens of species that were not listed among the species known during Darwin's time, make a laughingstock of the thesis.

The "creationists" are militant Christians who courageously do battle after battle in America to wrest the education system from the clutch of Darwinism. Unfortunately for them, the Biblical mythology on which they found their argument is hardly more reasonable than that of Darwin.

Creationists find themselves in a very awkward position when Darwinists cart out their proofs that establish, with procedures now more sophisticated than carbon 14 dating, that the creation of the world dates billions of years ago, and not several thousands, as the Bible would have it.

In Europe, the bestial tenet wields a fascination that seems irresistible, and it is easy to understand why: our father is a monkey, a fish is our forebear, and that's that. The nineteenth century in Europe saw the development of evolutionist doctrine in all domains.

Three great names took up the movement: the Frenchman Auguste Comte, the Briton Charles Darwin, and the German Karl Marx. Let us cast a glance at Darwinian naturalism.

The evolution of ideas, according to the philosopher Comte, progressed in three stages, the mythological, the metaphysical, and, finally, the positive. What is the basis of the positivism of French materialism? Facts, nothing but the facts, established by scientific experiment.

As to the third musketeer, the philosopher-economist-sociologist-historian-politician-ideologue Karl Marx theorized the history of human societies as the uninterrupted process of class struggle. Socio-economic Darwinism, Marxism has enjoyed a fate we all know well enough. In practice, economic politics has given the lie to the theory; the experience is of a magnitude and nature that wants meditating upon.

Curiously, Darwin was not convinced of the correctness of Marxist theories when he refused the German's request to write a preface to *Das Kapital*. Yet the latter seemed much inspired by the former. We must conclude that the solidarity that can be observed even among the wild beasts of the natural jungle does not exist among the ideologues of the jungle of bestial theories—each for himself and the devil take the hindmost!

4 Correcting the Copy

The buffeting of the nihilist and violently atheist winds of the last century continues to blow at the end of the twentieth, though by fits and starts, and no longer with the gale force of certainty that we encounter in the grand atheists of the past. Still, atheist rationalism has had its day; it is no longer as militant and virulent as it was in the Soviet Union, for example. With the collapse of the Berlin Wall, the entire structure of official atheism has fallen; only bestial Darwinism continues its song and dance of depraved and decadent mores.

As worthy evolved apes, homosexuals mass in the streets of Western capitals to claim official recognition of their rights. Homosexual marriage is established in several countries as legitimate and legal. If it is true that the churches are open again in Russia, the avenues of moral degradation are too, alas!

Who will dare to speak out against degradation and immorality? It is seen as change, as innovation, and change in itself has value. The key to progress, the innovative dynamic that makes the economy go, it is the province of the market, and thus of the world—since the world is a market.

Such is the logic of evolutionism—the philosophical and pseudoscientific Darwinian hypothesis about the general progression of modern societies—that maintains the dynamic equilibrium, ever accelerating in the race forward. The equilibrium of a bicycle: go forward or fall off.

Another dynamic has begun to swim against the current: at the end of this century, thinking heads revise and correct the copy of the thick-headed dunces of the past. Thus the "rotation of the days." With regard to knowledge and methodology, an epistemological philosopher like Karl Raimund Popper puts to the question the certitude of heretofore reigning ideologies. In the scientific arena, the Nobel Prize winner Ilya Prigogine, a Belgian citizen of Russian origin, exemplifies rational judgment with regard to the widespread notions of yesteryear that cradled—and still cradle—the infancy of immature reason.

Popper is a well-known English epistemological philosopher who died recently (1996). He leaves behind him a harvest of academic research that serves as reference for the élite European avant-garde. A great giant-killer of ideologies, he denounces the "falsification" of knowledge; prestigious constructs of the nineteenth century, such as Marxism and psychoanalysis, are for him false and scientific dead ends.

Psychoanalysis, that twin of Darwin's naturalist idea, emerged from the brilliant head of Sigmund Freud like Athena. It has since had serious after-effects for its author and his suspicious conception of "medicine."

Psychoanalysis brings together two streams of modern atheist thought: the greco-roman one that conveys a mythological symbolism from the distant past, and the bestial flood of Darwinian humanism. Psychoanalyzed man is, on the whole, but a cauldron of desires simmering with complexes. Only dreams and an obsession with death raise him above the stage of the infamous quadruped in the original jungle.

Popper's criticism does not cross the boundaries of theory, and psychoanalysis still awaits a counterrevolution to bring it to justice and adjudge it as a crime of *lèse-dignité* and a defamatory swindle.

Prigogine is often cited as a witness and called to the stand in the trial, now overt, of the great certainties that shore up the universe of modern ideas and that of the dynamics of the world; where is the world going?

The Belgian Nobel Prize winner, who published his book, *Les lois du chaos,*[3] in 1994, enjoys great respect in the milieus of both science and avant-garde philosophy. A chemist and physicist, he does not find in the universe the harmonious appearance believed in and thought to have been described by classical perception, but rather chaos and uncertainty.

His book, *La fin des certitudes,*[4] does not present a hasty conclusion based on a few philosophical conjectures or exotic fancies. The titles of his works say a good deal about the perplexity of one of the best brains of the West, but they say nothing about the scientific background of the chemist and physicist. His contribution to thermodynamics has advanced modern physics, and his works in chemistry have an important impact on modern biology. This brilliant savant proposes a new methodology for the sciences of tomorrow, even as Popper criticizes those of yesterday and today.

The two scholars keenly sense the upheaval introduced by quantum physics into the long-held notions of the material universe. The very foundations of reason and logic are shaken. If so much as one scholar has an idea that goes beyond the confines of his laboratory, the upheaval is such that he befuddles and undoes the human understanding comfortably based on dubious tenets.

The vanguard generation of thinkers is perplexed, frightened by mysteries hidden until now which divine Wisdom is revealing to researchers. In every domain, the unheard-of is revealed to them. Fundamental theoretical research, along with applied invention, goes forward at an accelerating pace. Intellectual and existential vertigo is still in its early stage, buoyed by powerful impressions. Let us hope that the embryonic state of things truly promises a birth, an opening of deaf ears and blind eyes.

The world needs to understand a message that gives meaning and significance to life and to the universe. Winning the modern world for *islam* means first of all removing blinkers and enabling blocked ears to overcome the pathological difficulty that intercepts the Message of God and censures the voice that wells up in each of us, whether savant, crowned head, or simple common mortal.

5 Uncertainties

A new dawn rises on the horizon of a humanity dismembered from its dignity by rapacious tenets. The perplexity of the great modern thinkers is but the first glimmer, but, just as day follows night, doubt is always followed by the search for truth. It is the law of alternation.

Here we shall follow the forerunner flight of a scientific swallow; Edgar Morin is his name. This great man of modern French thought is the founder of the "Sociology of the Present" and an author whose generous output includes a four-volume "method." He is positioned at the crossroads of several disciplines—sociology, anthropology, philosophy, biology—and has keen philosophical interests.

It is thus from a multidisciplinary approach that this man of science draws his inspiration in initiating a reform of modern thought, with the ambition of provoking a revolution in human knowledge that is comparable to the one Copernicus introduced four centuries ago with regard to the planets.

I take this forerunner as a mentor in order to interest those who pay no attention to anything that is not written in a European language by native speakers of that language. In order to put them in direct contact with an "authority" who is worthy of respect, I shall cite him several times.

> The great discovery of this century has been the fact that science is not the realm of certainty. It is of course based on a series of certainties locally and spatially situated. . . . Popper's work has been indispensable for understanding that a scientific theory does not exist as such except to the extent that it accepts its fallible nature and lets itself be submitted to the play of "falsifiability"—i.e. to the extent that it accepts its biodegradability.[5]

This last word, "biodegradability," is very eloquent. It is a term used by ecologists who are concerned with conserving nature by creating materials that dissolve upon disposal.

Darwinism, having become the unshakable creed in Europe, is the most pernicious wave of pollution in the sea of ideas; it awaits scavengers better equipped than the "creationists" to get rid of it.

Our author applies Popper's ideas to the classical sciences by dismissing the three methodological bases on which their certainty is founded. He does so while recognizing their concrete and efficient value.

> Classical science is constructed upon three pillars of certainty: order, separability, and logic. . . . The idea of absolute determinism (the order of the universe) has itself become the object of quasi-religious belief among scientists who forget thereby that it cannot be demonstrated absolutely.[6]

The chaos theory of Ilya Prigogine has come to overturn this ancient "belief" long held to be absolute truth. Quantum physics, and the baffling findings that derive from it, have only intensified the discomfiture of received ideas.

> In the sciences, the separation between the observer and the observed, i.e. between us humans as we consider phenomena and the phenomena or objects of our knowledge, had the value of absolute certainty. Objective scientific knowledge implied the elimination of the individual and of subjectivity. The subject would be a disturbance, a noise.[7]

But this is no longer true in the light of modern quantum physics.

> Well-known experiments on waves and particles, concerning the nature of the latter, have shown that these behave sometimes like waves and sometimes like particles, sometimes continuous, sometimes discontinuous.[8]

These famous experiments show that the subatomic world is both variable (sometimes this, sometimes that) and susceptible to the attitude of the experimenter: exit the Cartesian principle of separability. Still more iconoclastic is the assault of these forerunner scholars on the holy of holies of classical science, logic, the soul and conscience of rationality. The third pillar of the certainty of classical science, logic, is upended.

> Induction founded on a significant and varied number of observations permitted general laws to be derived. As for deduction, it was an implacable means for leading to the truth.[9]

If the ability to guarantee the truth by means of these two methods of reasoning has now been put in question, what is one to say of their being ill-used by an ideology that pretends to be "scientific"? Darwin jumbled the givens by making copious and abundant observations, only to appeal in the end to superficial analogies and hasty deductions: man is a monkey!

Haughtily unaware of the cutting edge of science, neo-Darwinians triumphantly add a string to their bow by citing geneticists who have shown that 96% of the genetic endowment is common between men and certain species of monkeys. This is the sort of "scientific" argumentation in circulation on the market of dupes, the market of falsifiable, throw-away, and biodegradable ideas!

6 Considering Complexity

Complexity is inherent in human nature, and the ever more accelerated complexity of reality believed by classical scientists to be immutable—as the order of the cosmos and evidence of an inflexible determinism—stupefies the leading edge of modern science.

The cognitive approach of scientific rationality cannot pretend to embrace the world of the senses and instincts, the social world pulsing and throbbing with human reality. The hypertrophied rational competencies of the scholar may hide his negligence to embrace the whole of humankind. If our scholar is also a merchant of illusions, driven by an idea in the back of his mind to fabricate in order to shore up a baseless tenet, you get a clever falsifier able to mingle the vile and the sublime in order to prove the unprovable.

One cannot go far with atrophied sensory faculties and a conceptual structure recognized today as unfulfilled and biodegradable: we will need other resources than the logic of rationality to imagine the complexity of cosmic reality. We will need the opening of a divine source to give meaning to life and to the world. The incoherence and limitations of thinkers in the face of complexity come from their seclusion within the rational. Still, the fact that the epistemological value of modern knowledge has been called into question is already in itself the promise of an opening. Morin continues:

> It is admitted today that one can arrive empirically, through rational and empirico-logical means, at these contradictions. Moreover, Kant showed that on the horizon of reason looms a number of fundamental *aporimes*.[10]

An "aporime" is a problem that is virtually impossible to solve.[11] When we admit that there are fundamental insolubilities we are not far from admitting the necessity of opening ourselves to other resources than reason—but how can we go beyond rational logic to open ourselves to something else?

Our mentor admits that there is no other solution than to open ourselves, but his problem does not touch on the fundamental question of the meaning of life, and thus his conclusion remains on this side of the threshold that separates the universe of faith from that of the circular reasoning that chases its tail in despair, unable to overtake itself.

> We can confront the problem not by dreaming of entering into a new logic that will permit us to integrate the contradictions, but by showing that we would have to jump through an endless series of hoops between our traditional logic and the logical contraventions necessary to progress to an open rationality.[12]

The author can multiply the hoops as many times as he likes; he remains a prisoner in the hoop of rationality. The irrational frightens minds honed by the rational. They are trapped in the complexity of accessible reality by their cognitive faculty and they cannot get beyond it. How could they, without the help that comes from God?

Elsewhere in his work, Morin speaks of the "three udders" of complex thought: in order to contemplate complexity, one must first "respect" the "tissue" of which it is made. Then, one needs a "strategy for dealing with the uncertain," since the way is strewn with uncertainties. Lastly, it is necessary to leave the closed system, since "we live under the sway of ideas that form privileged, coherent, and consistent closed systems that take no account of occurrences."

Here we part company with Edgar Morin and his confrontation with uncertainty in order to listen to the voice of another European thinker who appears to leap over the threshold of rationality with the means of rationality itself.

7 Can One Speak of Modernity and God at the Same Time?

"A little science distances us from God, but much science brings us back."

This maxim of Pasteur is taken as the motto of Jean Guitton's book, *Dieu et la science,*[13] a book we shall cite at length here, God willing.

Let us first of all pause to consider two definitions that are essential to marking the boundaries between two domains, that of science, with its rational instruments, and that of philosophy, with its complexity and rationalist uncertainties; since the book published under the aegis and patronage of Guitton, an eminent French philosopher and one of the great Christian philosophers of our time, is in fact the result of a dialog between Guitton and two scholars in theoretical physics and astrophysics. Thus the necessity of a twofold definition.

"Rationality" is the character of the rational. The "rational" is what is based on reason, deduced from reasoning rather than empiricism, and determined by calculations or reasoning. "Rationalism" is the doctrine according to which everything that exists has its reason for being and cannot be considered as unintelligible in itself. It is further defined as the doctrine according to which human knowledge proceeds from a priori principles independent of experience.[14]

We shall not get very far with the definition of rationalism, since it figures in every philosophical system, and the philosophical systems from antiquity (e.g. Socrates and Plato) to the present consist of an inextricable forest of systems of controversies and contradictions.

We shall retain only two observations useful for our argument. The first is that scientific intelligibility, based on experiment and verification, but otherwise put to the question as we noted above, is different from philosophical intelligibility, both in method and in object.

The second observation, subsidiary to the first, will bear on the deliberate ambiguity contrived by those Islamophobes among us who, in the rear-guard struggle against Islamists, use the Arabic word *'aqlânîya* to translate both "rationality" and "rationalism." In this way the pseudo-scientific argument is triumphantly brandished in the Islamist's face: you speak about the *ghaïb,* the irrational, of God; you aren't *'aqlânî.*[15] And if you aren't *'aqlânî,* you are necessarily obscurantist; you don't believe in reason! Pillory the obscurantists!

In such a climate, and to remove the difficulties we encounter in our relationships with ideological modernism and technological modernity, it is urgent that we ask good questions. Elsewhere, as the reader may well have observed, this work is dotted out with many questions; it is because this method helps to lay out problems and avoid misunderstandings.

Can one not speak of God (may He be praised!) without renouncing the scientific and technical means modernity offers us?

Must we abjure our faith and embrace the methodology of doubt and biodegradable mythology in order to enter modernity?

To speak of God in these modern times exposes you to suspicion; it tends to ostracize you, particularly if you are known in the world of science. That is why such great names as Popper, Prigogine, and Morin—men who dare to cast scientific "certainty" into doubt—do not, however, explicitly pose the question of God (exalted be He!).

The pressure is strong, and the great French philosopher Guitton himself feels the need to cover himself with the genius of Pasteur, that giant of science and great benefactor of humanity, in order to speak openly—if timidly—of God (exalted be God's Name!).

A disciple of the great Bergson and a member of the French Academy, Guitton is considered to be the heir of the intuitionist philosophy of his teacher. Bergson bases his spiritualism on the method of the immediate knowledge of duration and of life by means of intuition. This means the kind of immediate perception that does not proceed by reason or the methods of reasoning.

The French spiritual heir of a great master meets, in the space of a book, two scholars formed by scientific discipline and rigor: Grichka Bogdanov and Igor Bogdanov.

Philosophical rationalism open to the irrational sits down at the table with rationality entrenched behind the principle of verifiability that believes that nothing exists that cannot be seen under the microscope or the telescope or in the logic of one's calculations.

The book that brings the academician and two scientists together asks, in this last decade of the 20th century, the question of God: can we think of God and science at the same time? Can scientists accept working on the hypothesis of the existence of a divine Master of the universe who is neither calculable nor demonstrable?

The pressure is great, since the convictions of atheism are once again on the defensive and were recently expressed—with a serenity that seems to be unvisited by doubt—in the words of Jacques Monod, the Nobel Prize-winning French physician who died in 1976. The one who elucidated the mechanism of genetic regulation at the cellular level passed away without even having thought of shedding light on the mystery of his own existence:

> Man knows, at last, that he is alone in the indifferent immensity of the universe in which he emerged by chance. He knows now that, like a gypsy, he is marginal to the universe in which he lives: a universe that is deaf to his music and indifferent to his hopes, his suffering, and his crimes.[16]

Another Nobel Prize winner, the American Steven Weiberg, a theorist of great value, writes with the same despair, "The more we know the universe, the more it appears pointless and strange to us."[17]

8 Questions

Philosophers' insights, however spiritually convinced at the outset, lose their freshness and force by being formulated and reasoned. The *fiṯra* of which the Qur'an speaks, and which I translate as "innateness,"[18] has no need of formulation nor reasoning to perceive the truth of existence: it is a feeling, a meaning inscribed in the primordial tissue of the human being. It is the direct force and the immediate quest of the Creator when the intuition of philosophers wanders around the created universe as one beats about the bush.

By leaving the door ajar to the primordial question, just being astonished at this marvelously arranged world is already a great step toward absolute truth. The great thinkers, savants of uncertainty, drag on at great length before this innately natural response; like Monod and Weinberg, they are occupied with seeking an outcome that will imprison them.

Our academic co-authors, rather than asking the principal question—Who made me human?—Content themselves with asking relevant questions such as: Where did the universe come from? What is reality? What are the relationships between conscience and matter? Why is there something rather than nothing?

These questions stand at the boundaries between science and philosophy and bring to the latter new ideas about the material universe, the object of physics. Guitton and his two colleagues easily traverse the boundaries between the ideal universe of philosophy and the perception of modern physics, by which the material is revealed to be a simple idea.

A great revolution is announced, and Morin is not the only one to speak of it. Consider these remarks by the three authors of *Dieu et la science:*

> We are now at the edge of a revolution of thinking, an epistemological breakthrough the likes of which philosophy has not known for centuries. It seems to us that beyond the conceptual path opened by quantum theory there emerges a new and radically different representation of the world.[19]

This great revolution overturns philosophical ideas as well as scientific certainty "in a way that erases the boundaries between mind and matter. Thus we have decided to give it the name of "meta-realism."ÊÈ

The boundaries between mind and matter having been abolished, the possibility of asking about God presents itself. The question is to be posed with caution: revolution or no, the way is still littered with the skepticism of a Weinberg and the pessimism of a Monod. We had best be prudent.

> Nonetheless, certain harbingers suggest that the moment has come to open new paths across deep knowledge, to seek beyond the mechanistic appearances of science the almost metaphysical spoor of something else, at once near and strange, powerful and mysterious, scientific and inexplicable: something like God, perhaps.[21]

Perhaps? The intuitive spirit does not dare to speak out more firmly despite the formidable support of the new science. In the modern West, defying the taboos is still too risky. How difficult it is, even for a Guitton, to find the means of sharing his disillusion with a culture saturated by skeptical atheism and snug in its sufficiency:

> That is what we have sought in this book. By virtue of the displacement philosophy and religion have undergone under the formidable pressure of science, it was impossible to attempt a description of reality without appealing to the most recent ideas of modern physics and, little by little, we have been led toward another world, strange and fascinating, where most of our certainties about time, space, and matter were nothing more than pure illusions, much easier to grasp, of course, than the reality itself.[22]

At the edge of science's formidable pressure in its applications to information technology, the bewildering discoveries in every domain, and particularly in that of genetics, we find fundamental theory and research. Where philosophical intuition is joined by the most recent scientific discoveries, we enter once again the sphere of the rationally unknowable; another logic is needed here.

> If you agree to enter into metalogical thinking, if you yield nothing before the unknowable, if you admit that the unknowable is at its very core the course of modern science, you will understand why the most recent discoveries in new physics overtake the sphere of metaphysical intuition. At that moment you will better grasp in what sense Einstein, the last of the classical physicists persuaded that the universe—reality—was knowable, was mistaken. Today, on the strange and shifting frontiers asserted by quantum theory, all physicists, without exception, experiment with an agnosticism of a new kind: reality is not knowable, it is veiled, and it is destined to remain so. Accept this conclusion and you discover that there is an alternative solution to physical oddness: logical oddness.[23]

The authors continue by setting forth the only certainty and the only logic that is left to them: reality is scientifically unknowable, forever veiled, it simply does not exist.

> A logic of the odd? One might very well base this new conceptual edifice on the most powerful yet also the most upsetting concept of our century: quantum theory. With it, interpretations of the universe that make good sense, such as objectivity and determinism, can no longer be maintained. What shall we choose instead? That reality "per se" does not exist. It depends on how we decide to observe it. The elementary entities that comprise it may be one thing (a wave) and, at the same time, another (a particle). At any rate, reality is, at depth, indeterminate.[24]

The materialist vision of the world is scientifically false, and the physics of a genius like Einstein is brilliantly surpassed:

> Every year brings a harvest of theoretical reshuffling concerning the borderlines of our reality, the infinitely small and the infinitely large. Like cosmology, quantum theory continues to push back the limits of knowledge, until they brush against the most fundamental enigma: the existence of a transcendent Being, at once the cause and the meaning of the great universe.[25]

The agnosticism common to the scholar and philosopher may be the threshold of astonishment and expectation of a light that will come to dispel the darkness and lift the veil that prevents modernity from seeing clearly and finding meaning for itself. Much science leads back again to God, Pasteur said. But rational science has thrown in the towel and given up in desperation before the unknowable reality of the universe.

The sole source of information that remains is Revelation. It alone can help us ask—and answer—the right questions about existence: Why am I here? Where am I going after death? What should I do? How should I behave in view of the Life after this? What ethic should guide my action in society?

9 Revelation and Prophecy

What is Revelation? What is Prophecy? I capitalize them in order to distinguish the divine from the profane.

What else can tell us what Revelation and Prophecy are but Revelation itself? Science's new receptivity, a return to certainty by means of healthy uncertainties, will facilitate communication with the intelligentsia, even as the multimedia network can carry the Message of the Revelation to all azimuths.

In the Sûrah called Consultation (*Shûrâ*), God informs us:

> It is not given to a mortal that God should speak to him through any other means than by Revelation, or from behind a veil, or by sending him a Messenger (angel) who reveals to him, with God's permission, whatever He wills. He is sublime and wise. Thus We have revealed to you (O Muhammad) a spirit (the Qur'an) coming forth from Our ordering. You had wisdom neither of the Book nor of the faith. But We have made for you (of the Qur'an) a light by means of which We guide whom We will among Our servants. You yourself guide toward the right path, the path of God the Master, of that which there is in the heavens and on the earth. All things return to God.[26]

Thus Revelation is the Word of God addressed to a chosen and blessed person by one of the three means cited. Moses is the exception to whom God spoke without intermediary, as we read in the Sûrah of the Women:

> We sent you the Revelation, as We did to Noah and to the Messengers who came after him. We also made Revelation to Abraham, to Ismael, to Jacob, to the Prophets of the twelve tribes, to Jesus, to Job, to Jonah, to Aaron, and to Solomon. To David We gave the Psalms. Of some of these Prophets We have told you the story, of others We have said nothing. It is certain that God spoke to Moses directly. All the Prophets have announced (the Message) and given warning. This is so that after the coming of the Messengers, no peoples can have cause to argue before God. God is powerful and wise. God is the witness Himself of that which He has revealed to you. He has revealed it in full knowledge. The angels bear witness to it as well. Is not God's testimony enough?[27]

The blessed procession of the Prophets of God is presented to us; some of them remain unknown to us. These were neither wonder-workers, soothsayers, nor the enlightened such as all eras and all societies have known. Imposters, the evil-minded, though they amuse their crowds for a brief time, do not reach the universal nor found the great religions that stake out the history of divine guidance.

The chosen one of God, a simple mortal, but a saintly mortal, is the first to be astonished when Revelation surprises him. Our Prophet Muhammad (grace and peace upon him!) tells us his fear when, while making a spiritual retreat in the cave of Hirâ, in the mountains of Mecca, he saw the archangel Gabriel give notice to him of the Message: "He took me and gripped me with such strength that I suffered from it."[28]

The angel ordered him to read. Being illiterate, he did not know how. Three times in a row the angel gripped him mightily, before communicating to him the first revealed Sûrah, *Al 'Alaq,*[29] by which God let him know who is his Creator, and the Creator of the world.

Oh, my brother, my sister! If you have the good fortune of being able to read and understand Arabic, the language of the sacred, the Qur'an is available to you, with its authentic content and perfume preserved from any falsification. It is there for you, God's Message to humankind for all time. If you have some other language, let a good interpretation—I do not say translation, for God's Word cannot be translated—serve to support you provisionally until your heart is penetrated by the light of faith.

Such is Revelation; what then is Prophecy? The Prophet is a man to whom God has sent Revelation in order to make him His ambassador among the creatures of His that are endowed with reason. He lends men credence by means of miracles. The miracle becomes an integral part of his Mission, as supernatural proof of its veracity.

The Prophet Muhammad (peace and grace upon him!) said: "There has been no Prophet who was not gratified by such miracles as were capable of bringing people to the faith. To me He gave (as a distinct miracle) the Revelation (of the Qur'an). This is why I hope to have the most disciples on the Day of the Last Judgment."[30]

All the other Prophets (grace and peace upon them!) received Revelation. Some of them passed on a teaching that their disciples consigned to writing long after their death, and hands less certain have more or less altered and deformed. The Qur'an's particular and inimitable character is that it has remained intact and is thus authentic.

One of the greatest reasons that drives disciples to alter and deform the Message of the Prophets is the all-too human penchant for mythologizing the life and teaching of great men. The most glaring example is that of Jesus Christ. After the death of his faithful holy Apostles, deviations resulted in the divinization of the Holy Prophet Jesus (grace and peace upon him!). The miracles that God conferred upon him are so prodigious that he came to be made into a god on their account. His birth alone is a unique miracle, and his daily life was stocked with miracles; thus certain Christians did not hesitate to make a god of him.

In the Sûrah *Al-'Imran,* the Qur'an reports Jesus' discourse to his people:

> For you I fashion clay in the form of a bird, I breathe upon it and it flies away with God's authorization. I heal the blind and the leprous. I raise the dead, with God's authorization. I know what you have eaten and what you have stored away in your lodgings.[31]

10 Making Sense of Life

The first phrase revealed in the Qur'an, this miracle accorded to the Prophet Muhammad (grace and peace upon him!) informs us that it is in the Name of God the Creator that the one sent by God should *read* the Revelation. A few verses later it is intimated to him that humankind returns to God after death. Throughout the sacred Book we find forceful and reiterated warning against leading our lives as unrighteous egoists opposed to what is good.

In reading the Qur'an we are soon made to understand that to believe that this mysterious universe is the work of a Creator is not enough to give meaning, significance, and direction to our lives. When we say that modern science has lost its certainty, when we feel sorry for ourselves and wonder whether life has meaning, we are moved by mortal anguish, not by gratuitous curiosity. Mortal anguish and my future after death form the core of the question.

To know that I am God's creature is the point of departure and powerful anchoring of my faith in a Future after death. It is also the source of inspiration that my sojourn here below and my actions in the world are not merely blind groping.

The Qur'an is replete with four major themes:

1. God is our Creator.
2. Humankind returns to God after death.

3. The Prophets are humankind's Messengers and models.
4. Our sojourn on earth is to be rewarded or sanctioned.

Nothing takes the place of attentive, patient, and assiduous reading of the Qur'anic text for all who seek Knowledge and intelligibility through the path of Revelation, once science and human philosophies have proved disappointing and have been given up.

The first verses of the Sûrah *Al-Mu'minûn* (the faithful) embrace the entire life of mankind both here below as well as in the Future, as the result of the examination of his sojourn. Listen:

> Blessed are the faithful who pray with humility and who abstain from what is futile, those who offer the gifts of zakat, and who follow sexual discipline.[32]

After enumerating the moral qualities and the acts of worship that qualify the faithful for eternal happiness, an explanation of human origins and his arrival on earth is taken up in an arresting summary:

> We have drawn man from the essence of the earth. We have made him from a drop of sperm deposited in the sure haven of an organ. We have transformed the sperm into a clot of blood, the blood into an entity of flesh. Finally, we have given him form and stature. Blessed be God, the best of creators![33]

The evocation of the genesis of life is always bound to that of death and a return to life:

> After being created, you shall die. Then you shall be raised up on the Day of the Last Judgment.[34]

Life here below is an Ordeal to be overcome. Life thus has the meaning of being an examination to be undergone:

> Glory to Him who holds the Power and Who is Omnipotent. Glory to Him Who created death and life to prove you, so as to distinguish those among you who shall do the best work.[35]

Life is thus an examination consisting of trials and difficulties to test our manner of working. Objects, ideas, the cosmos, and the world's hustle and bustle constitute so many circumstances and difficulties in my path.

The great Ordeal in this time is to avow, without stumbling, without doubting the wisdom of the divine Plan, the formidable rupture of standards between the modern world, so rich and developed, and the poor and weak world of Muslims. Modernity—and Islam's resistance to its incursions—provides me with the occasion to do good work, indeed a noble work.

In our days modernity witnesses a frightening development in the domains of science and technology. The most frightening of all this progress is genetic engineering, the laboratory manipulation of cells and genes that make scholars believe they can create plants, animals, even humans, at will.

This mad advance of science and technology is a Test; it is a foolish rush that Sûrah *Al-An'âm* explicates for us. Peoples forgetful of God are put to the Test; alternatively, epochs of fortune and misfortune follow one another until the day when individual death or the collapse of a civilization brings an end, here below, to the life of all that seemed indestructible.

Like a breach in the wall of what was heretofore unknowable, an Ordeal is put into practice by Providence: what was impossible yesterday is today's triviality.

Oh man, perched over your microscope, you create nothing! Wake up! The cell and its nucleus, along with the genetic system were not imagined and fabricated by you, so far as I know. Poor unknowing manipulated manipulator! Was it you who gave substance, life, intelligence, and imagination to that marvelous instrument that is your brain? One cut into your cerebral instrument and, bang, it's a vegetable!

Verse 44 of the Sûrah *An'âm* teaches and instructs us:

> When they forgot Our instruction, We opened wide the gates of all things to them. They were deafened by pleasure, rejoicing in what We had enabled them to do; then We caught them up by surprise and threw them into dismay.[36]

Test after test, the individual and human societies proceed ineluctably toward death. Happy are those who are not deterred from the truth by enjoyment or misfortune. Happy are those who maintain the will to please God and do good works to attain their reward; for the Qur'an teaches us:

> Let those who search after this ephemeral world be satisfied with what We willingly concede to them. For such individuals We reserve the Hell into which they shall fall, covered with shame and error. As to those who search after the happiness of the Life Hereafter and whose striving after goodness flows from faith, they shall be received by God.[37]

11 The Law: The Way

Faith is certainty. Faith translated into action requires, beyond the impulse of the heart, an intention, a tireless search for the occasion of doing good. Belief in God and in the Last Day is but a sterile act of will unless it is accompanied by acts, that is, actions guided by a pure intention, a quickening will, and discipline.

Islamic Law is called *shar'iya* in Arabic; this means "the way."[38] The faithful, submissive to God, follow a way, a disciplined path, a method of life. Among sworn or ill-informed Islamophobes, however, the term evokes cruelty and a thirst for blood.

For such persons, *shar'iya* is inhuman. Since hands have been atrociously cut off by rash regimes—regimes without consideration for the care with which *shar'iya* informs the Islamic penal code—a ready argument can be had to condemn *islam* and its Law as a savage practice.

Such ill-intentioned or misinformed reductionism would wish to ignore (or would not know) the fact that *shar'iya,* the way, covers the entire normative field of individual and social life. For those who wish to know nothing, it is summed up as a penal code practiced as if by improvisation. The distressing usage made in certain Muslim countries of punishments instituted by *shar'iya,* with virtually no care for the circumstances under which the Law is to be applied, serves only to deepen the misunderstanding.

The Qur'an and Sunna (the teaching and practice of the Prophet) are the two sources of the Law. The Sunna shows us, in high degree, a gentle human Prophet, a Prophet who shows people the way, who teaches them how to act and how to seek salvation.

If penalization has its place, it is within the limits and structures of a peaceable society where crime must be punished—within the framework of a society that recognizes the rights of its citizens as much as it exacts their duty.

Of the Qur'an's six thousand verses (6,236 exactly), only thirty are devoted to ordinances repressing crime, thirteen alone speak of judgments and controversy. The rest is Guidance. The rest develops in man a solicitude for his Future after death by showing him the edifying example of the Just, and by commending uprightness and earnestness to him.

The rest—virtually the whole of the Qur'an—is devoted above all else to the relationship of man and his Creator, and the good work necessary during this life in order for him to perfect himself and merit eternal happiness.

In light of that relationship, social order, peace, and war, the sharing of goods, as well as the collection of moral, economic, political, and family principles are couched in a spirit of tolerance and a respect for life. Giving and forgiving—not cavil and hatred—are the conditions of the Islamic regulation of social life.

At the head of the objectives envisaged by divine Law stands the concern for achieving a salvific life of good work. The preservation of life, reason, moral social relationships, and property are vital objectives for insuring social peace and order, without which no constructive work is possible. Thus the sanctions prescribed by the Law form a railing, as it were, along the path leading to God.

Just as in a state of law where justice is the business of a human jurisdiction concerned with order and peace, so God, Who wants societies of faith to be ruled by order and peace, establishes His Law that sanctions thoughtless disruption and neutralizes all who abet disorder.

Nonetheless, the Law does not rest upon the same principle as human jurisdiction, nor does it derive therefrom. The revealed truth to which Muslim people adhere is its guiding principle, not a legal system imposed by constraint, by a power that monopolizes physical violence and coercion. Herein lies a great difference.

Firmness is required in every policed society, and Islamic society is neither a cloister of monks nor a garden of delights. The individual's course of salvation cannot be pursued in the midst of social turbulence; society must be governed by laws. Whether the fundamental law—in modern terms, a constitution—or partial laws, each segment of social life needs legislation that is renewed and adaptive.

The fundamental principles enunciated in the Qur'an and Sunna are the pillars of jurisdiction, but they do not cover every detail of social, economic, or political life. A large space is left open to legislative effort to put the Law into practice and to adapt it to changing circumstances.

One procedure and one qualification are required of the Muslim jurist that guarantee that the spirit of the Law is not betrayed and that explicit and clear resolutions are not transgressed. The initiatives of juridical effort—or Ijtihad—have their limits, but literalism and slavish following are as much impediments as the necessary and independent choices of jurists of the past.

A juridical system that is paralyzed and chained to the jurisprudence of the past, well short of the Qur'an and Sunna, cannot respond to the modern needs of a globalized economy and the international constraints that bind nations together. To isolate ourselves in our norms and close our shutters for fear of contrary influences will not get us very far in the "global village." On the other hand, to bend unconditionally to the dictates of the powerful institutions of hegemonic states is an even more foolish choice!

The desirable framework we need to participate positively in the modern world and escape the traps of globalization is that of multilateral Islamic solidarity. We need to throw up a blockade around our Law and defend it. The day is coming, if God wills it, when the selfsame Law will be the spirit and mortar of an Islamic fraternity that will abolish the artificial borders of the nation-states that imprison Muslim peoples.

12 The Cultural Wash

Modernism lies in wait without, with its claws ready to set on us and pierce us deeply, deforming our ideas and monopolizing our feelings. We can resist external influences by mobilizing endogenous forces, but what can we do when those forces are drawn down and immobilized by the lethargy of the very societies in danger of losing their identity? What is to be done if acculturation puts you in tune with a disheveled world that cares nothing about your reason for living: your faith, your mission on earth?

We need to begin by humbly settling down to the task of forming and reforming ourselves. We need to educate and inform with all patience. We must not hope to change people's attitudes and states of mind with a wave of the hand. To go about things abruptly will not allow us to share our ideals and have our convictions accepted.

This means that the action of the Islamic state must face the cold reality of a modernism that attacks us; we are not going to achieve any positive results unless the warmth of compassion and the helping hand of benevolent associations lend their assistance. The material and moral impoverishment our societies suffer from call out as much for social justice as they do for educational reform. Material decadence is the mother of moral and intellectual wretchedness.

Modernism inundates us with its libertine culture of uniformity. Even in the heart of the West, nations jealous of their cultural identity and their independence cry "Stop, thief!"

At the francophone conference held in Vietnam in the second week of October 1997 we could admire the faultless logic of President Jacques Chirac. It was he who put the world on alert against one-standard cultural imperialism, and, without naming the civilization of the hamburger and Coca Cola (names that have become common because of the will of economic domination and cultural standardization), he exhorted French-speaking countries to reclaim with him the francophone "cultural exception."

Chirac also announced on this occasion an institution capable of encouraging former French colonies into clustering themselves at the cultural bosom of the French motherland. How curious, this spirit of cultural neocolonialism—forgetful as well. As if the people of Vietnam could have overthrown two powerful armies in one decade by calling any other culture than their own!

The notion of "culture" having been introduced, I pause in order to examine this freewheeling term. Just what is this hackneyed cliché that can form and deform you, tell you what to do, what not to do, and how to think? What is culture? As a notion, "culture" has dozens of definitions—

each school of psychology and anthropology, each ideology has its own. Let us review a few conceptions of culture entertained by our European cousins.

The French hold literary and artistic creativity to be cultural values, along with an appreciation for its patrimony—written, painted, and sculpted; knowing what is useful and what isn't; the production of images, of personæ; a taste for refined expressivity and a way with words. Of God and of life's meaning—nothing.

For the Anglo-Saxons, culture is attached to a style of living, an anthropological bent, myth, practical savvy, landscape painting, and *tea time*. Of God—no mention.

The Germans have ready cash for a culture where historical myth rubs shoulders with practical efficiency, where civilization and power are symbolically conjoined, where the Germanic communities feel a sense of superiority to others. No word here of God, of the sense of my life and what will become of me.

For all of them, you are cultured on the whole if you have acquired a curiosity-shop of knowledge and are programmed to keep consuming cultural goods. Such a culture in no way informs me about the meaning of my life and my future; I turn the page to search for my homeland elsewhere.

I search for a homeland for my mind and heart—but not under the black cloak of the tenets of bestialism that lie at the base of pagan cultures. I seek it in the Revelation that alone answers my primordial questioning.

The acculturated intellectuals among us, who have a nearly carnal relationship with the West, fall in with its cultural ukases, its official pronouncements. The West, Western culture, Western speech, Western fantasy, Western art, Western certainty: these represent their only lights and landmarks, their sole truth. They are satisfied with the answer modern culture provides, if by chance or intellectual shamelessness they ask, "What am I doing here in this mad drudgery called life?"

André Malraux is a French man of letters combined with an engaged intellectual, a revolutionary adventurer, and a statesman and glorious companion of the great General de Gaulle—in short, a monster as sacred to modernity as he is. This illustrious man of culture defined culture as follows (I cite from memory): "Culture is all that tells me what I am to do on this earth."

Is it existential angst that drives this great mind to content himself with cultural nothingness as an answer to a desperate question? He was de Gaulle's cultural minister; was it his last thought—or rather, the epigram, rightly or wrongly attributed to him—with which he framed his disillusioned testament, with the words, "the twenty-first century will be religious or it will not."

Turning our back on culture, what is it we prefer—to be uncultured savages, frustrated, wild, knowing nothing of the world, stoners of modernity?

That would be to dodge the Test, to refuse to bring the Message to modernity so as to bring it to *islam.* We could scarcely be convincing or be accepted to the forums of dialog unless we were abreast of what is happening in all spheres of global reality, beginning with the cultural.

We have nothing against people's cultures unless they seek to acculturate us and brutalize us with the mindless hubbub of modernity. In the midst of the expansion of an unfettered American culture and the domination of Western knowledge, *islam* is not going to represent itself as the absolute negation of everything the other side thinks and teaches. But to put the brakes on to the imposition and playing out of the stratagems of acculturation, it is necessary to launch a lively denunciation of its pseudoscientific tenets. Let those who will, understand this; and let those who insult the future mock at this.

In order to regenerate and pump up the vigorous sap of faith in the hearts and minds of our young generation, we must first of all point out to them what is evil. The bestial tenet which takes man for an evolved ape whose only aim is to get on well and enjoy life, this is the basis of all the ideas to be cast away; the tenet and the culture it inspires are to be combated and filtered with a care for cultural ecology.

The distracted flight into futility which modernity merchandises must be renounced. We must free ourselves from its cultural incantation, so morally wretched and heedless to human suffering; we must consecrate our efforts to fighting misery in the world.

How to be other than an invading culture wants to see me—a culture that nibbles away my life and debases my will?

Notes

1 Sûrah 8 [*Anfâl*]: verses 22, 55.

2 TN: Not 1830, as in the original, where the title is given as *De l'origine des espèces par voie de sélection naturelle.* The work concerns primarily the evolution of coral reefs; the Imam's description overlaps the contents of Darwin's *Descent of Man and Selection in Relation to Sex* of 1871.

3 [*The Laws of Chaos*] (Paris: Flammarion).

4 [*The End of Certainty*] (Paris: Odile Jacob, 1996).

5 *La société en quête de valeurs* [*Society in Search of Values*] (Paris: Ed. Laurent de Mesnil, 1996), p. 217. All citations here are drawn from this four-volume work.

6 Op. cit., p. 218.

7 Ibid., p. 222.

8 Ibid., pp. 222–23.

9 Ibid., p. 219.

10 Ibid., p. 224.

11 TN: The term in French is *aporie*, the definition of which in Larousse is cited by Yassine: "an insoluble contradiction in a reasoning." The *OED* gives the cognate "aporia" as a rhetorical figure expressing fundamental doubt. "Aporime," or "apore" is closer in meaning to the French. All stem from the Greek aporia, "not accessible, impassible."

12 Ibid., p. 226.

13 [*God and Science*] Ed. Grasset (Paris, 1991).

14 TN: The definitions are based on those of *Larousse,* as Yassine indicates.

15 TN: *'Aqlânîa,* from *'aql* ("conception, understanding, mind, intellect, intelligence"), is defined as "rationaliste; rationalisme" in the *Dictionaire Arabe-Français Larousse,* where *ghaïb* (> *ghâba* 'hide oneself, disappear') is defined as "invisible, mystère [divin]."

16 *La société en quête de valeurs,* op. cit., p. 209.

17 Ibid., p. 210.

18 TN: Further translated as "character, natural disposition, instinct, nature."

19 Op cit., p. 18.

20 Ibid.

21 Ibid., p. 16.

22 Ibid.

23 Ibid., p. 12.

24 Ibid., p. 21.

25 Ibid., p. 23.

26 Sûrah 42 [*Ash-Shûra*]: verses 51–53.

27 Sûrah 4 [*An-Nisâ'*]: verses 163–66.

28 The two [*hadîth*] collections of Bukhari and Muslim.

29 TN: Sûrah 96, "The Clot of Congealed Blood," also known by its first word, the imperative *iqra'* ("proclaim [aloud]," "read," "recite," "rehearse").

30 Bukhari and Muslim.

31 Sûrah 3 [*Al-'Imran*]: verse 49.

32 Sûrah 23 [*Al-Mu'minûn*]: verses 1–5.

33 Sûrah 23 [*Al-Mu'minûn*]: verses 12–14.

34 Sûrah 23 [*Al-Mu'minûn*]: verses 15–16.

36 Sûrah 67 [*Al-Mulk*]: verses 1–2.

37 Sûrah 6 [*Al-An'âm*]: verse 44.

38 Sûrah 17 [*Al-Isrâ'*]: verses 18–19.

39 TN: The latter has the form *shâri'*; the root of both is *shara'a*, shown as two separate entries in *Larousse Arabe-Français.*

VI. *Being*

1 Forming and Being Formed

As we have repeated throughout this work, "the rotation of days" is one of God's laws by which eras follow one another in the unfurling history of civilizations. This is bound to favor Muslims over a fairly long term, since Muslim demography is galloping to approach one-half of the world population within the next few decades; it is expected to reach 40% by the end of the 20th century. Demographic vitality is a sign of life and a very significant indicator; in the West the age pyramid is the inverse and has become a death alert.

To skeptics whose view is ill formed and ill informed concerning historical vicissitudes, the alternate swing in favor of Muslims is a sweet compensating dream, a self-consoling mechanism of oppressed peoples. With all due deference to skeptics of whatever stripe, God is the Master of what is afoot, of what is being prepared between days and nights. Glory to Him!

Despite its apparent skepticism, the modern world is preoccupied with the Islamic phenomenon and its accelerated resurgence. It knows full well that one day Islamists, called forth by Muslims long abused, will come into power here and there. The crime instigated in Algeria largely by the West may perhaps prove a foil, a lesson, so that such tragedies are no longer repeated.

What will Islamists do once they come to power? Will they wear themselves out with vain demonstrations of force, to flout the West uselessly, and to thwart the stratagems of such blind power with its current possibilities, heedless of a tomorrow that cannot be recalled once wasted? Or will it set itself to the noble fundamental task of forming and informing the younger generations?

Bringing modernity to *islam* will begin within Muslim nation-states, their economic and political fields devastated by a Westernized and acculturated élite whose passions are a historical wrong-way affair. Of course, some of these Westernized élite will make up their minds to rally the new forces courageously; not everyone's case is desperate.

In any case, violent revolution and Stalinesque reeducation should play no role in the program of Islamist power—no more "cultural revolutions" à la Mao.

The institutional power of a re-islamized state should be ratified and enabled by the goodwill of a revivified and mobilized people with a view to forming and informing its disabused youths, to encourage them—this time confidently—to roll up their sleeves to do the work required to address so many bleak situations.

Schools and universities will be beehives buzzing with educational activity. Mosques, sanctuaries and havens of the faith, must become again the geometric locus of education; around them should radiate a spirit of seriousness and faithfulness to the Law of God (praised be He!).

State effort and the benevolent gift of the people will be linked to reestablish the bar and reinstate a sense of character—of *fiṯrah*[1]—in minds made destitute by the teaching of a pernicious acculturation. It should provide help to all to open a new era and change ways of thinking that have deviated from the truth. There needs to be a great deal of gentleness and love, but the hand stretched forth in love will be firm and resolute.

Fiṯrah is a Qur'anic word that denotes the psychological core of the human being. This core, this profound sense of identity and deep innate nature, is the place where faith and trust in God repose. Deformed as it is in the cultural and familial milieu of the acculturated among us, it awaits the prompt and friendly aid of the faithful whose life focuses on the mosque.

The younger generations, put on their guard against the typhoon of bestial culture, will easily respond to the appeal. Childhood is the principal stake of the future; it should be the object of our solicitude and care so as preserve the *fiṯrah* in its freshness, despite the dry and barren winds.

Islamists must understand that they will not come to power with an arsenal of repressive laws, but with a capital of love and energies of sympathy. They must devote themselves to the delicate work of raising, preserving, caring, and helping. They will find sure allies on the ground: men and women of faith who are ready and confident. An ally even more sure and confident, that will open up to friendly overtures and will respond to the appeal of generous sympathy, is the innocence of childhood.

The disposition of childhood to be formed and informed according to natural aptitude is demonstrated by Muhammad (grace and peace on him!), God's apostle, who said: "Every newborn comes into the world endowed with an innate sense (*fiṯrah*). It is his father and mother who (by their educating influence) make a Jew, a Christian, or a Zoroastrian of him."[2]

The Holy Prophet makes reference to the Qur'an and invites us to read verse 30 of Sûrah *Ar-Rûm.* The interpretation is addressed first to the Prophet and then to every reader of the Qur'an:

> Set your entire being to the faith with utter faithfulness, following and obeying the primary nature with which God has endowed humankind.[3]

It is clearly an exhortation to a righteousness of will and to moral and spiritual equity. If the influences of family, associates, and culture do not favor such equity and work to turn primary nature from its original end, education will have to correct the wrong caused by the ambient circumstances.

There must be a concerted effort between Islamic government and a well-wishing active public to set attitudes straight and dispel the fog. There must be a consecration without gradation and reservation for the sake of an Islamic future and the actions to secure it. We must wipe away the moral inertia and indifference of worm-eaten generations and delicately discourage acculturating militantism, since education aiming at reinstating the ancient faith is bound to clash with that which destroys our Muslim nature. But only for a while!

2 Unhappy Childhood

The disfiguring effects of secular pedagogy will not be the only threat to the effort to win children back to *islam.* Economic and social misery generates moral decadence and spiritual decline. To seek to restore the people's *fiṯrah* and to educate them in moral and spiritual righteousness will be a vain enterprise unless the material roots of evil are attacked.

Without first attending to the day-to-day needs of childhood, announcing a rehabilitation program on the level of ethical values is merely a stroll through dreamland. Priorities, some more urgent than others, will clamor for the attention of any newly constituted Islamic government. The most urgent will be that of guaranteeing children a future by rescuing them from poverty and responding to their distress.

In Muslim countries we have not reached the wholesale destruction of childhood that is found in the streets of South America or the jungles of sub-Saharan Africa. The commercial exploitation of children and their enlistment at age nine in militias is, fortunately, not the lot of poor children among us; still, the threat is one of degrees.

The spectacle of children in tattered rags living in the streets as victims of criminal gangs is pathetic. Television exposes the disgrace of the young people of Rio or Calcutta, youths abandoned to begging for their daily bread, for a handful of coins to buy a dose of cheap drugs. The spectacle of the adolescent engaged in drug trafficking is as frightening as that of the African child led to war with a Kalashnikov on a sling and singing of death. We are not there yet, but we are running in that direction, God help us!

While our situation has not yet reached such lows, our streets are more and more teeming with idle youths, out of work, coasting along, contaminating a childhood rejected by an inhospitable and inefficient educational system. Among us, glue sniffing and its petty trade are in currency. The big trade is already recruiting, and the world masters of that sad business have their go-betweens and clients among us.

Other agents of destruction ceaselessly undermine Muslim societies. The saber-rattling of Saddam, for example, has left in its wake a people in complete deprivation, lacking food, prey to disease and total wretchedness. Worse still is that Iraqi children suffer martyrdom. A recent report shows that a quarter of the children are in a desperate state. A quarter of Iraqis for generations to come will be physically and morally handicapped.

Another example is the Palestinian children of the *intifada.* The drama of Palestinian childhood is presented as a political phenomenon. The image of a child fallen under an Israeli soldier's bullets no longer tears at anyone's heart. The media rarely speak of the shameful calamity suffered by our children. Yet they cannot say enough in denouncing "integrationism" and supposed Islamic "terrorism."

Two aspects of humanity are the object of particular Islamic solicitude: children and women, mothers and their children. The protection of children is on a par with that of the family, and the family is above all the mother. The condition of women and the family should take priority as a preoccupation of an Islamic government and benevolent organizations.

Defaulting on this front would be the equivalent of admitting powerlessness and giving up. There can be no nobler cause for mobilizing Muslim peoples than that of defending the oppressed and the weak of the world. Well-regulated justice begins by equity at home. From an Islamic perspective, justice for children is tantamount to justice for oneself. To concern ourselves with the plight of the child here and now is to take care of our Future.

In twenty-three places the Qur'an exhorts the faithful to help the orphan, and it compares the abandoning of the orphan to that of the faith. Typical of the Qur'an on this subject is the Sûrah called *Al-Mâ'ûn* that I interpret here:

> In the name of God the All-merciful and most Compassionate. What do you make of the one who does not believe in the resurrection? Such a one bullies the orphan and repulses him, and he provides nothing for the care of the starving. Woe to those who, while praying, are distracted from their prayer; those who put on great airs, but refuse assistance to those in need.[4]

Clearly the hollow piety of devout egoists with unfeeling hearts reeks of hypocrisy; it has no place among the values of *islam!*

What definition might be given the status of the orphan in this modern era, guided not by altruist sentiments but by sordid individualism? Childhood without family and without resources, abandoned in the streets of the great capitals of the South, deserves priority in our concerns.

In a renewed Muslim society, respectful of Islamic norms, we are not acquitted of our duty by merely having put a tiny coin in the hand of an unfortunate child. We are no more acquitted when we found a squeaky clean orphanage and install a chain gang to work in it.

The duty of a man of faith, of a truly pious woman, toward unfortunate children is to deny oneself and become personally engaged in serving the needy. The duty to rise personally to the needs of the sick and to undertake the daily needs of the weak and abandoned is not fully satisfied except by extending a hand—one's own—and giving one's time and money.

3 On Being a Muslim Woman

As in every orderly human society, the stability and well-being of the family are aspired to in the Muslim society. The central pillar of that stability is the woman.

What does the Qur'an have to say about the Muslim woman?

The Qur'an sketches an ideal portrait of the faithful, man and woman, in the Sûrah called *Al-Furqân,* the Criterion. Eleven moral and spiritual qualities required by the model of the faithful are crowned and completed by the well-being of the family and the society:

> The model servants of God walk humbly upon earth and do not wish to lose their time in vain controversies with unbelievers. They spend part of the night prostrate before their Lord, praying that God may spare them the torment of hell; and they spend a reasonable part of their incomes on charity. They never call upon false gods; they never kill; they never fornicate; they never bear false witness; nor do they frequent people who are occupied by the frivolities of life. They listen attentively to the Word of God.[5]

The final verse represents a model for faithful women and men, pious at prayer, appealing to God with the hope that He will grant their requests:

> Lord God! Give joy and contentment to us in our spouses and children, and make of us a model and guide for the pious to follow.[6]

Such is the importance in *islam* of family happiness, and such is the role of the Muslim woman, namely, to be the pivot of family well-being.

This "woman at the hearth" is the opposite of the insignificant and oppressed creature that one sees these days in our societies, stunted by illiteracy and weighted down by unjust macho traditions. *Islam* and its Law and its model for woman have already delivered the Arab woman—during the time of the Prophet—from the abyss of injustice where she suffered martyrdom.

It is urgent to deliver the contemporary Muslim woman, fallen again, perhaps even lower than her pre-Islamic sister, and to draw her up from the abyss of injustice and negligence where she languishes. Our era is perhaps no more merciful toward women than one in which a depraved and inhumane father could cruelly bury his newborn infant if by misfortune it was found to be a girl!

The misfortune of today's Muslim woman is twofold. She lives torn between the unfortunate situation in which local masculine injustice has placed her, and the Western model whose apparent freedom attracts her. She will metamorphose into an imitation of the European woman as soon as she has the means to do so. She will do this if she belongs to an "evolved" social stratum fashioned by one-sided formation or school in a foreign establishment; the rest of the female population vegetates in ignorance, not daring to imagine the least bit of change.

The two, the "emancipated" woman and the other, are ignorant of all the rights that true *islam* grants them. The veiled young women of *Islam* who disturb the schools and universities of France by their presence, and who shake off the yoke of injustice among us, are the vanguard of a new consciousness.

Under Islamic Law, Muslim women have the right—a right that backwards traditions have confiscated from them—to choose their husbands, not to accept a suitor without conditions (including the condition of not marrying a second woman), to ask for divorce, to work and assume social and professional responsibilities, and to dispose freely and independently of their income.

A woman's right to instruction is limitless, as well as her duty to participate in society's efforts to emancipate itself and to liberate the Muslim nation from the fetters of custom and moral depravity. In other words, she has the right to be a complete human being on her own, worthy, living in propriety!

Numerous rights are prescribed to Muslim women under the Law: the foremost of them is the right to have the means and the time to worship the Lord and to participate fully in the pious work of the community in the time made available to her among her personal duties. Unlike the view of the Church, the Law does not see in her a creature without a soul in league with the devil and responsible for man's original sin.

The Muslim woman should become informed of her rights; conscious of them and well informed, she should be able to reclaim their application. No one else need do these things for her. A solid share of material and moral rights will free her from ancestral servitude and will allow her to devote herself to her duties. The good work required to rescue Muslims is arduous; it will take the hard-working goodwill of everyone, women and men side by side, associations rivaling one another in good works.

Competing in good work is one of the conditions of the Test. Do we not read in the Sûrah *Al-Mulk*[7] that God created death and life in order to test us and know which of us will do better works? An Islamic government can only clear the road and smooth out the difficulties: it is the joint effort of men and women to take to the field and act, to invest themselves and to persevere.

The feminine touch is more than a complement to masculine decisiveness: her delicate sensitivity and motherly love are irreplaceable, indeed decisive in the effort of change in order to bring about "the alternation of days." The decisive hand of an Islamic government can and should stop the hemorrhaging of a wounded society, but what other than feminine compassion can gently tend its physical and psychological wounds, soothing with healing balms the effects of so much suffering?

4 On Being a Western Woman

We have been drafting a sketch of what should be the condition of the Muslim woman. Here we shall make a few observations about the condition of the Western woman.

If that bestial tenet were true—if men and women were nothing but evolved apes passing through this life without direction and meaning—it would be an insufferable injustice to refuse them the right to cull life's desirable fruits to the maximum. Woman would then be man's paradise, her body the object of legitimate masculine coveting.

The tenet is the basis on which the conception and practice of the feminine role in the modern West are built. Strengthened by this false "truth" and comforted by the obvious inferiority of the woman's condition in our society, the West looks down its nose on us and falsely judges the case, making *islam* woman's enemy, and Islamic law an iron collar around her neck.

Listen to the judgment of an unbiased European, stigmatizing "the propensity of the West—feminist, but not only so—to take remarkable shortcuts in its analyses." François Burgat denounces one of the most facile and one-eyed shortcuts that the West takes in its ideological analysis of the condition of the woman in *islam:*

> The most classic (shortcut) consists of reducing the entire dynamic of ideological repositioning in the South to a mobilization "against women," to shutting them up in a ghetto analogous to misogyny, indeed to apartheid, erected along absolute explanatory principles. Poor wretches of bearded villains attaching what amounts to a *hijab* over the tearful faces of tender girls.[8]

Further on we read: "Isn't the 'woman question' really one of . . . the Western view of Islamism?"[9]

The clear reasoning of this impartial analyst does not proceed from the same principle that we do, nor does he take into account the bestiality of the Western conception of woman, European or Muslim. But his condemnation of "ghetto analysis" is a compensation.

With another Frenchman, we shed light on Western machismo and the bondage of Western woman. The demographer Jean-Claude Chesnais, cited in an article by Michel Godet, affirms that

> In varying degrees, the intimate drama of intellectuals who seek to reconcile career and family life touches, in reality, the women of all advanced societies, which would include Japan, China, Southeast Asia, American and European Hispanics, or Muslim women in Europe or North Africa.[10]

Western woman is outspokenly superior to her counterpart in our societies in the areas of instruction, productive activity, and economic independence that shelters her from need, whereas a woman here is at the mercy of men in these areas. But such superiority does not prevent Western woman from living a profound individual and social drama.

The Westernized élites among us deplore the lot of the Muslim woman in our underdeveloped countries. They are right, and so are feminist intellectuals who decry the scandal and misfortune of feminine misery among us. But there our point of view ceases to be the same.

They crow about overtaking the "cultural retardation" of our society vis-a-vis Western societies, while we find their blind mimicry, and the spiritual aberration it leads to (which is critical here) brings us directly to the social and moral dilemma of women in the advanced countries. Take whichever "ghetto" you like!

The so-called "progress" our Westernized militants crow about is only a decoy. The "progress" of the modern woman is of a curious sort indeed! Rescued from the brutal servitude of men, she is cast as their fodder, the consenting object of their desires, a painted doll, a wax doll, a rag doll!

The natural calling of woman in advanced societies is not only frustrated; it is systematically assassinated for sordidly economic reasons—and for licentiously sordid ones. Woman's pride lies in begetting the human race and perpetuating it. If this function is suspended or opposed, she finds herself profoundly unbalanced, as is also the society she lives in, a society that, for want of women who mother families, is in demographic danger of disappearing altogether. It is the drama of modern woman, about which a specialist will be addressing us soon.

But first let us note what it means to be a mother in *islam*. Bukhari and Muslim record the following teaching of the Prophet Muhammad (grace and peace upon him!):

A man came to question the Prophet, saying, "Which person deserves the most of my generosity and gratitude? The Prophet told him, "Your mother." Three times the man repeated his question, receiving the same answer. Only the fourth time did God's Apostle tell him, "Your father."

This indicates the precedence *islam* gives to the dignity of motherhood, honored as the child's protector and as woman and spouse.

Some Western observers and acculturated militant feminists among us anticipate the coming of an Islamic government—more probable now than ever before—with pity and scandal at the prospect of its treatment of women; they do so wholly ignorant of the teaching of *islam* and its attentive solicitude for women at every stage of their lives.

Its solicitude for mothers is great, since the mother is the very symbol of life, and life is sacred to *islam*. Even a non-Muslim mother has the right to be honored. The daughter of Abu Bakr, the Prophet's closest Companion, received a visit from her mother, who had remained a pagan. She consulted the Prophet regarding the attitude she should show her; the Messenger of God advised her to welcome her mother and be generous with her.[11]

5 On Being a Bad Mother

J. C. Chesnais assesses the condition of women in advanced societies from a standpoint that is purely utilitarian, though pertinent and instructive for our purposes. Though he is inspired neither by any love for *islam* nor for any intention to defend Islamic Law, he shows us how motherhood can be corrupted, and how motherhood as a calling is being asphyxiated in advanced societies:

> In the corporate West, pregnancy is borne with guilt, since it upsets the functioning of a tool of production like some kind of anomaly, a professional mistake, indeed, a betrayal, an infidelity to the employer.[12]

The Westernized women among us who insist on defining themselves within the coordinates of the model our author is deploring have even more need of the "mental revolution" he calls for:

> It is a matter of denouncing as absurd and suicidal the implicit consensus of today's social partners: growing socialization, at the cost of the elderly, and growing privatization, at the cost of the young. What logic will impel the collective to subsidize the growing number of the formerly active? In the name of what principles should inter-generational solidarity be anything but ascending (today's workers toward those of yesterday) rather than descending (yesterday's workers toward those of tomorrow). Only the chain of rising generations creates the future.[13]

French demographics demonstrates the suicidal absurdity of an economic organization that, operating on the principle of maximum exploitation of women's work, refuses to assume the costs of pregnancy and, in finding the woman culpable, saps the foundations of society and threatens its very survival.

The alarming consequences of such an attitude are being felt more and more, and the aging of the population, linked to fewer hours of labor, points to the imminent dawning of a major crisis. Solidarity among the generations collides with corporate selfishness and the built-in dilemma of unemployment: retirement claimed early and the progressive thinning out of a youthful workforce able to finance these retirements.

Hope for growing life increases the responsibility of women toward the elderly as the ongoing drop in the birthrate threatens these same persons with winding up one day on the street, for want of a growing generation to produce sufficient wealth to finance social security.

We cannot therefore replicate the social categories of others in thinking of our future. If for women the spiritual consequences of acculturation are always more disastrous on the personal level, the consequences of the condition of the modern woman can just as well be destructive in the social and human domain, as we noted above.

Even if our problems are not those of "advanced" societies, at least not yet, we should heed the lesson so as not to pursue a dead end. The demographic decomposing of "advanced" societies is diametrically opposed to the formation of an age pyramid that is too broad at the base. But the logic of development, and the difficulty of controlling birth in a positive sense, will lead us to a similar situation if our women are seduced by the Western model. Our plan for society should not aim servilely for a future that matches the present of others, as an African sage has said.

Our guide in the European demographic desert attributes the dependency of the elderly and the waste of the younger generation to a distortion of the birthrate. As a fault of this state of affairs, "the potential network of aid to the elderly is going to contract, creating a demand for public services. . . . It will be less and less rare for a woman in her fifties to have to care for grandchildren (out of work) and, at the same time, two generations of elders."[14]

In advanced societies, the woman's calling has been deflected from its natural course for economic reasons. Add to this sexual license—what you would expect of those who conceive of themselves as naked ape—and you reap a poisoned social harvest: the breakdown of relationships between ascending and descending generations for want of family stability, i.e. the lack of women as good mothers, i.e. for want of a family.

When woman, the keystone of the social edifice, forsakes her function so as to become a tool of production and an object for consumption, we should not be surprised to find general deterioration and delinquency:

"The toll of delinquency," writes Michel Godet, "is twice as high on the children of single-parent families as on children raised by both parents."[15] A single-parent family means a broken or divorced couple, above all, children born out of wedlock.

Godet concludes his article on a pessimistic note:

> It is true that everything is being done to make free unions, even parental bachelorhood,[16] more attractive economically and fiscally than marriage. The figures for France are amazing: more than a third of childbirths are out of wedlock, and fewer than half of the women under 50 years of age are married (two-thirds in 1986).

He ends with this cry of conscience:

> What are we waiting for to restore to the commitment of marriage the encouragement it deserves? In the absence of that volunteer family-politic, we continue to speak of "recomposed" families in order to conceal the fact of their breakdown and programmed death once there are no longer enough children to start families.[17]

6 Post-modern, Post-moral

Atheistic modernism considers sexual restrictions and the family as a central social value to be an antiquated discipline; in permissive modern societies, any discipline of this kind is considered an insufferable intrusion on personal liberty. Restrictions of this sort are thought to be an out-of-place austerity in an era that has rid itself of rigorist religions.

Just why post-modernism is—can only be—post-moralism is better explained by Westerners themselves. The philosopher and sociologist Gilles Lipovetsky is looking for a compromise between the outmoded rigorous logic of the past and a lax, permissive morality. Listen to him dialoguing with the ideas of these troubled and troubling times where the wisdom of a philosopher doesn't dare overstep the limits of a chic, better-class, and politically correct pragmatism.

> The third phase in the history of morality, what I call the 'post-moralist,' breaks off and, at the same time, pursues the process of secularization set into motion in the 17th and 18th centuries. For a society to be post-moralist would mean that it more readily aroused desires, ego, happiness, and individual well-being than it called forth the ideal of self-denial.
>
> Our culture is no longer dominated by the imperatives of a maximal sense of duty, but rather by happiness and subjective rights. The culture of the sacrificial ethic, broadly in force until the middle of this century, has been liquidated.
>
> Our consumerist mass-communication society has stopped systematically promulgating difficult commandments; it now functions outside the concept of duty, beyond any corrective moral obligation or discipline. Such is the post-moralist climate of the new democracies.[18]

We note that the author opposes individual rights to collective duty, selfishness to abnegation, ease to discipline, gratified desires to sacrificial giving. These are the hallmarks of a society that no longer has ideals, a society composed of individuals without absolutes to aspire to. Post-moralist societies are societies without moral moorings, societies at the end of evolutionary progress overcoming all sense of morality in order to behave more and more like monkeys.

> "Post-duty" societies, with their utilitarian hedonist cult of the present, contribute to the dissolving of formal environments and the self-control of individuals; they undermine the meaning of effort with short-term gains (speculation rather than production), and they invite the transgression of ethical principles (corruption, secret kickbacks, fiscal fraud. In the USA, one taxpayer out of five defrauds the Internal Revenue Service).
>
> Even as habitual social safeguards are dissolving (Church, local economy, political party, family, school), the ghettos are growing with fatherless families, illiteracy, drug trafficking, violence, and criminal extremes. For an entire segment of the population, the post-moralist era generates a ruthless sort of individualism, on the take, unstructured, without a future.[19]

Pessimism and deception—or the lucid thoughts of a wise philosopher? In any case, the testimony is very useful for us who suffer in our ghetto of underdevelopment, to similar woes, aggravated by poverty and material wretchedness. Are we going to be able to cure our grave ills by blindly following the Western model, especially now that we have seen its reality exposed? Where are we going to fasten ourselves to our ideals, our truths, our final purpose, at the core of a modernity rich in means and empty of meaning?

It is not enough to feel a certain satisfaction, by way of consolation, when reading the signs of decline of an impious civilization. What counts is learning the right lessons. The testimony of Westerners about themselves is proof that there exists at least in the West, for the sole use and good of Westerners, the freedom to think and express oneself. In itself, this freedom constitutes an inestimable value; we envy them for it!

Grappling with the complexity of what he is asking, the sociologist-philosopher-anthropologist-biologist E. Morin concludes his query into meaning with a modest proposal: fraternal solidarity among people, a community in place of a disintegrated post-modern society. Societies said to be advanced live without any other ideal than the selfish and hedonistic satisfaction of individual desires. Crumbling societies, without bonds of altruistic feelings, have similarly squandered their ideas.

Western scholars like Morin extol a change, a reform, in the search for the kind of solidarity that will save humankind from catastrophe. Revolutionary totalitarian ideology no longer has a place in a conceptual universe that is embroiled in complexity and specialized to death. One's human value and that of others is undiscoverable:

> The profound feeling of a destined community that binds together the idea of solidarity and brotherhood. . . . A very complex society grants many

> liberties, a good deal of play to individuals and groups. It allows them to be creative, sometimes delinquent. . . . At the level of extreme complexity, society disintegrates. To stop that happening requires some measure of authority. But, supposing that we would wish the least possible coercion, the sole bonding remains the feeling of a shared solidarity."[20]

A sensational claim. But it remains to be seen where such a feeling would come from. Clearly, the philosophical scientist, a rich professional in the exchange of ideas, lets escape from his lips a cry of passion doubled with a cry of alarm: how to stop the process of aberration in the freedom to play and to destroy itself without using some "measure of authority"?

Is it, with Morin, the dilemma of a sociological philosopher converted to reformism, or a post-mortem critique of a revolutionary Marxism with which the author has long crossed swords?

7 Religion and Modern Solitude

Edgar Morin, elder scholar, initiator of the "sociology of the present," is not alone in seeking a unifying principle to gather together the scattered state of individualism; others, dealers in ideas, express the anguish of disintegrating post-modern societies and criticize their society in less considered terms.

Jean-Marie Guéhenno is a professor of politics; with a good deal of bustle he announces the end of democracy and that of politics. He acknowledges the return of religion and considers that "religion of the imperial age inherits the functions that were filled by the state in the institutional age: rather than uniting, it divides. . . . In a uniform and homogenized world, religion allows us to escape to universal abstractions and rediscover, in the archipelagoes of modern solitudes, the sense of our uniqueness."[21]

Guéhenno's thoughts challenge us directly to explain how and why we might win the modern world for *islam.* Let us lend an ear to hear, as with the elder Morin, the rustling of hope for a community life with a human face where one could take refuge far from the anonymity of the post-modern crowd.

We will hear as well the intense rejection, by an intellectual disabused of "universal abstraction" and "globalization," of the market values current in the market of modernity. Rejecting this "imperial" age and being disgusted by it is within the thinker's range, but change seems unrealizable:

> Almost no one today dares to call himself a 'conservator,' since no one feels certainty about the principles that deserve to be conserved. Meanwhile everyone confesses that change is the rule in an imperial age and its princi-

> pal engine. But everyone understands that "change" escapes human mastery.[22]

Such men, distressed by change, anxious and incapable of changing whatever happens, are bogged down in their petty occupations, void of meaning, without principles or ideals:

> Organization man can scarcely allow himself principles; all he needs are his reflexes. A man of little faith, he could hardly afford to appear cynical. One simply expects him to tend to his inner emptiness with cheerful briskness.
>
> A man of little direction, he should, in a sea of signs without significance, become a sign himself. [. . .] With characteristic ease he acquires certain associations that link him to a well-identified clan: he plays bridge, is an Alpinist, a golfer—it doesn't matter. By means of the sport he follows, the car he owns, the club in which he holds membership, or his religious affiliation, he goes about acquiring bits of identity, fragile little staffs carried away in the general movement, to which the shipwrecked of the modern world cling.[23]

Without a rallying point besides the clubs where he gathers certain "bits of identity," without solid ground in which to sink roots to escape the shifting sands of change undergone without meaning, post-modern man furnishes his interior void and his leisure time by affiliating himself with a religious sect, a mainline club or one on the fringes, or—if he is not so exclusive in his choices—he goes online and joins the network of international communication.

Whether marginal or in permanent communication with numerous anonymous counterparts, he drowns in images and information. He is outfitted for killing time in the boredom of his electronic solitude, navigating aimlessly and bobbing from site to site in the immensity of the cold and forlorn desert of multimedia.

Where can he find authentic heart-to-heart communicating? Where will he find convivial companionship in whose bosom he can rekindle his heart?

From a distance our Western thinker watches the Islamic rebirth and attempts to assess it in light of his own preoccupations, unable to free himself from *a priori* judgments and prejudice. He sometimes finds Muslim fundamentalists to be unprincipled "triflers in ideas" without a plan, and sometimes copycats and plagiarists all too familiar with the free-and-easy methods of syncretism. Still, they have a few strong points:

> Islamist fundamentalists—and Hindus, for that matter—breathe down their conquering energy on societies already profoundly disoriented by ill-mastered economic modernity. The contrast between our disabused weariness and the revolutionary determination of Islamists frightens us, as if, after the death of Communism, Islamism might offer a new global political plan,

one even more dangerous since we will have lost faith in our own democratic universalism.

Our witness does not hide the weariness of Europe's elderly societies, nor the fear that the exuberant youth of *islam* inspires in them. It is the contrast of a historical situation whose causes and effects Guéhenno reveals while engaging in his two-edged critique:

> Politics is going to die in the richest societies, to be reborn, in virulent form, borne by religion among the poor, left stranded on the side of the road by the integration of the relational age.[24]

Islamist strife inspires our critic's evaluation of the ambition of Muslim victims of imperial injustice:

> This ambition, built on the failure of politics and from the marriage of politics and religion, will have an impact on Islam perhaps as profound as that of the protestant Reformation on Christianity. It has not yet finished branding its mark on history.[25]

This superficial comparativism, while on the one hand enlightening us by witnessing the state of affairs in post-modernist society, does not, on the other, state an effectively ambitious reason for the Islamic plan. Let us consult our references, our sole true lights.

8 Ignorance and Violence

The word *jâhilîyah* conveys a standard of judgment between *islam* and what is contrary to it.[26] Found four times in the Qur'an, *jâhilîyah* thunders against disbelief, malgovernance, the abasing of women, and the virulent fury of pagan tribalism.

Every era has its own *jâhilîyah,* its own form of tribalism, disbelief, malgovernance, profligacy, and injustice. Going to the word's root, I translate as Ignorance and Violence—I capitalize so as to draw attention to these salient and permanent aspects of *jâhilîyah.*

Jâhilîyah exists wherever humankind is ignorant of the purpose of its existence, wherever societies (whether nominally Muslim or no) are ill-governed, where woman is treated vilely, where violent instinctual passions win out in disputes, not the spirit of fairness.

I consult the Qur'an and the teaching of the Prophet in order to draw upon Knowledge and learn the duty of nonviolence. I write Knowledge with an uppercase and do the same with Science (in the singular) so as to shift from a conceptual universe we have long heard of to quite another universe.

The word Science does not have the same sense as what I have meant so far in speaking of vanguard scholars and philosophers whose multiple certainties of fact and whose notion of the concrete has been dispelled and volatilized to the level of the theoretical. Latter-day savants, desperate for some means of solid, absolute knowledge, resign themselves to stumble about, passing from scientific discipline to philosophical system in the quest of absolute truth more and more fleeting, more and more out of reach.

We who have faith by the grace of God (may God be praised!), we speak of Science and Knowledge to express the revealed Truth, proceeding from our principles and with recourse to our notional system, that of the Qur'an.

The question, dear brother, dear sister, is not, "What Knowledge can Revelation offer us?" The question is knowing if we are ready to open our minds to listen, if we have the time to listen and if the anguish of being touches our hearts. But if we have deliberately arrested our choice, comfortably ensconced in our position, in our sanctuary of selfishness, all our chiding is beside the point.

If you think you are merely an ephemeral dragonfly, an empty shell, no attempt to convince you to read the Qur'an is going to be anything but an insufferable annoyance. But that shall not prevent me from insisting yet again; human compassion and the weight of the burden of responsibility every Muslim carries in his conscience will not allow me to be discouraged.

What the Qur'an teaches us, and what our primordial nature—our *fiṯrah*—allows us to respond to as the most natural thing in the world, is that I am not here by chance and for nothing. The second rung of Knowledge: the Qur'an communicates Great Information to me that embraces my life and that accompanies me from birth to my passage from this ephemeral existence on earth to the Life Hereafter, there to answer for my acts and to be rewarded or punished *ad æternam.*

The simplicity of this Knowledge, the modesty—or great yearning—of its Information may give rise to laughter or banter from their thick heads, padlocked in their smug self-sufficiency: to dare to speak of such things with well-informed minds—what *naïveté,* what foolishness!

The skeptic's ferocious teeth are razor sharp, while conformist faintheartedness erects insurmountable barriers to dam up this "evil literature," unless some spiritual thirst is aroused among rationalists desperate of finding meaning in life or death, allowing them to be amazed to be there, to liberate them from the cultural shack in which they are held hostage.

The stridency of the criticism of unbelievers will not matter, their ignorant and violent arguments be reckoned to the unconsciousness of their impaired natures, satisfied with an animal existence, without metaphysical anxiety.

The foils with which our imagination or our lack of courage ruffles us are merely chimeras guarding the entrance to nightmarish grottoes. Unjustly attributing to Islamists the bad case represented by the example of tribal warfare in Afghanistan, and the atrocity of the slaughter in Algeria, is a master stroke in the dossier of the slayers of *islam.*

A mistrial is under way in the tribunals of the West, at which *islam* is being tried by a judge who is an interested party, where the prosecution is corrupt and the counsel for the defense is in the bag. It is a formal verdict, without appeal: *islam* is principally culpable, *islam* is synonymous with fanaticism, obscurantism, and terrorism. I will spare the reader the interminable cavils of this parody of double-standard "justice."

The West—having sent enormous armies into the field during two world wars, having permitted itself the use of nuclear weapons, and whose economy prospers in part through armament trading—is acquitted of blame, while *islam,* the perfect scapegoat, is accused of violence at the sound of the least firecracker.

Muslims, nationals of Muslim countries or members of Muslim tribes, are neither the first nor the last people to break their promises and betray their principles.

I am not about to defend the reprehensible actions of any desperate man discovered to be a Muslim (or of any organization that claims to be Islamic) that reacts with violence to an unbearably unjust situation. Violence, whether or not legitimate, is not one of the precepts of our Law.

The principle of nonviolence is indisputably one of Islamic Law, and we proclaim it loud and clear. The politically effective nonviolence of a Ghandi, and the good-naturedness of the Christian who offers you, sanctimoniously, the "other cheek" when you slap him on the other one, have no correspondence to the nonviolence of *islam.*

Defending the Message is another sacred principle that in no way runs counter to the ones enunciated above; the model of the Prophet, who justly battled thirteen years against tribalist madness, provides the example of nonviolence.

In the course of fifty affronts valiantly borne, and in the rules of the art, he has given us the example of unshakable resistance against all aggression, but without implacable fury or excess: in all these affronts, the total number of those killed on the field of battle was 900 on both sides.

Prisoners were set free, with or without ransom; they were never killed or tortured. Women, children, and the elderly were always spared and humanely treated. The Prophet forbade the armies of *islam* to cut or harm vegetation—to harm the environment, in modern language.

In those times, it is true, there were no Stalinist organizations with Kalashnikovs to mow down people with diabolic efficiency such as we know. There was no weapon that could incinerate, in the twinkling of an eye, a city of several million inhabitants. There were no chemical weapons to despoil the environment for decades afterwards and have genetic consequences. In the earliest period of *islam*, no modern technology outdid itself year in and year out at the industry of death.

What played no role in the heart and intention of the Prophet and his combatants was the pagan surliness and rancor that today animates the raging folly of modern violence: every twenty minutes a Southern child or peasant steps on a land mine buried under the soil of his land. Experts say that there are 110,000,000 land mines in poor war-torn countries such as Angola, Mozambique, or Cambodia. There are 0.0 under the soil of the producing countries, though there are millions in their warehouses, awaiting export.

The raging folly of modern violence is on a par with the ignorance that blinds men's minds and transforms them into wolves. Modern science, mother of efficient technology, itself a driving force in producing the instruments of death, is in the service of pagan ignorance. The *jâhilîyah* of the days of the Prophet had nothing at its disposal like the monstrous arsenal of sophisticated modern violence.

Our Prophet left instruction concerning *rifq* clearly enunciated in the Hadith, such as this one recorded by Muslim in his collection:

> God is lenient and loves leniency. Thereby He accords by means of *rifq* [the result] that cannot arise from violence.

The word *rifq* is rich in connotations.[27] To translate it requires evoking all its senses in the Qur'an and in the Hadith, as well as its living illustration in the example laid down by the Prophets (grace and peace upon them!). Among equivalents we may adduce: kindness, sweetness, tolerance, goodness, giving, forgiveness, gentleness.

9 On Being Worthy

In its world politics and its program for reform and for reuniting a disjointed Muslim society, an Islamic government should be guided by the teaching of the Prophet and the example of his sweetness and *rifq*.

With the firmness necessary for any change, compassion and understanding should smooth the edges and promote human dignity. It will be necessary, as a priority, to treat qualified heads, rich in experience, with respect, those who are frightened by what is happening in Algeria, those who speak in whispers of packing their bags in anticipation of an eventual seizure of power by Islamists.

The sons and daughters of the Muslim nation will all of them need to find in the shade of an Islamic government a protected space where they can develop their talents, and where their contributions can be appreciated. Aside from the recipients of a legacy of lies, every good intention should be judged on the basis of competence rather than in terms of a past that is over and done with.

The effort needed to leave behind our present situation, with its difficulties on all counts, should inspire us to manage our human resources. There is a large gap between principled intentions and action during crises: the witch hunt is the first resort of vindictive conquering minds. The temptation, though dictated by vengeful bitterness, should be avoided like the plague.

We must turn the page; we must be open to forgiveness and forbearance. The example of the Prophet (grace and peace upon him!), who granted his former torturers amnesty on the day of his triumphant entry into Mecca, should it in itself suffice to drive us to maintain the moral high ground and negotiate with those of rebellious mind, those with a penchant for violence, so that each might amend himself and join the common effort of reconstruction.

The bad example—the Satanic example—is that of Bolshevik revolutionary violence and Chinese reeducation. The victims of Maoist re-education during the "cultural revolution" have yet to be reckoned; as for the Soviet Empire, the chilling figures speak of 80,000,000 dead. "Chilling" indeed—as if the suffering, the killing, even if it were a single human being, could ever be justly expressed by toting up numbers.

It is said in the Qur'an that the assassination of a single human being is the equivalent of the murder of all of humanity. How atrocious, then, is the bloodbath in Algeria—how contrary to the precepts of our Sacred Book!

The Stalinist gulag is one of the worst Satanic illustrations of the violence of *jâhilîyah.* The worst, if such things can be measured, is the inhuman savagery of the Nazi concentration camps, which the adjective "diabolical" hardly begins to qualify. Putting living beings into ovens is an unspeakable act. The number of Jews who suffered martyrdom under Hitler hardly matters, when a single innocent victim would be too many. The image of horror of the extermination camps will ever remain graven on the forehead of ignorant and violent modernity.

Oh yes! The Jews have a right to our commiseration, as human beings, like every oppressed person on earth. Even if the West encourages and supports Jewish Zionism to expiate for past crimes and to preserve its interests, present and future, among us and against us, the Jew as such should not be the object of our hatred, particularly if he is a convinced and outspoken anti-Zionist. Jewish anti-Zionist associates indeed exist.

After World War II, the U.N. declared the defense of human rights to be its principal task. That is a good and honorable intention, even if its principles have been undermined in practice since the beginning. Since its foundation, the Security Council has been the mainspring of the U.N., dominated by the five major powers, i.e. the five that possess the supreme weapon of violence. Muslims should seek alliances in order to reform the institution along the lines of greater justice for unarmed nations.

The human-rights intentions of *islam* are on trial: would an Islamic government respect them?

It is an obsessive question that is asked of *islam* in the doubtful conditional mood of tomorrow rather than in the indicative or simple past (or any other tense)—and it is asked primarily of the repressive regimes in our countries that are responsible for flagrant human-rights violations.

The scriptural texts of the Qur'an and Sunna are not enough to convince the intransigent who gorges on his anti-*islam* prejudices; he wants tangible proofs. The West, with a beam in its eye, wants to point out the mote in the eye of the other. The West, from its glass house, throws stones on the houses of others.

U.N. officials lay much stock in its thundering pronouncements and grandly worded texts, but their selective character of their application is all too evident in practice: should a Westerner, especially an American or Israeli, fall under the bullets of a patriotic resister or a criminal terrorist, the Western media send up flares of mortal danger, while the Security Council takes the matter in hand.

In Bosnia the Serbs were allowed to carry out their ethnic cleansing program and exterminate Muslim populations before the U.N. risked timid intervention. The scandal of Bosnia is another wrinkle, hideous and indelible, in the face of modernity and all its violence. This monstrosity will not be eradicated by the slap on the wrist of an international tribunal, a tribunal of shame. The crimes of history are not expunged like that!

Human rights are imprescriptible in our Law since they emanate from a sacred divine order: "We have honored Adam's progeny."[28] This was revealed to us in our ignorance so that we might treat men and women not only with fairness, but with the respect due to a creature worthy of birth and being.

At the time of the Prophet (grace and peace on him!) the Jews of Medina, who incessantly betrayed their covenants with Muslims, were conducting the casket of one of their people and passed before the Prophet, who was seated with his Companions. The Prophet stood up to show respect for the funeral procession, under the astonished eye of the assembly. Questioned about the reason of his gesture, the Prophet explained, "Is it not a soul?" This practical lesson was given to teach us that the dignity of a human being derives from being a human, and no other consideration.

The first human right is to know the meaning of one's life and the existence of the Creator. All the other rights gravitate around this pole. It is why the first duty of every Muslim in a Muslim society is to strengthen this right. That is why public abjuration of the faith is inadmissible.

Each is free to retreat to his own individual ghetto of disbelief: the Inquisition is not a Muslim invention, nor is the torment of conscience allowed any longer in *islam.* But to claim the right, guaranteed by Holy Secularity, of shouting one's renegade convictions from the roof, is to sap the fundamental strength of a society. Each is free to drink the dregs of the poison of his disbelief within the four walls of his house, so long as the social space, sacred in *islam,* is preserved.

Is not the betrayal of one's country punishable in every civilized society? The Muslim society is founded neither on the right of blood nor that of land, but on the capital right and obligation of being both submitted to God and a member of a community. To parade one's non-respect for God and His Law in a society that has chosen allegiance to God and to His Law as the foundation is high treason.

10 On Being a Muslim

What can I do to reintegrate *islam* if I am a Muslim by nationality and the bonds that once bound me to the faith of my father—whom as a little child I used to watch at prayer—come unraveled, if barely vestiges still remain?

How to initiate myself to *islam* if I am the product of a secular society indifferent to matters of faith, and some vague attraction to *islam* calls out to me to learn more, perhaps even to attempt to practice *islam*?

Under the cloak of the sovereign Will of God (may His Name be glorified and magnified!), the first step should be yours. The Prophet (grace and peace upon him!) records this divine promise: "Whoever comes to Me with slow steps I shall go to meet with rapid steps."[29]

One must first take the time to meditate profoundly and be assured that this vocation—in the root sense of the word, that is, a calling from the heart—is not simply a fantasy. In an era when our time is colonized by the multimedia, this first step is already proof of the earnestness of our quest.

No time! No time! This is the leitmotiv of what we have become, our minds blunted by the instantaneous, unable to concentrate. We must detach ourselves from the false sense of urgency in our lives and devote the time necessary for deepening our ideas and feelings. We must sit ourselves down and ask ourselves, forcibly and earnestly, "Where am I going?"

At this stage, reading the Qur'an, and reflecting long and hard on it, will allow us to rescue ourselves from the daily bustle and cast a deaf ear to the hullabaloo of human babble to listen with the ear of the heart to our sacred language. Let us not be put off by the illogical incongruities of translating the Arabic language of phrases from the Qur'an into profane modern languages. If we have the good fortune of being able to read the original text, let us penetrate the music of the sacred text by chanting it aloud. If we lack the patience, a long and patient consultation of one "translation" or more will perhaps put us in harmony with God's Message, with the help of His grace.

While carefully maintaining our family and social engagements, it is imperative to put an end to any and all evil company we may find ourselves in. This does not mean isolating ourselves in a hermit's hut; but we must have the courage to cut short our habitual complacency, without transgressing the bounds of courtesy and genuineness. Abandoning disturbing friendships is not an easy matter; we will have to bear the jeers and taunts of inveterate characters who seek to detain us by picking quarrels with us.

We must overcome our reluctance and lower the barriers. We must bear up without violence under annoyance and real harm, look straight ahead, without taking refuge in evasive attitudes for fear of being demonized or slashed to pieces. Reconciliation with our Creator will be taken as a betrayal in the ranks of our habitual acquaintances, who are used to seeing us under aspects other than that of men and women repentant before God.

We can expect our former friends, still rooted in their habits of dissipation, to display fierce opposition to our initiative to dismantle their ranks.

Oh my brother, my sister! I am outlining here the sorrowful path, both psychologically and socially, of anyone who aspires to travel the path to God. The first step toward God is costly: if you can't pay the price, don't expect me to offer you a discount. If you can't face forward and strike out toward your goal without worrying about prejudice and suffering, bewail your insignificance and content yourself with an infantile sort of life, wan and without history.

I have put before you the Prophets and their Companions as immutable models of courageous behavior, about whom you have read in the Qur'an—those the Qur'an recounts again and again to try the truth of your vows, and to encourage you.

Pass the solitary test of detachment and you will then have to seek an encounter: you will need to go toward another companion and there make a place for yourself. You will need to adapt yourself to another environment, and adopt it. Nothing will take the place of a meeting, of spiritual "companionship." Companionship is one of the most essential notions of *islam;* in the path of the penitent, God often places persons clear of heart.

The mosque is without doubt the ideal place to find an ideal companionship. At the threshold of the mosque we bid farewell to the world's trivialities to enter into communion with the sacred. Five times a day the ranks of the faithful, among whom we take our place, will be for us a privileged place where our soul will open to receive the streams of the spiritual, as befitting the house of God.

Prayer is the central pillar of *islam,* and group prayer is twenty-five times better than solitary prayer. Fasting during Ramadan, *zakat* (charity), and pilgrimage are obligations which a Muslim is bound scrupulously to fulfill, so as to lend credence to his profession of faith. The first obligation is that of pronouncing the formula, "I bear witness that there is no god but God and that Muhammad is his Messenger;" but this counts for little unless praying five times a day and the other obligations are respected.

Some protest at every turn, "We are all Muslims," but you have never once seen them prostrate before God. Is this consummate hypocrisy or a distressing ignorance of what it means to be Muslim?

Those people ought to know that *islam* is not some cultural plaything to be worn by a professional Islamologist specialized in the art of reviewing juridical schools and disentangling divergences and intricacies of the Islamic past. Being Muslim by birth and nationality does not exempt you from Islamic obligations—praying, first of all, five times a day, always.

Let no one be fooled: the well-being of our soul depends on the sincerity of our engagement. Our spiritual elevation depends on the self-discipline we are able to impose. Prayer, like the other acts of worship and the totality of moral virtues a good Muslim should practice, calls for a determined ascesis. You are either able to assume your own rehabilitation, or you are hardly more than a mollusk in human form.

Those who have internalized the Western model of living willingly submit themselves to a daily ritual and a code of conduct. Their time is compartmentalized and regulated. They are utterly occupied by the state of their health and physique. They run to the doctor with the slightest ow-ow. They will pay any price to maintain their physique. Why are they unconcerned about their moral and spiritual health? Why do they ignore the sickness of their soul?

Because they are modern, secular, big league, and vaccinated against fanatical sermonizing, thank you very much!

At the mosque, oh my kindred souls, my readers—there you will find the crowd of the faithful. Batter down your sufficiency and abandon your highfalutin' manners! Mix with the common of the faithful and expect no preference if you happen to have some social distinction. In God's house, all are His servants; humility is learned from the humble. Seek in the mosque an encounter, a lightning rod that will put you in touch with other souls like your own, athirst for the truth.

Islam is an ascent, it is not a stationary state. The first rung is that of the practicing Muslim, attentive to fulfilling the obligations the Law prescribes for every Muslim. The second rung is that of the *iman*, a higher degree, where worship and moral rectitude are on a par. The third degree, *ihsan*, is the springboard for the great spiritual journey and its infinite space. A spiritual guide is needed for the highest degree, since the path is long and the way is full of snares. A spiritual guide, a tutor, is required until the plant of the spiritual being takes root and grows in strength.

I have spoken of rungs and degrees, I ought to have spoken of bricks and floors, since the image of a building that is being built slowly but surely is more apt. You cannot build on a void and with nothing: the progress on *islam*'s path to moral and spiritual perfection is a construction, and the fulfilling of the obligations of its Law are the bricks and cement, with prayer foremost.

Have confidence, kindred souls, in uncertain encounters. At the mosque, particularly in the mosques of the Muslim diaspora, you will find erudite Muslims learned in the matter of diatribes who will talk to you of the Law and the books in dry terms, emptied of their core substance. Take of their words of Knowledge of the Law but do not let yourselves be enmeshed in pointless quarrels and sectarian rigidity; you'll never be done with them. You will also run into sufis inebriated with "spiritual" ecstasy; take to heart their advice to love God, and ignore the rest.

In your prayer, beseech God to choose a companion, a school to guide you and assist you on your path to Him. Do your utmost to search the horizon for the Lord, knocking tirelessly at His gates. He alone is the hope of those who seek the truth. Seek it, my brother, my sister!

For the troubled unbeliever, the integrist sermon is ended!

11 The Purpose of Being

Are human societies able to change direction and master their future, or are they condemned to suffer the changes imposed by the logic of global progress in the world? In other words, should Muslims undergo modernity as some sort of historical fate, with all the moral and social consequences that entails, or can they free themselves from the embrace of modernist constraints?

In *islam*'s view of the world and humankind, humans have a mission in this life and a purpose for being that is radically opposed to what modernist views assign them. In modern societies the individual is an end in himself, the satisfying of his desires and needs is the society's *raison d'être* and his purpose amounts to respect for rights and the laws regulating a perpetually changing social life.

In the progression and organization of advanced societies, moral values have only a marginal role, if any; the ideal of the Islamic society to be reconstructed considers moral and spiritual values as both motivation and goal, the underlying reason for being of both the individual and the collective.

Will *islam* be able to rise to the challenge and appropriate to itself the modern means of development and science without losing its soul, or will it, under the economic and political constraints of globalization, have to follow in step with the world and abandon its primary goal along the way? Given that flexibility and adaptability to the new are the characteristics of every advanced society, while rigidity and fixity are synonyms of death, we must be on our guard lest the change of material conditions make us lose our course as Muslims and kill our souls.

Modern sociological analysis recognizes the influence of ideology on the orientation of human societies, an influence that is less and less certain as market values supplant other values. As a condition for change, whether for good or for ill, the Qur'an requires psychological and intentional change in people.

We will need to take a glance at the central notion of modernist ideology, the individual, and at that of the Islamic ideal, in which the faithful concentrate on their future and on perfecting themselves morally and spiritually by doing good works.

In large measure, change in individualist society responds to the desires and material claims of the individual, while change along the ideals of *islam* will have to be made in continual resistance to selfish materialist drifts and in service of the spiritual aspirations of the faithful.

My dictionary defines an individual as a human being in terms of exterior, biological unity and identity; as a particular being, different from all others.

So this is a being that is characterized above all biologically, of singular particular identity. His passport in life is above everything else his biological individuality. In Western societies the individual has acquired substantial rights, inalienable natural rights due to his worth as a living being, wrenched from society at the price of fearful historical struggles and bloody revolutions.

The individual in Western societies benefits from the rights guaranteed him by the social contract, in the form of a constitution. The Law concedes and guarantees him political and social rights, such as membership in the electorate, solidarity, labor, and so on.

These rights represent conquests resulting from successive changes: political revolutions, industrial revolutions, wars, sexual revolutions, technological revolutions, social and collective revolutions. The individual in advanced democratic societies is framed by a system of education that produces and reproduces good citizens aware of their rights and active producers of goods of all sorts.

He is protected by a system of justice that guarantees his rights and freedoms. He lives securely (though this is rather relative now that unemployment and organized crime have become the daily bread of developed countries). He lays claims, he demands, he consumes; his wants and tastes are in fact the engine of the economy and the political benchmark. His opinion, managed, researched, polled, and, for every purpose, solicited in daily opinion polls, is the measure of the truth of the moment in a world short on reference points.

In the Islamic society to be reconstructed, the faithful will be guided in their political behavior by other values radically opposed to the moral emptiness and nagging egoism of the individual that demands and consumes. In our life and mission, the Absolute requires of us the practice of giving.

Such a giving personality has to be trained. Just as the systems of individualist modernity command and make conditions for the good, well-thinking, and amply consuming citizen, so the system of schools, courts, information, and government in the land of *islam* must work in unison for the Islamic paradigm to be adopted in the hearts and minds of all, in their morals and their social relationships, in their work, and in their conception of the place and role of women. A life of involvement in charitable and humanitarian enterprises must be encouraged.

The Qur'an gives this portrayal of the perfect faithful member of the fraternal community: "The faithful are brothers."[30]

In the same Sûrah, the Qur'an spells out the spiritual and altruistic qualities of the faithful, qualities that condition and prove that they are truly brothers; the gift of self and of possession is the proof that belies in its absence each one's profession of faith:

> The faithful are none other than those who have faith in God and in His Messenger, those who do not doubt, but give generously of their goods and their persons on the path of God. These are the true faithful.[31]

The qualities of heart and mind, the acts of worship and giving, piety and altruism all redound from the same intention, that of pleasing God and helping one's neighbor. The same thrill the faithful feel in their hearts at prayer is translated socially into giving:

> Are not the faithful truly those whose heart thrills at God's slightest calling, (those) whose faith blossoms in their hearts at the recitation of Revelation, (those) who put their entire trust on their Lord, (those) who fulfill their prayer and spend generously (on the path of God) of a part of the goods We have allotted them? These are the true faithful; theirs are the higher degrees in the presence of the Lord, theirs is forbearing pardon, theirs the munificent endowment (of paradise).[32]

12 An Islamic Covenant

Such qualities can only result from education. Reorienting a society, broken and divided between a majority that clings to its Muslim identity and a fringe touched more or less by the virus of alienating acculturation, is above all a matter of reclaiming education and the means of communication.

It will take generous and persuasive patience to mobilize goodwill for teaching, spreading literacy, and instilling a spirit of forgiveness and enthusiasm in young people who are not deceived by their worn-out elders without horizon. There will have to be a consensus, in which all Muslim people will take part, in order for a torn-apart society to become reconciled with itself.

We hear a lot about consensus these days around here, and much is said about a transition to democracy, but neither consensus nor transition gets beyond the doorsill of the offices where coalitions and splinter groups command and countermand in the culture of professionals of the "consensus culture," a mysterious trade where only personalities co-opted by power know the ropes

After years—after a quarter century, actually—and after the corridors and the dungeons where a steady diet of secularist thinking has confined us, we propose an Islamic pact that will reconcile the power-monopolizing élites and the people, a pact that will strike harmony between them, that will allow the élites to avow and prove their allegiance to the *islam* of which they pretend to be the legitimate spokesmen.

The offensive and much touted slogan, "we are all Muslims," ought to reveal quite transparently what lies behind it. The secret palaver, the thundering declaration served cold to the people, should yield place to a frank and public dialog where each political party, each fragment of the civil society taking shape, each voice excluded under the rule of political charlatanism, can speak up, without exclusion, without esoteric sects and conspiracies.

The people will have to hear, unpacked, the secrets of the historical betrayal that has emptied our moral and material resources, and that has given free reign to a level of corruption that has become the normal way of life for corrupt administrators habituated to graft.

In order to raise the consciousness of people treated until now as minors, we will need a frank and public exposé of what has long been hidden, as a prelude to active participation of forces paralyzed by a lack of confidence and by waves of bitter deceptions.

You who protest, "we are all Muslims," should get moving to prove to yourselves and to the people that you really are. Until now, it has only been during electoral campaigns that you have beaten the drum and made spectacles of yourselves in all your highly charged excitement. Try, for a change, another method: be reconciled with the truth, in all sincerity and serenity.

Let us try to talk truth in an open forum, let us give the people the chance to judge us, on this side, Islamists excluded and kept out of circulation, and on yours, the Masters of democratic Ceremonies. The "national conference" formula invented by the Africans, and similar national covenants practiced from time to time by the Arabs, have merely served to disguise the wounds suffered by our countries, victims of the corrupt oligarchies that fostered their purulence.

Let us give the people the occasion and leisure to understand the games we are playing and the realities our appearance conceals. The people will take part in reconstruction, confident and, for once, knowing full well why.

"We are all Muslims"? Well and good! We shall sincerely be the first to celebrate the day we see you act according to the slogan you chant. As for you champions of Lady Secularity, we are quite aware that not all of you have become strangers to the *islam* of your fathers and mothers. We are committed as well to saving every likely competent participant tomorrow in the reconstruction of society. Far be it from us to enter into that spirit of exclusion that drives some among you to cozy up to supporters (both in and out of the country) by assuring them of your loyalty in order to attack fundamentalism.

Our aim and intentions are the opposite of yours. To you we propose an Islamic pact that gets us all to rally to the truths of *islam*, in confidence and transparency, brothers in solidarity, obedient to God, all of us, and generous with our persons and goods in the common effort.

God (exalted be His Name!) needs no one to defend his cause, but we, poor sinners, heroes of the Resistance and former convicts of illustrious causes; tomorrow we will be wrapped in our shrouds, frigid corpses Muslims lay out in the Muslim mosque for Muslim prayers. Which will it be there, stretched out powerless, delivered to the embalmer, poor thing: a true Muslim—or an ex-hypocrite, ex-militant, ex-office-seeking ex-liar (to himself and to others)?

Where is the militant of yesterday, today's tamed accomplice? Where are your sacrifices and ours, my Brothers, to censure the false and proclaim the truth? Militants once, sincere in your convictions, under the Marxist banner: what has become of you?

Redeem yourselves, dear kindred souls! Return to God, raise the banner of *islam,* honor, and pride of your glorious and pious forebears!

13 Instability

We take a great step toward an Islamic future when we recognize and admit our past mistakes. It is a serious miscalculation, a defect both intellectual and moral, to believe that we can build something solid and lasting while lying to ourselves and erecting an overhang that is unsupported by the truth of *islam* and the reality of a Muslim people ever faithful to God.

What remains and withstands is built on the bedrock of values. In contrast to "disenchanted" Western societies, ours, thank God, is laden with divine favor. It is constant in its faithfulness to God; apart from the acculturated and denatured fringe, it is penetrated by the divine. Weary skepticism and unbelief do not graze our spirits. Therefore the certainty of those politicians among us and their misappreciation of *islam,* that allows them to assimilate to it the role of religion in the secularist Western culture, makes them spout unthinking slogans.

In secularized societies, religion is a tolerated private affair; our politicians quickly draw the parallel and conclude that you can just declare yourself a Muslim like everyone else, relegate being a Muslim to the private sphere, and thus your individual faith doesn't concern anybody else.

But it does! There can be no instability in relation to *islam.* You cannot shore up your identity by abandoning the Muslim norm for other conventions; in *islam* the individual act of faith is inseparable from political action. Individual faith and collaboration for good are both proof of membership in the Muslim community and the stuff of that community's cohesion.

Not to take that into account results from either the fundamental deceit proper to hypocrites or disbelief cynically assumed and acted out—or both at once. The ladies and gentlemen who call themselves Muslims like everyone else take the trouble to appear in white robes at the mosque during official ceremonies, praying before the cameras. These same photogenic pious types drop their immaculately white daily habits, once night has fallen, to hit the local bar, where they go drinking and dancing like all bad drunken and depraved Muslims.

Doctor Jekyll in white robes publishes a piece the next day in his party journal affirming his attachment to *islam*, after having been seized by his nightly demons, and, setting aside his pen a few columns later, becomes Mr. Hyde in his panegyric of liberties that *islam* does not recognize.

If common dancers and drinkers sin against their values and break their commitments, the responsible politician and the opposition militant ought to be models of virtue, of unquestioned moral probity. They ought to set the example by their healthy private lives so that they may earn our confidence.

Faithfulness to the values of *islam* is not satisfied with declarations, showy ceremonial appearances, and journal articles: it takes action. For this reason the Islamic pact we are proposing to get us out of our rut should grow out of public debate and the prelude to engagement followed by deeds. Neither the serene quietism of a pillar of the mosque nor the amorality or immorality of a hypocrite can serve as a basis for the future of the struggle for justice.

The future is menacing, as gloomy in the forecasts of futurists as it is to the eyes of any observer who is at all alert. The ultimate fate of each sinner is horrible if, in addition to his private wants, he lies to himself and to Muslims in spreading his facile slogan. The truth of the individual's faith and scrupulous regard for collective morality are the indispensable conditions for the ultimate well-being of each and the successful outcome of the Islamic project.

Muslim people should maintain a state of alert, besieged as they are by incommensurable difficulties: globalization brandishes its chopper and sets ultimatums to be carried out by its satellite economies, at the cost to them of poverty, social injustice, underdevelopment, bad governance, corruption; the trail of disgrace is long.

Competence and professionalism on the part of functionaries *au courant* with how things get done in the world is surely an important goal for a country in a poor state of development, but if these experts are not integrated in the society, if the men in power decide and direct without obeying any faith, any law, the society thus governed and administrated is headed straight for the abyss. So long as the men at the helm are without any compass besides their whims, there is no hope for development, no hope for a future.

Our foreseen concern and sincere compassion go to those who, today, consider our taking a stand—if some manifestation of it manages to come across—as a ridiculous intrusion and an insolent infringement on the political rights reserved to sworn secularists. Tomorrow, our respect for human dignity will be dictated not only by reckoning the general interest, but by the divine order: "We have honored the children of Adam."

No pious Muslim will ever tolerate a woman or a man, whatever their convictions or errors, to be treated like rubbish. The absolute basis of our Islamic values does not allow human dignity to be relativized, that is, betrayed. The drift of Western modernity should be a lesson to us.

André Comte-Sponville resigns himself with difficulty to the loss of the absolute, the foundation of meaning and worth. Here is how the wise Western philosopher deplores the moral drift of a permissive and lax West:

> Without an absolute basis—without a basis altogether—the existence of absolute value or meaning cannot be certain. . . . The stake, today, is to live in that relativism to which we dedicate the evolving of our thoughts and beliefs, without however foundering in nihilism.[33]

Out of apprehension, aware of what an unbridled conscience or tribal spirit might unleash, we insist on principles so that, when the moment arrives, we do not come to grief in chaos. The drama in Algeria is a manifestation of unbridled morality as much as the result of a sociopolitical derailment from which one would be well advised to learn lessons, whatever side he may be on. Those who lack foresight, driven to the brink by events, are always impelled to improvisation, excess, and, ultimately, to destructive violence.

14 Mobilizing

If it is applied with an open mind, sensitive to psychological and objective difficulties, Islamic Law will not make a priority of pursuing the sinners' peccadillos. The agenda of an Islamic government will never conduct meetings to discuss the opportunities for harassing women by obliging them to wear a square of cloth on their heads; decency and good morals, notwithstanding their importance for us, are not the sole business of government.

Making public life moral is an issue for a general mobilization to which men and women (veiled or not) will be called; good dispositions will need to be encouraged and sustained. Muslims of good will, of both genders, will be invited to the mosque, where constructive encounters will take place, the locus of life and of participation.

The traditional role of the mosque will have to be reestablished; new life will have to be breathed into it. The mosque, a place of worship, the house consecrated to God, should once again be the focus of humming activity, instead of being a cloister open only during scheduled times of prayer. The mosque needs to be liberated from the role of a high place in official propaganda that the seculars who govern us have made it: for too long the Friday sermon has been the occasion of chanting the praises of power in the sleepy tone of a soulless litany.

The Prophet (grace and peace upon him!) inaugurated his activities after his exodus to Medina by constructing a mosque. He took part in this work with his own hands. Like everyone else he was covered with the dust of his work. This was to underline for us the strategic importance of a mosque in the life of a Muslim community concerned with the participation of everyone in the common work.

The quarters inherited by an Islamic government from its predecessors are numerous. Nationalized and entrusted to functionaries who are little motivated and unenthusiastic, these premises will have to be turned once again into hives of activity.

In the day of a Muslim who lives according to Islamic norms, certain times are consecrated to prayer, preferably in the mosque. Other daily activities should not encroach on times for prayer.

> Prayer remains for the faithful something prescribed at fixed hours.[34]

Friday, a blessed day, will be the day for assembling. On that day, midday collective prayer is an obligation that every good Muslim respects:

> You who have faith, when you are called to Friday prayer, hasten with eagerness to answer the call and leave every transaction. This is indeed best for you, if you but knew.[35]

With every transaction coming to a halt at a fixed hour of the week in order to answer a general call, the time of the faithful takes on the rhythm—five times a day at fixed hours—of the daily hours of prayer. This temporal discipline cannot be imposed by external authority; it is the expression of the disposition and the dynamism on the part of the man of faith and the woman of piety.

Modern man's time does not belong to him; jostled and squeezed by the time-clock of labor, he rushes off to find the freedom to devote his leisure time to satisfying his appetites, his need to play, have fun. The Muslim, well adjusted to his day and at ease with time, frees himself from servitude five times a day to find himself once again in the fraternally comforting bosom of his neighborhood mosque, ceremoniously joined to his brothers at a weekly assembly. Work and leisure are shared in joy and contentment with others, in permanent contact with them.

Daily toil and labor are not borne like some painful vexation, and leisure time is not devoted to benumbing play so as to forget the disgrace of living without knowing why. Modern men are only occasionally and infrequently disturbed by existential anguish as they give themselves over to their heart's content to killing time and forgetting the tragedy of a life that denies death, its absolute enemy.

The Muslim who lives *islam* to the full goes often to the mosque for prayers and peaceful contemplation, a holy place from which he leaves ready to defend his values and to earn his livelihood. The mosque is the place from which radiates the mobilizing energy necessary to arm the body as well as the will to continue the work of reconstruction. This is why it is of such importance to revive the role of the mosque and to free up the daily routine so that the faithful can be spiritually rejuvenated there five times a day. Without this reenergizing source at fixed intervals, straying from mindfulness of God and aberrations of uncontrolled duration will lead in the long run to laxity and carelessness.

Permanent mobilization and mastery of time are the traits of a collected individual and an alert society. The loss of control of time is one of the greatest cracks in modern societies, deplored by those societies' lucid critics, though they find no remedy for the "scarcity of time" and the difficulty of "living for the moment."

The phrase *habiter le temps* ("dwelling in time") was coined by the philosopher Jean Chesneaux, who published a book under that evocative title in 1966. That retired professor deplores the temporal air modernity breathes, which deprives modern man, with all his material means, of a simple lodging in the moment:

> We are time's orphans, and yet we are obsessed by time, thus doubly at a loss to exercise our democratic capacities in the time we have. On the one hand it is as if we are willing to risk seeing the fundamental link between past, present, and future dissolve altogether. Yet, on the other hand, we are overrun, drowned by the problems of managing time.
>
> Budgeting time, time-sharing, installment programs, temporal stress, time parameters: these constraints of time and inquiries into time weigh heavily on the social plain as well as in each personal life. Yet the society of modernity tends to value the throw-away, the clip, the zero delay, all of which degrade and atrophy our sense of duration.[36]

Notes

1 See verse 8, n. 18.

2 Bukhari.

3 Sûrah 30 [*Ar-Rûm*]: verse 30.

4 Sûrah 107 [*Al-Mâ'ûn*]: complete.

5 Sûrah 25 [*Al-Furqân*]: verses 63–68, 72–73.

6 Sûrah 25 [*Al-Furqân*]: verse 74.

7 Sûrah 67 [*Al-Mulk*]: verse 2.

8 Op. cit., p. 210.

9 Ibid., p. 211.

10 *Futuribles*, no. 202, pp. 68–69.

11 Bukhari and Muslim.

12 Cited by M. Godet in *Futuribles* no. 202, p. 69.

13 Ibid., p. 70.

14 Ibid., p. 71.

15 Ibid.

16 *I.e.*, the irresponsibility of male parents' abandoning their out-of-wedlock children to the abandoned mothers.

17 Ibid., p. 72.

18 *La Société en quête de valeurs,* already cited, p. 25.

19 Ibid., p. 26.

20 Ibid., p. 231.

21 *La Fin de la démocratie,* ed. Flammarion (1995), pp. 130–31.

22 Ibid., p. 113.

23 Ibid., p. 114.

24 Ibid., pp. 125–26.

25 Ibid., pp. 127–28.

26 TN: "Ignorance, paganism" (< *j-h-l* "be ignorant, not know").

27 TN: "Goodness, benevolence, mercifulness, courteousness, sweetness, mildness" (< *r-f-q* "be accommodating, good, kindly, sweet toward someone; treat someone with kindness").

28 Sûrah 17 [*Al-isrâ'*]: verse 70.

29 Bukhari and Muslim.

30 Sûrah 49 [*Al-Hujurât*]: verse 10.

31 Sûrah 49 [*Al-Hujurât*]: verse 15.

32 Sûrah 8 [*Al-Anfâl*]: verses 2–4.

33 *La Société en quête de valeurs,* op. cit., pp. 130–31.

34 Sûrah 4 [*An-Nisâ'*]: verse 103.

35 Sûrah 62 [*Al-Jumu'ah*]: verse 9.

36 Chesneaux, op. cit., p. 107.

VII. *Having*

1 Globalization

The threatening character of the new political order and economic globalization announces an offensive on all fronts by the great ruling power against all the underdeveloped countries who will suffer from it more than wealthy nations.

This politico-economic aggression demands that we mobilize all our forces to face it.

The word "mobilization" belongs to the incantatory lexicon used by our politicians to shake off the torpor of a people who do not want to move, having lost confidence in Westernized élites cut off from their roots. The word is taken up and inserted into the electoral platforms of fabricated or prefabricated parties comprising agents who are neither élite nor Westernized—except in their manners and bad habits.

Although the word no longer works in the abracadabra of unmasked politicos, mobilization is for us an urgent necessity and an ardent obligation for reestablishing broken lines of trust and giving renewed worth to one's pledges.

At the dawn of independence of our countries, popular enthusiasm had reached its apogee; an immense hope sparked the energy of a generation ready to sacrifice its efforts to build a future of dignity in imitation of the nationalist pioneers who scarified their lives for independence. A young generation, with their heads in the clouds of enchanting promises, pickaxes in hand, built bridges and leveled mountains in order to pave a road to the future.

It did not take long for their enthusiasm to wane once the oaths of fidelity were betrayed and the class newly come to power gave itself over to extortion. Entire generations, refusing to bow down before such hypocritical despotism, opposed the tyranny and underwent still worse affronts. Unfortunately, revolution and sacrifice had no other point of reference than the nihilist ideology of atheist socialism. Those who revolted were no better than the corrupt class; each was as bad as the other: the one side for its hypocrisy, the other for its declared secularism (and actual atheism), and both were in opposition to the values of *islam*.

In order to give direction once again to a society lost between two propositions equally unattached to our values and equally deceptive, we shall have to mobilize yet again with renewed spirit, saving what is still recoverable so that we can take up once more and with confidence a movement that miscarried. Since the damages are great, we will need a resolute determination founded on morality and made dynamic by the faith of the faithful. We shall have to be united in our effort in the face of the approaching threat, unless we want to run off into the uncertain.

The fate that knocks at our gates is called globalization. Countries like ours—underdeveloped and given to the wrangling and hesitation of politicians occupied in fighting over power and its privileges, ever ready to change hats—will be its first designated victims.

We are going to listen at length as two European experts describe for us the menace they apprehend for their own rich and solidly organized country. This will allow us to measure the danger to which we are exposed and which we will have to face. Hans-Peter Martin and Harald Schuman, two German journalists, describe the present and future situation of their society and designate as well the enemy they reproach for this state of affairs.

We always prefer to let Westerners speak about their modernity, out of a concern with being accused of exaggerating. Our Islamic point of view will thus rest on objective statements and direct witnesses. Who is attacked by globalization? Listen:

> It is no longer profiteers who are being attacked now, but so-called "social spongers": it is now being claimed that protection for the elderly, the sick, and the unemployed should be left to individual responsibility.
>
> In the United States, where half the citizens, particularly among the common classes, no longer vote, the new Social Darwinists have won a parliamentary majority. And they have undertaken a partitioning of their country according to the Brazilian model.
>
> The next victims of this unstoppable logic will be women. In Germany, the Christian Democrats charged with domestic problems have already decided to enact salary reductions for pregnant women on sick-leave, a measure that gives rise to apprehension among the salaried class as a whole.[1]

Our two German witnesses, whose system of government is the very model of a strong and stable democracy, claim that a strong German government must face American aggression. The enemy, for our two authors, is indeed American hegemonism, when speaking of globalization:

> The existence of governments capable of facing up to the new moneyed International, and of acting by undertaking certain reform, is threatened with the sanction of capital flight. The only nation today that could, on its own, call forth a change in direction is the economic and military superpower of the United States.
>
> But at this time the chances of seeing America launching an initiative to curb market forces for the profit of all peoples are practically nil. On the contrary, it can be expected that future American administrations will enact (apparent) solutions of a protectionist kind, seeking to procure commercial advantages for their country at the expense of the others.
>
> This will in no way contradict American tradition. The American image of self-sacrifice in helping the rest of the world solve its problems has

never existed in fact. American administrations, whatever their stripe, have always behaved virtually exclusively according to what they considered their national interests. So long as it was necessary to fight the East, "the Evil Empire," there was a need for Western Europe to be stable and prosperous in order to oppose the attractive face of capitalism to communism. But Washington now no longer has any need of Europe to play that role.[2]

2 Justice and Injustices

A nation that is less sure of itself, teetering on its foundations, and bogged down in contradictions, cannot undertake decisive fights. It can only be saved by collective volunteerism and the mobilization of all its forces to face the unleashed forces of the global market. An Islamic mobilization of all our forces is our last resort, the last plot where we may be able to reorganize our defense and undertake a way out of the trap of the moneyed International led by an arrogant America that is not about to lessen its stranglehold.

The economic trap we have fallen into, and the social Darwinism which is for us its bitter fruit, threaten and will continue to threaten our life, not only in terms of a social peace that is precarious enough, but also in terms of our very survival as a nation. Still, we were not born yesterday; our weakness is not congenital—as a thousand-year history makes clear. The divine rule of the "rotation of days" and the logical nature of things will not make an exception in our case.

So long as we transgress Qur'anic Law by breaking the divine laws that direct the progression of humanity, we will remain the class dunce, no-accounts in the fierce competition that no longer hides capitalism's "attractive face." Our sickness presents itself in the symptoms of underdevelopment, the poor distribution of goods and services, injustice of all kinds, and generalized corruption coolly claimed as a mode of governing.

These symptoms, extremely serious as they are, should not conceal the source of the illness. Little tricks—a constitutional mini-reform here, a little electoral law there, no sooner enacted than betrayed—is not going to be able to rescue us from the abyss. Our illness is curable only if we strike at the virus in ourselves; only then will the symptoms disappear. There is a way of climbing out of the abyss, provided we know how to neutralize the forces that drag us back down. Our cure and our escape depend on the trust we shall be able to place in God and in our values.

In a hundred-meter race, what chances would a one-legged runner have, jumping on a wooden leg? Our worm-eaten wooden leg is the system of secular laws that the managers of our societies are the first to break. Gangrene attacks the entire body: the selfish values of the secular skeptics at the head of our institutions and the imported laws with no base in faith are the double ruination of our societies.

A return to God, a covenant among the members of our societies by which God would be both their Witness and Guarantor, will permit moral and social virtues long devalued and out of circulation to break forth and become widespread today: integrity, solidarity, confidence, honesty, work well done, the given word, justice.

Justice and the rights guaranteed to everyone are the two conditions of social stability in the state of law. The community of faith must guarantee the vital minimum of fairness so that no one is harmed, and that all might take part in the common effort, assured of their security. The injustices wrought upon us from without are but the just punishment for the injustices we wrought on ourselves.

Only faith in God and respect for His Law, which is its solemn imperative, can reawaken our will and affirm our steps. Faith in God (may His Name be glorified!) is inseparable from respect for His Law. These two sacred links, which education and frequent mosque attendance will reinstate, will reunite our ranks in rediscovered confidence and solidarity. Confidence in God and in His Promise will back our efforts and guide our steps. Sure of our Guarantor and reconciled among ourselves, we will be prevented by God's Word from recoiling and beating a retreat before the great scourges of modernism such as globalization.

We read God's Promise in the Sûrah called "Light":

> To those among you who have faith and do effective good work, God has promised that He will make of you His lieutenants on earth, as He made of their forebears; that He will confirm the faith he has bestowed on them; that he will replace their fear with assurance of security, so long as they worship Me without associating Me with other divinities. After (this promise) those who aver their unbelief will be villainous.[3]

Thus it is a question of faith, of faithfulness to the One and Only, of worship, of fear dispelled, of assurance and security. The Promise is conditional; the condition is clear.

Still more explicit are the considerations accorded to the faithful attached to God by their oath of fidelity, and for whom justice is the first clause of their oath. The Sûrah called "The Bee" calls for the order and determination of a perfected moral society in which the worship required of the faithful is an integral part. The secularism that wants to separate the social sphere from any contact with religion could not better be given the lie than by these two verses:

> God ordains justice, good work, and generosity toward kinfolk; He proscribes baseness, reprehensible acts, and excess. He exhorts and counsels you so that you might reflect. Be faithful to the covenant you have made with God; do not violate your oaths after having solemnly sworn them and having called upon God to witness your good faith. God knows your actions.[4]

Strengthened by our solemnly contracted covenant, and with God as Witness and Guarantor, we will be able to apply ourselves to the difficult task of righting the wrongs of a significant part of the people. Establishing a new constitution enacted by an elected assembly and reshuffling existing institutions with a sense of greater probity, integrity, and justice, will allow a new dynamic to get started and will deal with questions of culture, society, political and economic order, and civilization, so long pending.

Nothing solid can be built on the void of an overhang. So long as we persist in importing wholesale the notions and values of others, we will never be anything but their pale copies, without soul or substance.

3 Capitalism's Impasse

Any imitation of Western capitalism that ignores the particulars and the final goals of *islam* will lead, not to an Islamic land, but to deceit and ultimate disaster. Without the moral bases of social, family, and political life, repeated reform efforts will be bound for defeat. The example of Western capitalist societies, whose ailments are exposed and denounced by their best thinkers, is edifying.

Western democracies search in vain for a means of reining in the corruption of their morals—corruption altogether. In Italy, the "White Hand" fails to put an end to the Mafia. In France, illegal manipulation of suspect funds is wiped from the slate by a majority vote granting amnesty to the party in power, as if morality were a statistical equation and a matter of parliamentary balance.

American schools have become the theater for armed confrontations between gangs of brats raised on a daily spectacle of violence, on the streets, and on the television screens. The Western hope of reforming public education has disappeared along with the dream of reviving a moral democracy.

In this chapter we have been attempting to lay out the problems of development; the moral relationship between having and money is the critical point we must deal with. Avarice and greed—characteristics of the immoral individual stigmatized in the Qur'an as a blind and immoral attachment to having—lie quintessentially at the heart of capitalism.

Let us first hear the moral judgment the Qur'an pronounces on arrogant types the likes of which we have been considering. Then let us examine the present condition of capitalist arrogance at the summit of its power under the name of "globalization."

> Have you not seen—(the pronoun refers to the Prophet and every good listener, to whom be peace and well-being!)—How your Lord treated the

people of 'Ad (no longer existing), of Iram (another punished people), the like of whose colonnades has not been equaled, of Thamud, who quarried rocks in the valley, and Pharaoh, master of the pyramids? They all transgressed the law of justice in the world and multiplied its losses. Thus your Lord struck them with stinging punishment. Your Lord is ever on the lookout.[5]

The case of modern capitalism does not differ from the examples evoked from the past; all the conditions are there: arrogance, waste, prestige and power, self-sufficiency. The colossal dimensions of modern disorders and globalized injustice call forth divine punishment proportionate to the crimes.

The Word of God is a warning addressed by Him to people of all times to hold them back and prevent them from falling in when they stand at the brink of catastrophe. Can modern capitalism, already at an impasse, take hold of itself and change course before the punishment it deserves strikes all of humanity? Is it in any position to take control of itself?

A physician's clinical examination diagnoses the advanced state of the illness that makes it difficult to treat. The doctor, Jacques Robin, is the author of a book called *Changer l'ère*.[6] This physician of the human body auscultates the heartbeat of capitalism and publishes a pessimistic diagnosis. We place it before us as something to be read attentively and as a concrete example illustrating the historic prototype of whose repeated tragedy the Qur'an recounts.

Today, when the capitalist market economy extends to the most diverse of human activities in every country in the world, whatever the level of its development, it leads to situations as inhumane (as communist economy) and comes to rest before its own impasses.

> First of all, the market's pretension not only to represent the entire economy, but to assure its self-regulation, does not stand up under examination. Liberal economists, the Anglo-Saxons in particular, believe they have the last word when they assure us, often arrogantly, that the market economy, guided by an "invisible hand," is best at deciding production and distributing according to the preference of the players. Twenty million new poor in the US, and above all, two or three billion casualties in the countries of the South suggest the opposite.

As a tool that produces billions of casualties in the world, capitalism has other functions as well, as our scandalized author continues:

> The market economy best serves the powerful and the best off. States treat the market economy as a tool in their global strategy, notably by using monetary distortions. Thus, manipulation of the American dollar weighs heavily, on balance, in global commerce, such as in the Uruguay Round; and, as everyone knows, the world agricultural market is in the hands of the North.

Next our physician, calling for a change in the capitalist era to one that is kinder and more just for humanity, outlines the most serious of the symptoms of the illness his patient is suffering:

> The third impasse is more terrible yet: the market economy finds it is incapable of controlling course changes. Crises to date have only been dealt with at the price of misery, violence, and war.
>
> Today, what we face is not so much a crisis of circumstances as profound technological and cultural change. Driven by information technology, the first of these carries with it an unprecedented production of goods and services with less and less human labor.
>
> The second calls into question the value of labor in social relationships. The inability of the market to distribute wealth in abundance through the information-market, the tendency of money to be a speculative tool, the rapid degradation of the environment through industrialization: everything shows that this ever-expanding market economy involves us in its own contradiction.[7]

4 Capitalist Waste

Who among our Westernized élite is asking where a globalized modernity that brings disaster to most of humanity is taking us. It is not hard to discover the identity of those behind the devastating results and the selfish principles that generate them. If, instead of honoring the principles on which the relation with wealth every Muslim and Muslim society depend, we close our eyes and submit to the harm unbridled capitalism inflicts on the economy; we remain easy victims; worse yet, we become accomplices in our own murder.

The disastrous results of capitalism without justice are syndromes of the irregularities and malformations proper to market economy. We can cry "Stop thief!" all we like; we will never capture the thief until we lay hands on the shameful disease of capitalism never questioned by the analysts, the congenital defect I call usury and the cult of the Golden Calf.

In the conventions of capital, all interest in excess of the legal limits is usurious. The financial laws of the central capitalist banks and those of international financial institutions assign a threshold to money below which interest rates can freely move so as to maintain microeconomic balance, thus allowing money to be sheltered, and enjoy a guaranteed return that is not threatened by risk. It is up to the worker and entrepreneur to knock themselves out to pay the interest and alone suffer the consequences in the case of loss.

The grand Keynesian dream linking full employment to zero interest rate has never come to pass, nor will it, so long as man remains a prisoner to his penchant for selfishness, and modern societies operate exclusively by calculating self-interest and capital gain.

Our Islamic principles exhort us to the individual virtue of charity and the social morality of justice and equity. In the Qur'an, giving is preached insistently, while demanding interest is stigmatized with singular vehemence:

> Of every expense that you make or vow (of spending) that you take, God has knowledge. The unjust shall find no help. If you give alms openly, so much the better for you! But it is better still if you slide them discretely into the hand of the needy one, for We shall value it as an expiation for your sins. God knows of your actions.[8]

Public and private giving is highly prized, in contrast to usury, which is presented as abject villainy and an unforgivable fault:

> It is not up to you (Muhammad) to guide them (toward the good path), but it is for God to guide whom He wishes. Every gift you give, give it for love of God; that will be to your advantage. For every gift of the best that you can, you will be fully recompensed.[9]

The two following verses insist on the same theme of generous giving,[10] before coming to the matter of usury.

> Those who consume the fruits of usury (who practice usurial interest) will not yet finish doing so before they are as someone Satan has possessed and made to struggle. And this is because they say, "What difference is there between trade and interest?" Now, God authorizes trade but forbids interest. Those of you who will be affected by the exhortation of your Lord and stop the practice will be able to keep your former gains, your affair is God's to judge. But woe to those who return to the practice. They will dwell forever in hell.[11]

This sacred verse opens for us a new horizon of hope, for we are in a situation similar to the era of transition at the time of the Prophet (peace be upon him!). The illicit present and future gains that we will have to let circulate for some time are as the misdeeds that God will forgive us, as we hope and pray He will. We will be restricted from circulating these gains once the reorientation and reorganization of monetary and financial systems in Muslim countries give a certain degree of independence from the capitalist International, official or private.

The Islamic banking institutions that work up participative investments linking capital with labor without the shameless exploitation through interest charges are still in a stammering phase of development: promising results, but little else. Even these few meagre results have to be wrested away from the hegemonic power of the international financial market by Islamic banks holed up in the crevices of the colossal global system. Still, such enterprise is not to be disdained; such banks announce the possibility of a saving way, paving the path for the day when Muslims will attain political maturity and a moral and spiritual awakening.

When that occurs, all Muslims will be working toward uniting their efforts and will begin to realize their important potential—potential that today is scattered and ineffectual. We will have to motivate our common effort with the will to escape God's anger; His Word puts us on guard against worshiping the Golden Calf:

> Oh faithful, fear God and abandon the remains of usurial interest (that you have yet to discover) if you would truly be faithful. If you do not, await battle with God and His Prophet![12]

Such is the horror with which Islamic Law regards the practice of usury. Timorous and disciplined in an Islamic society, money ought to circulate not by running behind an easy remuneration attributed to capital as capital, but with regard to its financial contribution to savers, entrepreneurs, and workers. A bank should earn enough to pay its administration, but it must not be allowed to play the role of voracious intermediary.

Let us hope that the way out of this Satanic labyrinth is not too far off.

5 What Development?

What kind of development befits a communitarian life based on the values of solidarity and mutual assistance that *islam* preaches?

Or rather, do we have the choice of borrowing another path of economic development than the one our present means and situation allow us? That is a more suitable question for the times as they stand.

The time in the mosque is serene and fraternal; we leave, take to the streets, go home, and it is the air of modern time we breathe. After recollection and prayer, the Muslim needs to roll up his sleeves and wear himself out making a living. The Muslim society will require a minimum of material comfort so that, in its bosom, the moral and spiritual comfort of its men and women can be assured.

Being Muslims does not dispense us from the rule of economics; a bad economy can only have an economic remedy. As it stands, the modern economy of the imperial age, dominated by transnational giants, leaves us only a few tiny openings we can slide through by concentrating our efforts and calling up all our internal forces.

The time still seems far off when Muslim peoples will weigh heavily on the economic scale, truly global and worldwide. Despite our petroleum and natural gas, despite all our material and human resources, our weight on the scale is insignificant, since we lack a consciousness of our identity and are laid low by the absence of one of the essential factors of development: justice in freedom and freedom in justice.

An Islamic government that announces its desire for independence and calls for justice will lose little time in becoming a target for the revilement reserved for spoilsports: economic embargo and financial restrictions will be the recalcitrant's first whip-lashings. Add to these threats the outrageous disproportionate external debt and its traumatizing effect, which no change of system is going to avoid, and you understand the absolute necessity for counting on God's assistance, and on all our forces, without exception.

There are shady fortunes stashed among us. Some injustices have been committed that, in the absolute, ought to have netted their authors example-setting sanctions. As such things go, however, our vital capital needs and the quickness with which money disappears are such that a well-advised Islamic government can only close its eyes and ears to overlook the source of illegal fortunes of the defrauder or marauder.

Economic amnesty is the sole alternative to economic debacle and failure. Past faults can be expiated under the form of taking active and honest part in developing the country. Let all be allowed to rectify liabilities by demonstrating constructive activity as proof of amendment.

Without disabling the existent economic apparatus, we will have to dismantle feudal economic lobbies. If the policy is to encourage the productive forces retained by an honest middle class, a few petty marauders can be overlooked. Wisdom and prudence alone will permit a twofold stake.

Separating the chaff from the grain is an operation that may be successful in a field of well-tended wheat, but not in the capitalist jungle. The duty of husbanding one's life, that of preserving the common weal, that of insuring one's country's economic solidity, all of these militate for an economic policy in which moral rigor is compounded with necessity, without so much as grazing its principles.

A Stalinesque extermination of the kulaks is not our recipe for burying the past, but rather, collective repentance before God in an atmosphere of rediscovered Islamic brotherhood.

Development goes forward by means of mobilizing and moralizing public life. The pardon and rehabilitation of property and men must not turn into sanctimonious laxity, however. Development does not obey order like some sort of military operation, but a new page open to pardon ought to make it clear to everyone that from now on no one will be able to diminish the law and escape unscathed.

The long practice of self-discipline necessary for an economic take-off, and the multitude of problems inherited from the era of lies, will require that public mobilization and moralizing be decisive and trenchant, after a period of reasonable amnesty. The urgent and vital need of productive investment and the coolness of foreign capitalists who turn up their noses and refuse adventures without sure guarantees will force us, even beyond the virtue of pardon intrinsic to *islam,* to tolerate dubious possessions.

Moreover, as necessary as foreign capital and know-how may be, they can never replace local investment and a local address. Hence the absolute necessity of managing men and possession. Let us be guided by the example of the Prophet, who amnestied his former torturers at the time of his triumphal entrance into Mecca.

A new legal framework must be set firmly in place that will outline an Islamic deontology in the domains of commerce, industry, and investment markets, so as to put a stop to barren speculation.

Local capital, under the government's watchful eye, should be applied to the essential task of earning society's living by confronting the tumultuous waves of pitiless international competition that brandishes over our heads the sword of the open market presided over by the augurers of the WTO [World Trade Organization].

"Sharks" swarm in the ocean of the current market; an open market will whet their appetite even more. The government must be able to guarantee investors' rights and manage the infrastructure necessary for development and favorable to it; but without global agreements, it will not be able to conquer the markets and convince its clients.

The government will have other fish to fry, and giant fish at that, since two crucial dilemmas remain for it to solve. First—and this is not the easier of the two—is the conundrum of a corrupt and teetering bureaucratic administration, slow and inveterate in the art of twisting the laws to suit itself. A battery of new laws, austere by definition, can only be applied once a profound reform of the judiciary and administrative personnel has prepared the terrain. The second dilemma is social and painfully real: to reconcile a private economy subjected to the cannibalistic law of competitiveness that forces businesses to lay off a maximum number of personnel, with the socio-economic imperative of preserving existing jobs and creating new ones to combat unemployment and insure a minimum of social justice.

It is extremely difficult and ticklish to coordinate a policy of general redress with a policy of development, in addition to a social policy under the whip of international financial insistence that dictates to debtor countries a line of inhumane conduct that includes, among other drastic conditions, the suppression of unemployment compensation.

Only God's promise allows us to escape despair.

6 A Favored Islamic Project

Although the Islamic community to be formed must rest on the bases of solidarity and a minimum of well-being for everyone, modern enterprise rests on other bases and pursues other goals, such as profitability and survival in the midst of feverish market competition. It has neither states of souls nor a philanthropic calling. Market constraints oblige it to practice "flexible employment," a euphemism for partial employment, disbanding, and unemployment.

How can modern enterprise be compelled to perform its economic role without abandoning its social function? How can government protect both investors and the social interests of labor? Two kinds of logic must be reconciled; the economies of Southeast Asia seem to be linking them together, with the aid of the governments that protect and defend one another's interests.

To escape from the orbit of the American world policeman and frustrate the strategies of the decisions taken at Brussels and Washington, we will need to find our inspiration elsewhere and adapt Asian wisdom to our situation and final goals. The necessity of bending to international norms need not enfeeble us altogether, as evidenced by the success of Asiatic economies that allows a minuscule Singapore to hobnob with the big players and send sparks flying like some fire-spouting dragon.

To be in a position to learn new management methods, business among us will have to unlearn bad habits, once it enters the field. In today's world there is no longer a Wild West for intrepid pioneers and consummate adventurers like those empirical self-taught captains of industry. Their place has been given over to management techniques; old-fashioned hardheadedness has had to bend to youthful managers capable of following the perpetual evolution of knowledge and methodology.

The "leveling" we hear so much about, and whose model is offered to us by way of assistance, is not going to happen without an independent mobilizing of our "human resources." The model of "total quality"—a label required for survival in an open competitive market—should be studied in its Japanese form, where the art of sales marketing is allied with a certain personal quality in production.

Post-modern, post-industrial enterprise in advanced societies has to be clever and inventive or disappear; there are no orthopedic clinics for economic lame ducks. In our underdeveloped countries we have even greater need of inventiveness and cleverness, since we enter the race with many handicaps, not the least of which being an educational system that is deficient and ill-adapted.

With the two German journalists we have already met, let us follow the feat of strength and agility that permits the cutting-edge economies of

Southeast Asia to maintain the purchasing power of their workers while favoring business—something our Germans appreciate and admire.

> All Far Eastern countries on the rise have without exception wagered on a strategy justly banned in the West: massive state intervention on all levels of the economic process. Instead of letting themselves be led like lambs to the slaughter of international competition, as Mexico has done, the dragons of state-guided expansion, from Jakarta to Beijing, have adjusted a diversified apparatus that allows them to control their development.
>
> For them, integration in the world market is not an objective but a simple means they make use of with prudence and circumspection.
>
> In all the Asian countries of strong growth, opening the economy to foreign markets follows the principle of the aircraft carrier invented by the Japanese. High tariff barriers on imports and technical directives block imports in all sectors of the core economy when their planners judge their own enterprises to be too weak to confront international competition and wish to maintain employment rates.
>
> On the other hand, authorities and governments set into action a full range of means, from fiscal exoneration to cost-free infrastructure, to protect export production. The manipulation of monetary rates is an important tool in this strategy. All Asian countries copy the Japanese model, and, thanks to the sales of their central banks, artificially maintain the external value of their currencies at a level below the actual buying power of those currencies internally. This explains how the value of average salaries in Southeast Asia corresponds to only a fortieth of West European values when converted at the official exchange rate, while in terms of their buying power they correspond to one eighth of the European level.
>
> The engineers of Asiatic growth intervene not only in the short-term capital rates of their financial markets; direct investment by multinational groups is also subjected to precise rules. Malaysia, for example, systematically organizes the participation of its own enterprises, national and private, in subsidiary group companies. This assures that a growing number of locally salaried workers acquire the know-how necessary for access to the world market. To raise the general qualifications of their population, all these states invest in addition a considerable part of their budget in an efficient system of education.
>
> When that is not enough, supplementary training leading to licentiates and diplomas assures the transfer of technology. Directives bearing on that part of national enterprise destined for the world market are further alert to insuring that a sufficient amount of the profits realized from exporting remain in the country and be poured back into the creation of national enterprises.[13]

We cite at length from Western analysis of a Muslim Malaysia whose Islamic majority has not handicapped it and of the little dragons who make the giants of the West pay dearly, first for the lesson and then for illustrating what state volunteerism can do to facilitate a supple change which harms neither labor rights nor creative and active enterprise.

7 Solidarity,[14] Poverty

Three institutions ought to preside over the progress of the economy to give it a framework, protect it, and lend it active force:

1 A competent government that is faithful to the principles and values of *islam.*

2 A trade movement independent of political management and solicitous of the public weal with active and wise patronage.

3 A charitable structure that can fill in the gaps and supplement institutional deficiencies.

The moral and legal authority of the government should be exercised with assurance so that everyone is dedicated to his task. The vociferations of a politicized trade movement will respond indefinitely to the evasions of a greedy management if the government that protects business does not speak out in favor of the justice its workers deserve. Outbidding and ceiling raising cannot replace a policy that guarantees the comprehensive and well-managed interests of all.

The machinery of impoverishing people, as I call imperial capitalism, leaves little room for maneuvering for weaker economies but it must render justice for the work force at any price. Justice to workers rendered with dignity and mutual understanding will prevent confrontations between the work force and management. Strikes are very rare in Germany, where negotiation and consensus are the rules of the day. They are symbolic in Japan; striking workers continue to work and act like family members. Strikers content themselves by wearing armbands as a sign of protest to put moral pressure on an abusive boss; this reduces tension and preserves a propitious social peace to the well-being of everyone.

The sense of solidarity between bosses and workers ought to be cultivated by being able to face external threats together. The dictates of international suits threaten not only global economies; each enterprise is threatened by bankruptcy and the loss of jobs. Our youth, unemployed and without hope of a future with dignity, have had their fill of suffering as a result of restrictions imposed by international financial institutions; the measures of structural adjustment are a painful case in point.

Social peace is necessary for harmonious development. Justice for workers is a condition that unstable political tightrope walking cannot insure.

Social peace and justice are the tributaries of an equitable distribution of economic surplus in a Muslim community respectful of the Law.

Zakat, a pillar of *islam,* is the obligatory gift set apart for necessary expenses to restore and maintain social balance.

Zakat is an annual obligatory appropriation on property in liquid capital and on the products of commerce, agriculture, and cattle breeding.

Zakat means purification and sanctification: liquid wealth should circulate and is stricken with anathema if it is hoarded and blocked. The mobilization of capital is therefore encouraged and the portion of *zakat* appropriated each year is made to encourage large and small investors to make their money bear fruit. The payments of *zakat* are set apart in the Qur'an for eight categories of the deserving; the poor and needy figure first in the list.

The eradication of poverty is the principal objective of *zakat* and of every system of familial, parental, and humanitarian solidarity. "Poverty leads imperceptibly to unbelief," says the Prophet (grace and peace upon him!), and since nothing can be appropriated from a broken-down economy, the struggle for solidarity and against poverty comes, with ardent urgency, by way of development.

The management of *zakat* payments will be entrusted to an administration of integrity and energy that will consider the broad picture and, instead of distributing the entire *zakat* in the form of assistance to the most destitute, will capitalize a portion of it and reserve it for productive investment. Small and midsized enterprises will thus be able to be created and their returns distributed to the poor who are capable of making a living by taking active part in those concerns. Thus the economic fabric will be strengthened and an effective means of eradicating poverty will be put in practice. Societies born of *zakat* will thus be able to participate in the effort of development by means of a substantial asset.

Before the second Gulf War, the money deposited in Western banks by the petroleum magnates was estimated at a trillion dollars. At the zakat rate of 2½% per annum, this would make close to 25 billion dollars. Injected each year into the economies of solidarity, instead of being spent on London casinos and cabarets, that amount would allow the enormous disparity in our societies between rich and poor to be set aside, and with it the source of social tensions—the source of the psychological and material discomfort of the deprived who look, powerless and frustrated, upon the shameless level of luxury our evil rich enjoy.

The goal of a competitive development of solidarity on the global market is to fight unemployment by creating jobs and opening opportunities for youthful and alert initiatives. The object is to provide society with the material means necessary to assure to the most deprived a home and the wherewithal to satisfy the fundamental requirements of everyday life.

Can there be a solution to the problems of development without a well-orchestrated effort on the part of everyone motivated and mobilized by a spiritual breath that comes from the mosque and reawakens the entire society with the warm sentiment of brotherhood, of concrete and effectual solidarity? The economic space where such an effort should be organized in terms of modern requirements should be permeable by the spirit of benevolence and take part in charitable action.

If the dizzying advances of modern societies over ours oblige us to be humble pupils of the know-how of others, where are we going to find the necessary moral and spiritual nourishment for our eternal well-being as individuals and our dignity on earth as societies and peoples? Where shall we seek our souls' nourishment if not in our values and in our Qur'an?

The human element, human competence, the integrity and the good will of men and women, are decisive factors of both development and solidarity. The foremost priority for development is education and apprenticeship, so that "human resources" can be fully prepared for meeting better tomorrows.

The Islamic solution to our problems—the most pressing being development—consists of persuading our financial ministers and departments that in serving the economic future of their country they are serving their own Hereafter. The flight of capital and grey matter, two vital ingredients, give rise to an incredible hemorrhaging that drains our very substance.

It will be essential to return to the mosque to read once again the Qur'an and listen to the sermon; trust in God and our solemn mutual covenant will restore our confidence and inscribe us all under *islam*'s sacred banner. Are we not all Muslims?

8 The Community Ideal

Unless we draw new strength from the intact source of our values we shall not get far—indeed we will know only failure and setbacks. Community direction and morality are at the very basis of the ideal organization of Islamic society, an ideal founded on solidarity and giving. Ever since the shock to the Muslim world of contact with modern Europe two centuries ago, Muslims have continued to ask themselves, why are they stronger than we? Why are they better organized and better governed than we? Why . . . why?

The distress into which comparison with the other has brought us has driven several among us—those who have received a Western education and whose dealings are Western—to draw a definitive judgment: the cause of what ails us is none other than *islam!*

This alienating judgment is now being doubted and the wave of bitter deceptions is bringing the best among us to examine ourselves and one another more profoundly. Even those who yesterday were not in the fray are today losing their assurance in the face of the burning questions still unanswered, such as the problem of development which has yet to come, and that of democracy on the road to which we are forever in transit, quarantined like the plague-stricken, busily playing one against the others for the amusement of the gallery in the farce called "Charters of Honor."

Returning to the mosque and to the Qur'an will put us back in touch with the ideal of life in community that has been absent from our lives but is ever present and intact in the holy texts and in the hearts of pious men and women faithful to God. The appeal of that ideal will be heard, ever more clearly, both as an invitation to meritorious individual work and as an alternative proposal for rebuilding our societies and restoring their equilibrium on the solid foundations of our faith and Law.

In *islam,* communitarian links are formed through giving and attentive service to one another. The community's vital nucleus is the family, conceived not as a narrow cell but as a social space comprising near relatives and extended kinship to whom we owe solicitude and care.

The quality of a civilization is measured by how it treats weaker members: children, the sick, orphans, the poor, the elderly, oppressed persons. . . . Statistics will belie our least pretensions to realizing much with regard to these categories in the actual state of affairs, but God's call and the ideals of *islam* mark out the horizon and point the way toward a communitarian life that is much better and more just for all dependent persons.

God decrees that His faithful make it their first priority to honor their mothers and fathers and to shower their kinfolk and neighbors with favors. Those miserable death-homes to which Westerners so blithely abandon their parents are directly antithetical to the warm welcome and embracing love God strongly exhorts us to show those who raised us. Ingratitude toward one's parents is a mortal sin from which all the faithful ask God to guard them. We are commanded:

> Your Lord has decreed that you shall worship Him alone. (He has decreed) that your fathers and mothers be treated in the best manner. If one or both of your parents living with you should attain advanced age, do not then say to them, "Huh!" nor treat them harshly; speak (instead) to them in respectful terms; take them under your protective wing, deferring to them out of compassion. Say, "O my Lord, show them both the same merciful grace they showed me as a tiny child. Your Lord knows the depths of your souls; if you demonstrate your goodness, He will pardon your sins so long as you are faithful and prompt to repent. Give your next of kin their due (of tenderness and assistance); give to the poor and to travelers (in distress). Do not lavish away (your possessions), for those who do so are Satan's brethren.[15]

I shall return soon to the matter of squandering and the Satanic brotherhood of squanderers. But before that, let us insist on the mother-virtue of all goodness: our faith. Let us recall that the cradle of the faith, after our pious mother and father the model of righteousness, is the mosque and the school associated with the mosque, a powerful source of assurance at the heart of the community.

The five daily prayers are the occasion for the faithful to access the spiritual and moral resources through contact with the community of the faithful. Maintaining the faith depends on such close contact among souls in purification, much as the same way that endless recycling and continuous formation are indispensable to the financial structures so as not to lose step in the march of progress.

It is such therapeutic sessions, alongside and within the context of five occasions of common prayer, that we may consider as the nourishing compost of faith. I should say "sessions of faith"[16] to describe the seminaries, study groups, and roundtable discussions on the matting of mosques devoted to the remembrance of God and to mutual counsel.

Such resource sessions are actively counseled by *islam;* the Prophet (grace and peace upon him!) teaches that those who partake in "sessions of faith" become mutually fruitful and perfume their souls. These sessions are the manifestation of the community living out its spiritual sharing, anticipating the boundless gift of Paradise. They are occasions where moral health and peace of soul go side by side, a bathing pool of purification in fraternal love, a stepping-stone to a new beginning, far from the morass that reeks of selfishness and hypocrisy.

Authentic morality and sincere generosity, the progeny of true faith in God, will set us apart from the modern political "moral" display and show-off generosity described here by the French philosopher and sociologist, Gilles Lipovetsky:

> In the realm of media-charity, moral action depends less on ethical principles than on media coups. More and more, the media determine the priority cases that succeed in stimulating and directing generosity. They allow the masses an access to solidarity, but at the same time they disengage the individual; they are a powerful force for mobilizing altruism, but at the same time they make consciences guilt-free—one drama chases another in an endless consumption of charity show images—and they bring on an erosion of our ordinary duty to come to the aid of one another.[17]

Media simulation and moral erosion, charitable NGOs nonetheless do a remarkable job, to an extent that allows us to hope that one day Westerners will come to cooperate more closely with us in restoring our ruined vital common space against that life-crushing capitalist machine, so that not another child dies of hunger or is employed drudging away from morning to night for a laughable pittance.

Having

9 A Patrimony of Ruin

The moral erosion acknowledged by modern Western scholars merely exhausts Western societies and unsettle the bases of the values it still stands on. The ravaging effects of modernity, that great producer of useful and useless items, transgress all bounds and make an attack on the common patrimony of humankind. The destruction of the biosphere that it has been choking for decades and which it is violating at a frightening rate at the end of this century is one of its most formidable effects.

Under the hegemony of the *pax americana,* greenhouse gasses are beginning to produce global warming, threatening the flooding of countries at low altitudes such as Bangladesh; it has already caused periodic cyclones and chronic famine. The ozone layer has been punctured, and humankind is deprived of the protection it affords. *El niño,* that destructive meteorological phenomenon, is perhaps only the first of the monsters to come that will be born to the marriage of the abject selfishness and unspeakable mindlessness of Western consumer societies.

The fallout from the growing excesses of twenty-five percent of human society plunges the rest of humanity into wretchedness and will soon enough constitute a wall against which the progress of the growing planetary economy must crash. The wall can already be detected in warning signs which, alas, warn and alarm only a handful of ecologists with a vision of the future.

In vain the Greens stigmatize the methodological devastation of our planet and the pollution has now reached the stratosphere, which has become a dumping ground for space-age garbage: among those who control the political will of the great polluter countries, no one can decide to rein in the devastating madness. America refuses to sign the accord for the progressive diminishing of greenhouse gas emissions, just as it refuses to sign an accord intended to stop the production of antipersonnel land mines.

The Greens in many countries, alas, remain strangers in the eyes of societies of limitless consumption, as unreal as the little green men, and their warnings are no more worrisome than ridiculous "beep-beeps."

We who are short on development cannot, in the current state of our economic and political insignificance on the world chessboard, do much more than raise our protest in unison with the alarms of those who denounce the criminal assault. The mad race of the exponential growth of some and the bottomless misery of others can only lead to a collision whose shock-wave will strike with maximum force the very weakest: us!

Let us not be broken to pieces by underdevelopment. Let us remain mindful of the poignant urgency to develop our potential to the maximum, following the example of others, until humanity finds a way out of the ecological impasse that appears more and more inevitable. Meanwhile let us remain in solidarity with the protesters and respect nature.

The first victims of environmental destruction, we will for a long time remain, reluctantly, in the backdrop of the drama, superfluous in the sense of those who protest the desertification of the southern countries without being able to do anything otherwise; how are we to influence the course of events so long as we are underdeveloped, without a say in the matter?

The damage to the biosphere is frightening; stopping the massacre will require solidarity of planetary dimensions and concrete action. The deforestation of Amazonia, the overexploitation of natural resources, pollution of the air, land, and oceans by toxic waste of all kinds, climate imbalance, the scandalous distribution of the products of development among a minority who guzzle their food, sheltered in their comfy dwellings, while the majority suffers malnutrition or dies of hunger in slums and shantytowns—the massacre must stop!

The violence perpetrated by modernity against nature has a logical corollary in its violence against humankind. The victims of a Chernobyl are not going to stop at the tens of thousands of humans directly affected by the disaster; like the descendents of the people bombed at Hiroshima and Nagasaki, those of Chernobyl will bear the mark of the nuclear curse for generations.

This Promethean civilization aims at taming nature, subduing it so as to slake the insatiable desires of modern man; but it will only succeed in befouling nature and making it unusable for future generations. The brutal offensive against our living space is a direct offensive against humanity, and the destruction of nature amounts to breaking a biological covenant that each of us should respect for the other and for all living things.

The Qur'an fulminates against those who sow disorder on earth; fifty verses are devoted to the theme. Like the wicked and like usurers, disrupters of the relationship between the earth and its inhabitants are the object of divine malediction:

> Those who violate the covenant with God after having sworn to uphold it, those who break the bonds God has ordered to be preserved, those who spread disorder over the earth: all they shall be smitten with a curse; theirs the evil abode.[18]

While the eternal evil abode awaits the earth's corrupters, the divine sanction is already beginning here below, and, owing to the poisoners of the planet, gangrene is inexorably gaining on the once-green and welcoming globe. The face of the earth is besmeared, natural cycles are becoming more and more blocked, the seasons are out of alignment, the ecological balance is out of order, nature's mechanisms warped. The acid and sulfurous rains that fall on the industrial centers of the West and the thick blanket of black smoke that envelopes the rich capitals are foretastes of what awaits the whole of humanity who will unjustly pay the price of the excesses of the consumer societies.

The modern West, rushed and aroused by the noise of their publicity machines, produces too much of everything. Having satisfied the basic needs, other wants, induced by incessant advertising, force further production, further consumption, further pollution.

Too much information, too many excitements, too much of being incited by the media, all this turns people away from the Great Information that informs them of their Future and the Life Hereafter. And this, for us, is the most abominable aspect of the crime, worse than any drug, poisoning quite otherwise from those minor annoyances that damage only our physical health. The work of Satan pointed to by the Qur'an, that of squandering spendthrifts, is but an innocent peccadillo compared to the orchestrated campaign of that great diabolical work.

With regard to those who tear apart the common birthright of present and future humanity, our responsibility is great, especially now that genetic techniques are directly attacking human biology, human intimacy, our heritage as humans, the dignity of a unique creature that cloning manipulations try to alter by doubling and multiplying individuals a hundredfold. In the eyes of a mad modernity, a human is worth no more than Dolly, that unfortunate sheep!

We Muslim peoples too will effectively be sheep, following dumbly along the same path, unless we pledge all our efforts, once we have rounded the cape of underdevelopment, to condemn the moral foundations that permit and tolerate modern misdeeds and crimes.

Our duty, once we have mastered modern science, will be to call technology into question, along with the instruments of destruction that it produces. For it will be incumbent on us to take up the heavy task of imagining a future for humanity that is based on peace and dignity!

Notes

1 *Le Piège de la mondialisation* [*The Globalization Trap*], ed. Solin-actes sud, pp. 294–95.

2 Ibid., p. 229.

3 Sûrah 24 [*An-Nûr*]: verse 55.

4 Sûrah 16 [*An-Nahl*]: verses 90–91.

5 Sûrah 89 [*Al-Fajr*]: verses 6–14.

6 [Changing an Era], ed. Seuil, 1989.

7 *La Société en quête de valeurs*, op. cit., pp. 163–65.

8 Sûrah 2 [*Al-Baqara*]: verses 270–71.

9 Sûrah 2 [*Al-Baqara*]: verse 272.

10 TN: Sûrah 2 [*Al-Baqara*]: verses 273–74 (Y.A.) (*Charity is*) *for those in need, who, in God's cause are restricted* (*from travel*) *and cannot move about in the land, seeking* (*for trade or work*): *the ignorant man thinks, because of their modesty, that they are free from want. Thou shalt know them by their* (*unfailing*) *mark: they beg not importunately from all and sundry. And whatever of good ye give, be assured God knoweth it well. Those who* (*in charity*) *spend of their goods by night and by day, in secret and in public, have their reward with their Lord: on them shall be no fear, nor shall they grieve.*

11 Sûrah 2 [*Al-Baqara*]: verse 275.

12 Sûrah 2 [*Al-Baqara*]: verses 278–79.

13 Martin & Schumann, *Le Piège de la mondialisation* [cf. n.1], pp. 188–90.

14 TN: Translating the Arabic *taḏâmun* "group feeling," "social identity."

15 Sûrah 17 [*Al-Isrâ*]: verses: 23–27.

16 TN: *Assises de la foi* suggests as well the juridical aspects of Islam.

17 *La Société en quête de valeurs,* p. 29.

18 Sûrah 13 [*Ar-ra'd*]: verse 25.

VIII. Power

1 Discovering Our Future

Our indignation at outrages against nature should take the form not only of defending nature (which has intrinsic value in itself), but as an expression of the concern within *islam* to keep our habitat safe and secure, so as to free us from material servitude. The fanaticism that is destructive to nature is opposed in the West by another fanaticism: the moderate "Greens" and friends of nature are overrun by worshipers of nature, "integrists" of a sort for whom nature is an absolute value.

For the adepts of "deep ecology," the biosphere is a temple where every living being—including beasts, plants, and flowers—enjoys rights and becomes a fetish, a supreme value in itself. Fetishistic radical ecology sets up nature and living things as a normative instance, the inverse of the order wished by God, Who created every species of life for humankind. Our duty is to show our gratitude to our Creator Benefactor by using with moderation the things with which we have been endowed, without squandering them but also without animistic excess.

With regard to possessions in general, the relationship of humanity to nature should neither become excessively possessive nor acquire a naturalist aesthetic. It would be yet another injustice to humanity to reverse the roles and make a fetish of nature, for it would deprive us of the full enjoyments of God's benefits. The physical, moral, and spiritual well-being of humankind is the point of our existence; everything should contribute to its expansion, beginning with its biological maintenance, which depends on good economic, political, and social organization.

Modern individuals and modern societies base their relationships with nature on the utilitarianism of enjoyment. Modern political and economic institutions as well as the totality of the laws of modern society aim merely at material comfort; they know nothing about humankind beyond the biological dimension.

The future to be discovered for Islamic society will have to have another strategy in adapting the means made available to us by modernity to the rather different ends of *islam.* The political sphere is the chief arena where the future of an entire society is played out; its economy, its development, and its capacity to give value to its final ends against its shifting fortunes. Because of the power it holds, politics can influence and affect every aspect of social and private life.

The politics of society, industry, agriculture, education, and information, scientific research, development, and investment planning will have to come together as the heart of a global strategy that will determine priorities and submit the whole to the fundamental criteria of effectiveness joined with humanity's spiritual well-being.

A new start under the banner of *islam* will need a new conception of power and a new political organization. New ambitions will need a new order of things. Traditional society, atomized into individuals neutralized under the weight and grasp of absolutist powers falsely labeled as democracies, will have to yield to a vital participatory community. Islamic power will have a strong hand in this emancipation, this rebirth.

The secularist modernity that surrounds us is complex, drawing its inspiration from various ideologies that know nothing of neighborly love, faithfulness to God, or world justice. By the light of this modernity, the Westernized élites among us try in vain to form a "civil society" (an expression in vogue these days). They will only succeed in accentuating and aggravating the political exhaustion and indifference of the people who, more than these "ladies and gentlemen," are aware of the political stakes and the roles assigned to the players.

A new beginning, a new political order, will need to weave a new social fabric whose weft and warp will give material expression of faith in God and brotherhood in Him. It will throw in its lot with frankness and sincerity, get rid of the lies, and look to the men and women who purify themselves body and soul by praying to God five times a day for clearness of intentions and moral transparency to take the place of political opacity and hypocritical intentions.

Everyone, however, will have to take his part in working toward restoration. Since *islam* is not a doctrine of vengeance and settling accounts, all who were seeking meaning in their lives in the form of an outdated good citizenship or archaic patriotism will be offered the opportunity to prove, by their actions, that they are not carry-overs from an order that is dead and gone, and that their turnabout is not motivated by complacency and opportunism.

True repentance is pleasing to God (magnified be His Name!) and the tender reception of the penitent is the sacred duty of every faithful Muslim. It is not by a brutal and violent clean sweep of the past that an Islamic government can launch a new beginning, nor by smashing the economic and administrative machinery of bad governing, or the evacuation pure and simple of the political, administrative, and cultural personnel who have become mindless slaves or paid robots, well oiled and programmed.

We should not be less wise than Nelson Mandela, who fought apartheid courageously and suffered the horrors of prison for twenty years. This great man, now freed and the President of the Republic of South Africa, is leading the black majority of his country on the path of wisdom by making them forget six centuries of oppression at the hands of white racists.

A new era of reconciliation has begun in the openness with which competent and learned whites take their place in common service to the nation side by side with native-born Africans. A "Truth and Reconciliation" Committee has been charged with shedding light on the criminal past of the biggest fry, ignoring the lesser offenders so that all might amend their ways and take up their work.

Given the traps the modern world sets, it would be risky, if not impossible, for anyone intending to cast free without the permission of the police of the moment, were it not for God's promise (exalted be the Name of God!) to favor His servant's efforts. The growing consciousness observable everywhere is the sign of a future near at hand, the declaration of a new fight: the fight for peace and in peace.

The political and cultural mess a government under *islam* is going to inherit will have to be deftly handled in order to face the future, to welcome it, rather, with all hands on deck. The human element is the principal ace; rebuilding anew is not going to come about through political speeches, nor by maintaining the cultural barricades behind which our acculturated men and women are enclosed, exhausted and hostile, and little interested in an Islamic plan.

2 "Modernize Islam!"

We must not lose sight of the divine Promise if we would have the courage and determination we need to take decisive steps to enter the labyrinth of external complexity and sort out our internal imbroglio at the same time. With our vision and ideal, we are not starting off smilingly into the void: the place has long since been pursued and laid siege to by the colonizing West which, since the 19th century, has been flying the flag of "civilizing backward peoples."

The colonialist motto has been reappearing since the liquidation of formal colonialism; now the Westernized élite make it their rallying cry to "modernize Islam." In the time of direct colonialism and the military and administrative presence of Europeans labeling themselves as "liberators," all one was allowed to do was to submit and keep quiet. Now that we are among ourselves and "we are all Muslims," it is no longer only military violence that is called on to silence and subdue the pretentious extremists who want to win the modern world for *islam;* the weapon of Western culture is also brandished in endorsing and justifying violence against Islamists. Specious education and disinformation second the action of the arm of the police.

In the physical absence of the former colonizer, the struggle goes on among us against *Islam* in the name of freedom of thought, of democratic pluralism outside of any Islamic norm, and of the right to be different—

like the right to call oneself a Muslim without having the conviction. The ideals being proposed and imposed are those of atheist rationalism, materialist notions of progress, and a secularism that looks down its nose at religion like some sort of allergy.

What the West has inculcated in the pupils of colonial schools has become a precious acquisition that allows small fry to become grand and swim about like sharks, seeking to harm people who are profoundly attached to breathing free.

By what ground rules are we going to put our plan for an Islamic society into effect when the tension between seculars and Islamists is not only of a political nature but also one that is profoundly cultural? What keys are we going to turn to open the many gateways that block our road to a stable future?

One thing is certain: the West is not going to throw open its arms in welcome to a government under *islam* as long as it can stand in the way of its coming to power. It is not going to roll out the red carpet to receive a delegation of Islamists. No, it is going to throw a monkey wrench into the works; it is going to side with dishonest operations, as in Algeria, to make it clear to us backward peoples that we do not know how to vote, if by imprudence the ballot boxes proclaim once again that Islamists have won. But one day, for the sake of peace, the West is going to learn that in reckoning long-term interests, cooperation with Islamists is the wave of the future.

Muslim countries are going down the barren slope of impoverishment; the statistics of bad management among the West's clients, "Muslims all," look bad. Secular functionaries are becoming more and more corrupt, never ceasing to discredit themselves. One day, Muslim peoples awakened from their slumber by the Islamist movement will understand that there is no recourse from widespread corruption, the burden of poverty and underdevelopment, bad governing, and crying injustice, apart from God and His Law.

There will be a massive vote, as there was in Algeria, for an Islamic government. Will the lesson there—the atrocious results of interrupting the electoral process—be taken to heart, or will the same unscrupulous strategy be repeated, with the same tragic outcome? And for how long?

Those who let themselves be persuaded to modernize *islam*—to secularize it and strip it of its values—are proceeding from a false premise: *islam* is not an ideology adaptable to harebrained whims. *Islam* is not an object easily encroached upon, by leaving behind Muslim people, bereft of their identity, to ruminate bitterly on heaven-knows-what kind of fatalism. *Islam* is God's Message; the "alternation of days" is one of God's Promises.

We will actively await our hour to proclaim the truth loud and clear, with all due deference to those for whom the word "truth" calls to mind some prerational barbarity and makes them itch to attack the villain. We will actively await our hour with serenity and nonviolence when we raise our voices everywhere that the sun will rise again, that an Islamic future awaits humanity.

Certain young Islamists are driven toward power as if authority quickly seized could take the place of the construction of the individual and organizational self. Impatient activism that leads organizations of desperate youths to intolerance and counter-violence and that engages in the logic of violence will only delay the arrival of better days. The divine law of the "alternation of days" takes its time.

Duration is one of the essential dimensions of such alternation; the Qur'anic appeasement of the Prophets and faithful of all times insists on active patience and resistance. But conceiving the project of *islam* for the duration does not mean bearing insults indefinitely; apathetic fatalistic torpor awaits those habituated to *dolce far niente* idleness.

Biding one's time means being alert to the political landscape, so as not to be surprised by events. But we must not wait for our secular political partners on the inside to grant us, one day, a place in the sun, nor for the West, united today to reject the Islamic movement, to return suddenly to more reasonable sentiments.

The West has durable strategic interests in Muslim countries, and pessimistic Cassandras of the Huntington kind do not stand a chance against Western interests by perpetuating Western Islamophobia. Already Europe and Russia are drawing closer to constructing economic links with Iran, rich in petroleum and juicy markets. The American Big Brother—the Great Satan of the Iranian revolution—is winking discretely at Iran so as not to be outdistanced by European competition. Like a big steamer, the bulky apparatus of American diplomacy is describing a wide arc to come round.

Despite all the snares and difficulties, we have the capital—God's Promise—and we have the key to an Islamic future: faith and good works.

3 Our Prison: The Nation-State

If you want to influence the progress of society you must first assess your position and calculate the extent of your potential trajectory. The borders of each nation-state within which Islamist movements circulate constitute the bars of a cage, of the prison that limits you, ties you up, and blocks your impetus.

Our ambition for a union of Muslim countries without borders flies in the face of the reality of secular dismemberment left over from colonial dividing-up. Muslims preserve the vague memory of the unity of the

Umma, and the nostalgic dream of a new era haunts their lucid moments, but the awakening is bitter when they open their eyes to find themselves cut up, diminished, and in perpetual evolution toward further division.

The demons of nationalism, a recent and modern form of tribal sentiment, lash at our minds and fortify one brother's antipathy for another. The nation-state, a Western institution born of the European wars of the 19th century, was imposed on us by colonial cartography. It has since become part of our mental furniture: a sense of worth derives from national identity, our geographical coordinates have become our address, and little local histories define the dimensions of our existence.

The mission of Islamists is to make hearts beat again with new faith, determine our cause and unite all wills to the work of reconstituting and reunifying. The desire is legitimate, the duty is sacred, the action is necessary for consolidating Muslim peoples in taking up the project of reunification in order to surpass the prisonlike narrowness of nation-states.

On the economic front where all decisive combats take place, the attack is made merely by ragtag troops of Muslims, scattered, disordered and underdeveloped; naturally their victories are imaginary. Enough self-flagellation! We must put back on the tracks a train as good as new. The mission will be all the more difficult, since the tracks that lead to development—our foremost priority—are planted with land mines and pitfalls. The universal goal of *islam* is our horizon, but in gazing at the heavens we must not lose sight of what is taking place under our feet.

If development is the priority of every government that is conscious of its responsibilities, a government under *islam* must maintain solidarity with the multitude of nation states that the Muslim world has become. It must be able to accept that necessity and work to insure cooperation without blustering about the legitimacy of the survival of tribal entities here or megalomaniacal dictators there. The West knows how to make allowances for things; it can make its democracies endure the necessity of cooperating with the devil whenever its major interests are in question. The example of the American protectorate in occupied Palestine—Israel, to give it a name—cries to heaven with injustice and hypocrisy.

Without injuring anyone's rights, and without lying, an Islamic government that rises from nothing and inevitably locks horns with Western hostility—while waiting for creaking diplomacy to come round—should not try playing any solos. If it is unsuccessful in its attempts to cooperate with the Muslim states under its wing in complete harmony, it should at least avoid provoking useless dissonance by picking a quarrel with its fellow Muslims. Oppositional Islamism can be allowed to denounce deviant regimes, but not a responsible government surrounded by enemies and weighted down with problems.

Revolutionary Iran was carried away from its goals by the fits and starts of a neophyte power; after eighteen years' experience it has learned to navigate masterfully the stirred waters of international diplomacy. At the end of 1997, Teheran hosted the summit meeting of the Organization of Muslim States, making the Superpower white with rage at having been unable to isolate Imam Khomeini's homeland.

The handshaking between the Imam's successor and the Wahabite Prince is a defiance to America, already distanced from its European allies in the race to reconciliation with Iran. The Saudi plays the benevolent middleman and offers his services to effect a rapprochement between two diplomacies up to now impossible to reduce to the same denominator. Surely he is doing this in response to a wink from his Transatlantic ally.

The overarching and scrupulous aim of an ideal *islam* should not let it be forgotten that there are on earth puddles of standing water and mud. It must tuck up its trousers to keep from getting them dirty, but still it must cross; responsibility entails a kind of servitude. It is human to be mistaken many times in one's life, but it is a sign of intellectual blindness and feeblemindedness to repeat the mistakes of others.

It makes sense to appear to forget the discords of the present, deep as they may be, in order to save the future. It is fair enough to sort the difficulties and allow time to take its course. Entrusting the long term to the long term is wisdom itself; what will it profit a megalomaniac, demon-possessed head of state to knock himself out trying to lure international revolution and embezzling Muslims' money left and right?

At the head of a government under *islam* there must certainly be technical competence matched by faith and moral integrity, but those in power must also be emotionally mature and mindful of the irreplaceable value of levelheadedness and of waiting for fruit to ripen. Fruits out of season are fragile; to every season its reality. The Islamist governments that will rise up everywhere one way or another must not compromise the future through haste and gratuitous backbiting. Gratuitous? Hardly: the government that goes about its business in bad humor pays dearly.

Muslim countries must consider fighting on the economic front a vital priority; each state, as it stands, must find the welcome that the future of Muslims deserves. The time for archaic survivals will pass, the false suns will be eclipsed, and the Muslim nation will be born anew, bearing the universal Message.

Where are we to find governments with the primary virtue of controlling themselves and doing without clamorous attacks, so that this rebirth can come to pass in harmony?

4 The Interior "Front"

I put "front" in quotation marks in order to dash any hope of seeing ourselves one day committing the political mistake that is both a moral fault and a default on our commitment to nonviolence, that of laying ourselves open to civil war like the one that rages in Algeria.

Did Algeria's Islamists provoke the tragedy? Did they wish it? Surely not! The unpardonable crime they committed was to have become so popular that they won the elections hands down, and so threatened to cast into the shade of oblivion the "heroes" of the only party which during the last three decades has been exploiting the country the way a private firm is exploited.

One day or other we are going to be the last moral and political refuge, and the people, outraged by the underhanded partisan maneuvers that have led the country into an impasse, will vote overwhelmingly for us. History does not repeat itself, the situations are not at all the same; sooner or later there will be ears attuned to our appeal to wisdom.

We appeal to clarity, since it is only thieves who fear the light of day. The dominant class among us is corrupt; it is time for it to pack its bags and go off to swallow its disgrace. We extend it a hand so that its retreat might be made in peace and with dignity.

The ballot box, the judicious and operational invention of Western democracies, has up to now been nothing but a trick and optical illusion here. We hope that it will cease to be a gadget that makes a travesty of the truth by accepting false evidence, and that the results of an election be respected however it turns out.

The free elections that exposed the truth in Algeria have hampered the military-partisan Old Boy "conglomerate" that insisted on keeping power even at the cost of sacrificing a population. Because of these criminals' interruption of the democratic process, the people, treated like minors and wards of the robber state, will for several generations have to pay the painful price of a historical crime in which the West has been shamelessly steeped.

For a long time now our hand has been held out to the political class here who have so far ignored us, though they have not yet wished to abandon the illusion of power that excludes Islamists from the political landscape. They continue to persist in imagining a democracy in which these "obscurantist enemies of democracy" have no part. Our outstretched hand will not be ignored forever; the people, weary of the long dark tunnel of an inept "transition" that never ends, will make another choice—one that will not please the gentlemen comfortably seated on their usurped armchairs.

Our proposal is simple: nothing short of a public debate open to all with no one excluded. Instead of closed secret meetings among the gentlemen on high, let us tell the people just what has been going on with the voting, what it can possibly mean to be Muslim without respecting a single Muslim norm, what sort of constitution it is that can be changed time and again—and why it is done, what can be the stake and scope of elections forever contested and taken back, and what purpose a "charter of honor" may have when it is used shamelessly to play the tragicomedy of consensus.

The people, the large majority of whom are illiterate—thanks to the politics of their benefactors—will have to know; they must be informed. Our simple proposal is to clarify matters, not to plot in the dark like criminal conspirators. The ballot box—that little marvel of democracy—must be allowed complete expression, so that the people can choose with full knowledge of the issues.

When the left or the right, both secularist, convince the people to vote for the secular "best choice," we will bow to the will of the Muslim people. We are not driven to seek power; political adventurism, especially the current conditions of general obstruction and crisis, is the equivalent of suicide. What do we want with a burden already too heavy that imprudent behavior would render still more of a risk? The politics of the worst is neither our game plan nor the object of our hopes, but things get worse year after year, and every day the people are further convinced that those responsible for their suffering should go.

A premature move on our part, ill-considered and hasty, would only have disappointing results. When a commercial enterprise goes under, the law requires that it divests itself of its balance, which the judiciary distributes. In politics, the verdict of the ballot box holds court, but what is to be done when there is no neutral authority—none that is not steeped in the liar's game of falsified ballots—that might guarantee and bind the disputants to the rules.

Once this authority is in place and has proved its seriousness and impartiality by its actions, we can then proceed to compete. The mandate the electors deliver to political candidates rests only on the confidence or lack thereof that the elector concedes and approves of with respect to his petitioner. Up to now, the electoral platforms produced by the political parties appear to be simple sales pitches at a thieves' market where everyone tricks everyone else; the first sucker is the elector-buyer, typically illiterate and unaware of the fundamental importance of the little slip of paper he slides into a little mysterious box surrounded by so much folderol.

Unless a serious undertaking respects the concerns of the client, it is found in error and is obliged to pay the damages caused by its failings. An authority of moral and political integrity and credibility guarantees the respect of the moral contract by virtue of which the elector, attracted by its promises, chooses his representative with confidence. The only authority that will be qualified to play that role is one that has never lied to the people nor betrayed their confidence or pillaged their wealth.

Vigilant care on the part of the guarantor-referee will have a twofold goal: the much mouthed phrase, "We are all Muslims," should be spelled out and related to a practical program that takes its sole inspiration from *islam;* that will assure all that we are speaking the same language. Islamists like us, for our part, will reassure our formerly secular fellow citizens, now really living out their Muslimhood, that we will respect the rotation of power so long as the truth declared at the polls is guaranteed to be put into practice.

But everyone is free to abandon the much mouthed slogan and offer the public the program of his choice. Universal suffrage will have its say.

5 Change

It is not an election victory or a turnover in power that we aspire to. A change of government or constitution is at best a response to critical conditions—an airing out of the atmosphere—until the vested political power can send in a team or a party to remake its brand-name image. The change of direction we wish to imprint on our society does not come about at the level of periodic shifts of political power nor to the short-term reforms of real or fictitious "consensual" democratic change-over, itself a contributor to the same system of thought and values that has brought us where we are.

Our goal is the kind of deep change that only a direct and continuous action, with the help of God, is capable of initiating or directing. The formation of political parties is such that the scent of electoral victory transports and ignites them. They are structured and assembled so as to play a role, either that of a majority in power or the opposition minority that stalks it and connives to overthrow it. We, however, are formed and organized for other ends; our horizon is broader, we watch from further on.

Our vision does not stop at the borders of the nation state where we feel boxed in. Our ultimate goal is the uniting of Muslim peoples in a single entity; the reunification of the *Ummah* is our duty. That may seem an empty dream, the Utopia of a visionary, but our Qur'an is the living Word of God that orders us to be a single nation, not several; the times favor our drawing closer, and economic necessities urge us. Projected over the long term and prepared by education and the mosque over several generations, what once seemed a Utopia becomes a reality when God permits it and when the form of its unitary organization is found.

Education is our profession and our means for changing people by getting them to adopt an attitude, a vision, a will that soars beyond historical contingencies and surpasses the narrow frontiers of geography, confined by the politics of Mr. So-and-so and the mindset of a fragmentary identity. Our vision and profession—by virtue of which we are united and organized—distinguishes us from political parties whose ambitions are immediate, whose sights are no further than that of a minister's portfolio.

Our plan is an enterprise requiring time and labor; profound transformation through education and persuasion can only come about after long gestation. And all the while we are competing with political parties entirely concerned with the here and now. Yet we must compete, since everything must have its beginning, and the greatest marathon departs from point zero.

The work of education and changing outlooks and attitudes is not a matter for improvising; inventing the future and the form of power requires not some simple election platform or elaborate government program, but long-distance vision and the plan for a society that meets permanent needs and the expectation of the justice *islam* affords its peoples.

That plan will have to be given form and consistency as our resolved will. The starting point will be a constitution that is sure of itself and does not veer in a different direction with every outburst like a weathervane that turns with the slightest breeze.

Our assurances never to hang on to power against the consent of the electorate will respond to the concerns of the political parties—whether or not they regard *islam*, and above all Islamic Law, as an envenomed legacy to be jettisoned. A guarantor-referee will take into consideration the obligations on both sides, and the first election can decide matters.

In contrast to a constitution from on high, we will have to elect an assembly representing the entire popular spectrum crowning a long public debate. No political entity or independent personality should be excluded.

To insure that a constitution debated in assembly and submitted to referendum not be merely a paper weathervane, an iron-fast juridical body would prevent a call for revisions every time a sudden whim or novel fad tickles imaginations. This guarantor authority will see to it that the constitution is rigorously respected. By "ironfast juridical body" I envision something at the raised level of a parliamentary majority necessary for reforming the constitution.

Thus secured against infractions of the basic laws, each party would take turns showing its competence and ability at running the business of state. Islamist "populism" and secular élitism will no longer be unbridled forces busied with demographic outbidding: you who only recently draped yourselves in your self-sufficiency and class privileges, and you who have just arrived on the political scene, whom the masters of the house find poor in experience—let's have some results!

The polemical jousting between Islamists and secularists will end the day everyone faces the wall and has lost the easy alibi that might rescue the argument. Like the intellectual in the civil society, the Islamist who only yesterday was pontificating and casting anathemas at the others will wind up meeting at the worksite, where he will have to give up his prejudices so that each one's true worth can be gauged. We greet such a coming together with all our heart and consider it the necessary outcome of the historical dynamic that thrusts a young and popular Islamist movement toward a politically brilliant future.

The residual political class that leads a rearguard action opposing any change has been disowned by the people faithful to *islam*, though illiterate for the most part. This old political caste is unaware of the obstacle it represents in the path of younger generations, better formed and more apt for serving the interests of a Muslim people. Flopped out in their armchairs, enduring years of insult, these puffed-up gentlemen—who are responsible for the hemorrhage that bleeds us white—will have to change in order for society to change.

6 Democracy? What Democracy?

Democracy! The word enchants, the password, the word that solves all our problems!

Democracy is Algeria's corpus delicti, put to death with euthanasiac pity, for fear that the enemies of democracy—those bearded fanatics and bizarrely costumed women—would commit an outrage.

The simple, blunt question that secularist democrats ask—(I specifically call them secularist democrats, since there are secularists who are not democrats)— is whether Islamists are for or against democracy.

Simplistic reaction-responses range from a slightly shaded "for" to a categorical "against." Democracy, essentially secularist in essence and birth, deserves from us a more nuanced answer—where our distinctions are not simply a way of begging the question. The reverse question—Are you for or against *islam*?—might do in a heated media controversy. But in a serious discussion, a two-way negotiation aiming at mutual understanding, the question should be asked in a poised and serene manner.

An Islamist the least bit alert is not going to be cornered into denying the importance of democracy as a system and procedure for managing social conflicts, and any secularist who hopes to win the favor of a Muslim electorate is never going to saw the branch from beneath himself by admitting that he is against *islam*. The moderate secularist might sincerely answer that he is for *islam*, understanding *islam* as one religion among the others, and religion itself as a private matter that has nothing to do with politics.

Instead of giving too much importance to the declarations of a fiery Islamist embroiled in heated controversy, and answering parry with riposte, like a court order, let us ask the Islamists to expound quite calmly on how democracy upsets the Islamic absolute. Instead of being mesmerized by democracy, that mythical bird in these parts, a bird that beats its wings on its home turf, a democrat should open himself democratically to the other and not impose his absolute, his singular notions, on another.

Let us begin our discussion by considering the testimony of authentic democrats speaking about the democratic ideal and what has become of it. Paul Thibaud, former director of the journal *Esprit,* relativizes democracy by demonstrating the degrading of the democratic ideal:

> Pierre Manent has illustrated modern relativism with remarkable clarity. He shows how relativism began by destroying religion, that it is now destroying politics, and that soon there will only exist that degraded form of politics called management, and that it is no longer concerned with values but simply with adjusting the facts, demands, and capacities. The politics of management is the upshot of the degradation of the status of truth in democratic society.[1]

Democracy, degraded at home to the level of management know-how, falls very far:

> Democracy is not skeptical, it has a very strong ethical basis; but it is always losing sight of that basis and having to recover it. There is a mechanism in democracy that keeps driving it to lose sight of its proper foundation.[2]

It is not our intention to initiate the trial of democracy. It is enough that we note here that democracy is, by birth, freedom from every absolute except its own, an enemy to every ethic that differs from its own. This radical exclusivity that democracy hides behind democratic toleration, pluralism [etc.] is a virulent mechanism that turns democracy against itself and drives it to destroy its own ethical basis.

Degraded to operational management and eroded by the friction of its machinery, democracy is on the way to losing its footing by losing its morality. The halo that once illumined its forehead no longer exists except in the imagination of its new fans here.

Professor Jean-Marie Guéhenno claims that democracy has fallen into escheat there and that its relatives here are hoping for a windfall, but the elderly aunt they thought was filthy rich is not even solvent.

> No one should be surprised that in "advanced" democracies the voters are voting less than ever, since most politicians have lost the respect of their

> fellow citizens, Japan being just like other modern countries on this score. The political man dreamed of by Enlightenment philosophers should have proved the bastion of truth in the society. . . . But to realize such an aspiration, the collective and democratic search for the general interest, he would have to bet that everyone is capable of bearing the truth in himself, and thus of recognizing it.[3]

The moment the citizens of a democratic country have renounced every truth, even the social truth of general interest, the democracy that formed the selfish citizen loses its right to the respect of the citizen as a non-truth.

In announcing the end of democracy, our critic seeks the means of finding a new wind for democracy by relativizing it as one small truth next to so many other truths. The status of absolute Truth and the elegant magistrate's cap the old dame's nephews want her to wear no longer jibe with her advanced state of degradation.

> Because it is the most accomplished model in the world where rule replaces principle, Japan is said to be able to both impregnate other civilizations and remain impermeable to them. . . . It accepts the "truth" of others all the more readily for not having renounced its own. Rather than truths, it has methods, owner's manuals. . . . Anything that "works" deserved to be taken into consideration.
>
> . . . along with national and territorial clearness, we have lost those founding principles that make us a society. At the very least we can hope, imitating the Japanese, to find in our memory and rituals the pale reflection of a society that no longer exists.[4]

Having drifted from—and lost—its principles, democratic modernity recognizes only what "works" and gets results as being meritorious.

Can democracy's way of proceeding respond to our need of exercising power without making us lose our soul, without running us down to the state of "advanced" modern societies that look for scraps of truths to reassure themselves that their moral decline is not yet complete?

7 Shûra

Our kind of "democracy" is called *shûra.*[5] What wouldn't one do to make oneself understood by a French-speaker with no other point of reference than his Western culture, closed to every idea, every word that has other roots? What wouldn't one do to get one's meaning across to minds that are mystified and alienated by a secularist culture gulped down willing or forcibly and assimilated to the point of becoming in itself the basis of some people's cultural metabolism? For such persons, any idea, any notion that departs from the secularist syllabus is the ramblings of a deranged brain.

Shûra, then, is "our democracy" while awaiting a fuller explanation—while waiting, ultimately, for experience to demonstrate the inanity of aborted attempts to acclimatize secularist Western democracy in an environment characterized by faith. What wouldn't one do to demystify the Westernization cunningly undertaken by encroaching secularist modernity?

On an etymological level, the terms democracy and *shûra* already manifest their radical difference. The two Greek roots *demos* and *kratos* mean "people" and "power" respectively; thus democracy etymologically signifies "the power of the people," the sovereign capacity of the people's elected representatives to legislate in their name, without reference to any superior authority. *"Shûra,"* on the other hand, is the Arabic word used in the Qur'an to connote "consultation," the work of interpretation, adaptation, and understanding to put into practice the revealed Law which men have no right to change.

Shûra and democracy belong to radically different reference points; the historical itinerary of democracy, a Greek word and practice, is utterly other than that of *shûra.* The first begins at pagan Athens and ends in "advanced" modern societies as a secularist practice, atheistic and immoral, while the second has its beginning at pious Medina and remained a dead letter for nearly fourteen centuries. Today it is both a vital need for Muslims and a divine system that forms a part of our Islamist plan. It remains to be put back into practice by means of a process yet to be found or borrowed from the wisdom of the people.

To put *shûra* into practice, the Muslim people who have to this point been resigned and obliged to consume the products of others—including cultural products—must break the yoke of docile vassalage to imported modern norms in order to embrace the normative principles of Islamic Law.

The burden of a long history of dictatorship, like the oppression under which Muslims suffer today, weighs heavily on their consciences and the political and social aspects of their daily lives. The dictatorship has had varied forms, from hereditary caliphates to more recent "progressive" regimes. Oppression today is exercised in the name of some cosmetic democracy that the secularist political microcosm succeeds in commercializing despite the carnival of electoral campaigns. Such carnivals repeated, along with lying claims of superiority, have done much to reveal to the people the hideous face of the Big Lie. The people have already begun to decipher with ease the hypocritical game of a political class that has lost all credibility, a game taken up or suspended at will at each constitutional mini-reform.

No one dares question such granted "democracy." The lower classes, overwhelmed as they are by illiteracy and misery, submit in silence; the civil society asks no further accountancy from "democratization" than the matter of paying its bills. One is anxious to see the end of a transition that keeps a democratic Eden shining.

As for the Islamists, they face serious challenges in getting secularist democrats to understand that the democratic rules of the game that have been imposed on Muslim peoples will never take root so long as they are at odds with the Qur'anic law. How can we explain to the secularists right among us—and "Muslims all"—that Western democracy cannot be grasped apart from the historical path that gave rise to it and developed it? In which language shall we explain to them that *shûra*, kept turned down low until now, cannot be removed from its Qur'anic context?

In the Sûrah called *Shûra,* the political cannot be disassociated from the social, which is an integral part of the religious, hence secularist embarrassment in wanting the domain of power and its organization to be separated from religious concerns. Just as a mind formed in a secular school is amazed at Islam's "mixing" of the two spheres, we are amazed at the oddness of separating private from public life and the mosque from parliament.

In the Qur'anic context of *shûra,* the organic division of personal, social, and political duties and virtues, interdependent and indissociable, mutually supporting, is much in evidence:

> However important the gift you have received, it is merely an enjoyment of the life here below. What awaits you in God's presence is better and more lasting if you are of the number of those who are faithful to their Lord and return to Him (trusting in Him). Those who avoid committing grievous sins and infamies, who forgive even in their anger. Those who answer their Lord, offer their prayer, submit their affairs to mutual consultation [*shûra*], put (the goods) We allot them to good use. Those who, when injustice is meted them, reply and defend themselves.[6]

"Mutual consultation" is inserted among nine virtues and duties that characterize the thought, feelings, and behavior of the perfected faithful and those of the community of the faithful. Faithfulness to God is inseparable from obedience to His commands; abstaining from evil is the corollary of toleration and pardon. God's call is heard five times a day in the voice of the muezzin, and the diligent response of the faithful directing themselves to the mosque is a virtuous duty situated along the plane of *shûra,* giving, and good stewardship in the attentiveness of the faithful jealous of their rights and ever ready to withstand and protect themselves against injustices.

Everything holds together; *shûra* cannot be taken out of its moral and spiritual context.

Modern democracy loves to be moralized; it has a great need to be preached to, and some of its best sons and daughters do so. This is because modern democracy since its birth has had no moral underpinning, no absolute truth. It was inevitable that the tender stalk would one day contract a parasite and wither away.

Transplanted in a foreign soil such as our societies, where it has been found since the beginning of the clash between two cultures, democracy refuses to take root—and nothing will make it do so, neither the ceremoniously signed "code of honor" nor the hasty reforms and constitutions whose editing is the province of Western theorists. The imported fertilizer has proved powerless to make democracy healthy and palatable in an environment that pays only lip service to it, like a good slogan for periodic consumption during limited terms. As such it is one of many hollow words coined to conceal reality.

By transposing democracy in space and time, and by trying to draw parallels between democracy and *shûra,* the only thing that has happened is the attempted smuggling of an exotic bird that is destined for certain death in a climate different from its own. The anachronism and climatic estrangement to which *shûra* has been subjected to by comparing it with modern democracy are certain means for exiling *shûra* to some ghetto of confusion and ambiguity in order to enthrone a subterfuge of democracy while democratic procedures might have been a school of apprenticeship instead.

Democracy could have been a school of apprenticeship if it were only a procedure—if it were not, with secularism, two sides of the same coin.

8 Procedure and Institutions

British "due process" (respect for procedure) is given as a guarantee in itself of the justice of any operation, especially one that entails juridical or political conflicts. "Procedure" is defined[7] as a "method or way to be followed in order to obtain a result." More particularly, in matters of law, procedure is "the collection of rules and forms that must be observed in instigating action justly, rendering a decision, and executing it."

That being the case, can democracy be reduced to a procedure aimed at obtaining concrete results and handling situations of conflicts of power? That is what analysts of "advanced" modernity and its system of government say.

Can *shûra,* a general principle of divine origin, be bent to democratic forms without its formal content amputating the content of its moral and spiritual dimension?

Let us ask the question another way. Can the Islamic system of government to be found and adapted to the needs of a modern society borrow certain rules and methods for institutionalizing and managing power without betraying its divine inspiration and shifting from its bases for the sake of formal requirements?

The functional and efficient truth of democratic procedure, when democracy is well propped in its native habitat, is undeniable; whatever the criticism one would address to democracy as developed, and now losing speed in the "advanced" societies, it remains the least evil way of running the commonweal.

Seen in this light, can we borrow the instruments of the democratic method to run our affairs? Are we authorized to do so?

Let us begin by consulting the Qur'an to know whether we have permission to borrow the instruments of democracy. The verse cited above, enjoining us to practice *shûra* as a virtuous duty alongside and in close association with solidarity with other duties, speaks of "their affairs."

The expression suggests both that all our affairs can and should draw benefit from mutual consultation and that our political and social affairs are entrusted to our care. God grants us the liberty to choose the best way to manage our affairs as a function of time and space, under the twofold condition that the normative principles of Islam are not demeaned and that *shûra*, as an Islamic duty, is not dissociated from its context.

Governmental responsibilities and the organization of constitutions in democratic regimes have developed according to a standard of competence and honesty that the democratic electorate is thought capable of judging. In an Islamic regime, still to be devised, only those men and women should be able to exercise power and run institutions who join to competence and probity the essential virtues that make a Muslim truly Muslim. The popular vote will always remain the judge.

The first Islamic government—I use the term for want of a better—functioned for ten years under the aegis and direction of the Prophet. Consultation, during the Prophet's lifetime and under his four successors called "rightly guided," was practiced without ceremony. The direction of public affairs in a tribal society with a rural and pastoral economy did not ask for much by way of the competence and organization that our modern societies or candidates for modernity require of the state.

After the blessed epoch of the Prophet and his four caliphs, public affairs fell into the hands of absolute powers—and bad governance continues: it has not yet had its last word even today.

Everywhere today, absolutist regimes dominated by secularists more or less hostile to *Islam* try to put on democratic airs. Sometimes they create instantaneous political parties whose popularity is as ephemeral as it is miraculous; sometimes a single party is divided into little formations to give the impression of pluralism—a major democratic attribute; and sometimes elections are organized where falsification, corruption, and deals of all kinds give rise to prefabricated parliamentary chambers. To create democratic appearances, constitutions are unhesitatingly tailor-made to create a 100% plebiscite or "reelect" the president by 99.9% for the Nth time before "electing" him for life.

In place of this weak democracy, warped and veneered like a nice fence erected around a sickening discharge, we hope for the institution of true *shûra* whose authentic roots and persons of integrity will insure us against fraud and will shelter us from the deformations that an ill-adapted procedure risks inflicting on the very heart of the undertaking.

Let us return to the instruments of democracy to consider whether any might be retained without fear of going counter to our faith:

- We have already spoken of the benefits of the ballot box to the extent that it expresses the true will of all the voters and is conducted transparently and legally under the surveillance of a proper and impartial guarantor-referee.
- As an explicit and interpretative expression of the Law, a constitution is a necessity.
- The basic democratic principle of the separation of powers does not conflict with any Islamic prescription.
- To put an end to corruption, clientelism, favoritism, and the peddling of influence, the authority of a transitional period, like the authority that issues from *shûra,* should be able to count on the efficiency and integrity of an independent and incorruptible judiciary system. This is of the greatest importance in a democratic state and under an Islamic government alike. By addressing a grave warning to a venal judge, the Prophet also puts us on our guard against the abuses of power that might result in a judiciary system where the judge was all-powerful.

It can be said straight out that a judiciary system that can be permeated by corruption is the Achilles' heel of power. Power carries in itself the virus of its congenital disease: corruption. As Lord Acton said, "Power corrupts, and absolute power corrupts absolutely." The judge who takes decisions in his own heart and conscience without referring to anyone holds an absolute power. For this reason the choices of judges in an Islamic government will have to be a matter of particular care.

The American system is excellent: elected judges are closely observed by the interested population, and they are recalled when necessary without anyone finding fault with the process!

- It is good to recall that the ideal of the separation of the three powers still remains an objective to be achieved, even in fundamentally democratic societies; the task for us will be even more arduous.
- Freedom of expression is one of the most desirable democratic institu-

tions. Nothing can take the place of a free and diverse press directed by professionals who are committed to exposing evil and denouncing it.

An Islamic press freed from the control that stops to examine it and put it under quarantine, as happens in secularist regimes, should, like every democratic press, play an increasing political and informational role as an educational, moral, and spiritual function. The rapid and varied evolution of means of communication by satellite and the information highway opens the way for *islam* to be carried far and wide and to set forth the truth of mankind's existence on earth. These technical means must be used to spread the Islamic Message around the world and present the Great Information in an intelligent manner.

- This will need to be done in order to achieve, reinforce, and create a profound meaning to human rights, rights which Western democracies make their creed (and also their weapon for destroying others who have other conceptions of mankind and human rights).
- Democratic process manages power by means of balances and counterweights; alongside each power a counter-power is placed to watch and control it. This is one of democracy's great assets.

The controlling mechanisms of an Islamic government will have to be institutionalized on the model of procedural democracy. But the institution of a morals police or of a tribunal for repressing fraud and unfair promotion will have to be preceded in an Islamic society by the education of every member of the faithful, men and women. Everyone will be educated so as to be able to distinguish between "blameworthy" and "praiseworthy," but the promotion of goodness and the repression of blameworthiness will not become the means for unleashing anyone on anyone else: disorder and chaos are the most blameworthy of all.

Democratic forms and methods, applied with precaution and discernment, cannot harm *shûra*; indeed, *shûra* needs them to take effect in the modern world. Only the other face of democracy—the religion of secularism—is unacceptable.

I believe that after what has been said thus far, it should be obvious that no one can be truly democratic without being inimical to any law that takes its inspiration in something other than democratic secularism—even as no one can be truly faithful to God by rejecting even a single article of God's Law.

It follows, then, that winning the modern world for *islam* puts an end to choosing between two religions: either you are faithful to God without restriction, or you waver between pillar and post, claiming "we are all Muslims." To win the modern world for *islam* does not prevent drawing on the wisdom of a people, so long as that wisdom is not foolishness, i.e.

does not counter the Law of *islam.*

Crucial questions remain: What will become of the existing political parties under an Islamic government? Will a partisan pluralism continue to have a reason to exist in an Islamic regime? What role do opposition parties—such as the prefabricated and tame ones—play in a secularist and "democratic" government, if not that of a tired "opposition" that in the main speaks out in favor of "consensual" agreement? That is merely a cozy situation for vilifying Islamists with impunity and keeping a sharp eye on them, especially when they resist the sirens of "consensus" and refuse to toe the mark. Islamists are easy marks for those whose hands are free and whose place in the lap of the tutelary government is secure, while their hands are tied and their mouths muzzled. What will their role be in an Islamic configuration?

In the democratic system, the balance of power owes everything to the existence of political and business organizations whose critical activity and rotation in power constitute the rhythm of political life. Public debate, the free expression of contrary opinion, as well as a diverse free press, aware of its responsibility, constitute the essential instruments to be borrowed from democracy.

The organization of Islamic power has much to learn from the peaceful manner in which differences are dealt with in a democracy. Pluralism will remain a natural gift that *shûra* should not only tolerate, but encourage as an indispensable means to active emulation in the course of service to the people.

Immorality and corruption seem to be two of democracy's inherent defects; actually they are the natural penchants of every political class. Power corrupts by its nature, whatever its form. A critical and transparent pluralism can only hold off evil.

If we propose at the start an Islamic covenant whereby every political organization takes its position and explains its choices and its conception of *islam,* there is nothing in this intention that would exclude anyone whatever. Every party's choice and program will determine its political future.

The Islamic covenant is an invitation to all to participate in a project of restoring an Islamic society; it is quite the opposite of exclusion. If by chance there are those "We are all Muslim" types who propose that the people should choose politicians without faith to represent them, let them say so clearly. Our duty to all stages of the transition, and beyond, is to disclose hypocrisy and point out deceit. From the moment that we are engaged in respecting the freely expressed will of the people, our only weapon will be the word, truth, transparency.

9 Appeal and Community

By "appeal" I translate the Islamic notion of *da'wah,*[8] that is, the proclamation of Islamic truth and the invitation of humankind to cling to it. *Da'wah* is a function of the mission of the Prophet (grace and blessings upon him!) as well as the duty of every faithful Muslim.

By community I mean the friendly conviviality and mutual assistance of a proximate society such that the Qur'anic ideals of brotherhood, charity, pardon, aid, and solidarity in the face of everything are the rules of a life lived voluntarily and with conviction.

The paradigm of the Islamic community is that of the Prophet's Companions at Medina. The image the Prophet gives of them as an example is one of the most beautiful recorded in the Hadith:

> In its mutual and brotherly love and helpfulness, the community of the faithful resembles a living body: the least suffering of one member of the body results in fever and insomnia for the whole.[9]

The ideal Islamic community has a center that facilitates mutual assistance and affirms the spiritual bonds of brotherly love: it is the mosque. Located in the midst of the neighborhood, the community mosque will be able to radiate over a limited territory, as is essential to its mission. Lodged in a place expressly constructed for it (or quickly arranged for the purpose), the mosque should be the central institution, present in every neighborhood: apartment buildings, government offices, workplaces, schools, etc.

Under absolutist regimes, the function of the mosque is reduced to a minimum. Apparently this geographic investment of vital space cannot be envisaged by absolutist governments for whom the mosque and its instruction are "enemies of reason and hotbeds of unrest."

In an Islamic society the mosque and the activities it enlivens form the central institutions in the service of which governmental institutions should be morally and spiritually subordinate, just as the body is subordinate to the mind. The government will administer the material life of the people, while the mosque will orient and nourish their spirituality.

The necessary complementarity between the function of government and that of the mosque will permit the faithful, scattered and preoccupied through the length of the day by concerns and their material livelihood, to find in an omnipresent mosque a haven of peace and moments of contemplation.

The centrifugal forces of markets and temporal negotiations should be balanced by the centripetal forces of spiritual reflection and prayer at fixed hours, five times a day. Otherwise the faithful would lose their reference point in the daily hubbub. Such language will seem obviously nonsensical to a modernist who has lost the meaning of life.

The Islamic ideal would want to invert the modern scale of values, so that moral and spiritual values would be more appreciated than the materialist values of wealth and influence. The Islamic ideal of the moral and spiritual perfecting of people during their sojourn here below, as active subjects with lively consciousness, will replace the modern ideal of the numbered and programmed individual citizen, overadministrated and overcharged.

Modernity deprives the citizen of his most sacred right, that of knowing God and preparing to meet Him, so as to cram him with throw-away and renewable products if he is the citizen of a rich democratic country, or, if he is the subject of a dictatorial underdeveloped power, to grovel in misery and want.

Democracy, which seems to choose its residence in well-off Northern countries, goes hand-in-glove with a certain level of education and income, with material life in high standing. The permissive culture that goes with such a level of material life and the enjoyment of democratic rights draws men downwards by flattering their carnal instincts in songs, films, shows, and whatnot. The only appeal heard in modernity is a bestial one; social links are limited to furtive professional contact in noisy supercities choked with smog pollution.

The habitat of these great polluted conglomerations in every sense of the word, as well as the centralized and distant administration, does not favor communitarian conviviality, the fertile locus of moral virtues and spiritual life. In a society with Islamic convictions, regionalization and local administration will respond perfectly to the requirements of communitarian living.

But these community links of solidarity and sympathy can only be woven of durable and sturdy stuff if necessary time, daily, is devoted to proximity in a propitious place that is none other than the mosque. Spiritually meaningful bonds are formed through permanent and heartfelt contact, through the contributions and interpersonal exchanges that favor mutual growth of mind and feelings.

This communitarian homogeneity is the dispenser of security by the solidarity of charity; it metes out material gifts as well as peace of mind and soul. But these are only the immediate results of the lasting brotherhood the faithful establish here below in the hope of sharing eternal happiness in paradise in contemplation before the face of God (glorified be His Name!).

The simple modification of the centers where decisions are taken will not suffice to solve social and economical problems, surely. The reform of the political system and its decentralization will not in itself bring about job security and work opportunities for unemployed youth if it is not also accompanied by a profound reform of attitudes and a sensitizing by which the political and administrative power participates fully and in complete solidarity with the central institution of the mosque.

Notes

1 *La Société en quête de valeurs,* op. cit., p. 200.

2 Ibid., p. 201.

3 *La Fin de la démocratie,* op. cit., p. 54.

4 Ibid., p. 55–56.

5 TN: *Shûra* "advice, counsel, consultation, deliberation, suggestion."

6 Sûrah 42 [*Ash-Shûra*]: verses 36–39.

7 TN: Yassine's definition is cited from Larousse ("*méthode, une marche à suivre pour obtenir un résultat; l'ensemble des règles et des formes qu'il convient d'observer pour introduire une action en justice, rendre une decision et la faire exécuter*").

8 TN: From the radical *da'wâ,* "appeal to, invite, convoke, hail, name."

9 Bukhari and Muslim.

Epilog

My intention in this book is to play upon all registers of human understanding, including sometimes the jostling of direct challenge, in the hope of awakening the heedless and honing a blunted will.

We have been given the unique good fortune to exist; to what are we going to devote that existence? To begin with, what is the point of existence—mine, yours, that of the universe?

Where and how shall we invest our lives, our energy, our time, our possessions, and our wisdom, for the greatest return?

My life-capital is an irreplaceable good; invest it badly and it's bankruptcy. The Qur'an uses such language, representing a person's life in terms of an investment, with reckoning, recompense, and insolvency. The worst among the losers is one who has lost his soul squandering his life in heedlessness of his Destiny, and his energy in pointless actions. My discourse on accountability speaks of man's naturally selfish preoccupations in order to arouse in him concern about his end and the primordial question of life's meaning.

An elementary step in spiritual awakening, concern for one's destiny after death, is a move in the right direction, one that, sustained by meditation and acts of worship, will lead man to transcend the habitual that glues him to the pell-mell of daily grind and that rescues him from his familiar environment and numbing routine.

Step by step, the spiritual ascent of the faithful opens before him undreamt-of horizons, his life takes on another hue, his actions another importance, his participation in the common work of the community gains new meaning. His vision of life and death changes, his aims and aspirations animate a will renewed to action, first as a prudent steward conscious of the importance of his relationships, then one who vows his action to God without reckoning, in pure gratitude. God becomes his sole preoccupation, the Law of God his only truth.

Every action vowed to deities other than God is an investment bound to fail. *Islam* now has greater need of faithful people than ever, need of their self-denial, their boldness, their wisdom, and their concerted efforts, in order for Muslim peoples to go forth along the road of their common well-being. My personal well-being depends on the effort I provide for *islam* to triumph, and for the Muslim nation to live and prosper.

Having come to the end of this book, I would be afraid of duping my reader who is faithful to God if I were to neglect to remind him of the condition without which his action, even if effective and useful for Muslims, will have no value for his personal accountability: absolute devotion to God. Vulgar intentions may well accompany an activism that is devoted to some ideological idol or commonplace ambition, but is not with action for God's cause.

• • •

Is there any means to be had to purify the soul? Some means of breathing lungfuls of fresh air, of feeling the sun's rays on one's skin, of breathing in the fragrance of a springtime of the spirit, of bathing in the Fountain of Youth?

To do this we must leave our spider's nest, come out of our dungeon, throw off our prison rags. For a means to be had we must go to the source. The standing water of the marsh will never evoke the feeling of having bathed, the company of listless and depraved characters cannot firm up our will to do good.

The source of truth is the Qur'an. This book began by inviting the reader to open the Qur'an and listen the Word of God; it concludes by repeating the invitation. Attentive reading of God's Book will illumine our steps if instead of feeling idle curiosity we open our will to know and to be.

The Sûrah called "The Cave" advises the Prophet to seek out a certain quality of person and to be patient in their company; let those who can understand this:

> Still your impatience (by remaining) with those who call upon the Lord day and night, desiring His Face. Do not turn your gaze from them to go looking for the false brilliance of life on earth. Do not obey those whose hearts We have rendered impermeable to Our Call, those who follow no passion but their own and whose behavior is extremist.[1]

The Qur'an bids us return to the mosque where the Name of God is called upon and where a spiritual flood irrigates the heart that knows how to wait patiently. The Qur'an instructs us to leave bad company at once, that which will snare us and keep us prisoners of the frivolous things of earthly life:

> Know that the life below is but a game, a frivolous amusement, vain attire, and proud rivalry, a race for acquiring wealth and children. (The life below is) like a rain-shower: the vegetation it brings charms those who cultivate it, then it fades and yellows, lo it is dry chaff.[2]

The Qur'an invites us to meditate the significance of our existence on earth and puts us on guard against the Satanic delusions that strew our path. It calls to man to make him return to himself and be astonished at the marvel of a creature that is his composed being:

> You, man! What is it that misleads you from your Generous Lord Who created you, shaped you, refined you and composed you in the manner of His choice? Yet (despite everything) you treat as a lie (the Great Information concerning) the resurrection?[3]

• • •

Throughout its hundred and fourteen Sûrahs, the Qur'an teaches us forcibly and in great detail about the Life Hereafter, and the call to man is preceded and followed by recalling the human condition:

> Does not man see that We created him from a drop of sperm—and lo he declares himself our adversary. He cites examples to us, forgetful of the fact that he is but a simple creature. He says, "Who will revive bones that have fallen asunder and turned to dust!" Tell him, "The same will revive them Who gave them life the first time. He is Expert in everything!"[4]

The Day of Last Judgment is to be dreaded:

> Humans! Fear your Lord and dread a Day where no father can rescue his child, nor can any child rescue his father. God's promise is truth. Be not deceived by the life here below, lest (Satan) the deceiver deceive you concerning God.[5]

On that day humankind will go forth without wanting to:

> Oh man, you who go forth inexorably and completely toward your Lord! You will meet Him surely. Whoever receives his writ (the balance of his acts here below) in his right hand will have his account settled quickly and shall return in joy toward his own. Whoever receives his writ behind his back (lamentably) will suffer distress, for he will burn in the flames of hell. Such a one had been full of himself (during his sojourn on earth) among his own, assuming that there is no return after life. But there is![6]

The end of the world, that of our sojourn on earth, is the concern of only a few in these modern times. Occupied as they are with fighting for subsistence in the South or for their excess in the North, humankind has neither the time nor the information to occupy itself with life after death.

In the North as in the South, people are uninformed of the inexorable end that awaits the world. It is an unfortunate symptom, a psychosis to be haunted by the fear of the end of the world in these modern times. Only ecologists fear that hot-house gasses may asphyxiate the world or that a nuclear catastrophe may make life on earth impossible.

The Qur'an speaks of something that resembles a cosmic cataclysm that will end life here below; above all it speaks of the post-cataclysmic. God, who created life and the cosmos that shelters life, unveils what will happen to life and to living beings to those among us who believe:

> I swear it by the Day of resurrection. I swear it by the soul that does not cease blaming itself. Does man believe Us incapable of reassembling his bones? We Who surely have the power to reanimate even the little bones of his fingers. Man would rather continue to treat as a lie the Information of what awaits him. So he asks (skeptically) when the Day of the resurrection will come. That day will come when sight will be dazzled, the moon eclipsed, the sun and moon united. On that day mankind will cry: "Whither escape . . . ?"
>
> But no! You love the fleeting life (here below) and forget the Life Hereafter. On that Day there will be dazzling faces, gazing upon their Lord. Other faces that Day will be overshadowed in their apprehension of catastrophe.[7]

• • •

Lord God, shed Your grace on Muhammad and his own, as once You shed it upon Abraham and his own. Bless Muhammad and his own as you have blessed Abraham and his own. You are Most Glorious. Receive our prayers. *Amîn!*

Notes

1 Sûrah 18 [*Al-Kahf*]: verse 28.

2 Sûrah 57 [*Al-Hadîd*]: verse 20.

3 Sûrah 82 [*Al-Infiṯâr*]: verses 6–9.

4 Sûrah 36 [*Yâ-Sîn*]: verses 77–79.

5 Sûrah 31 [*Luqmân*]: verse 33.

6 Sûrah 84 [*Al-Inshiqâq*]: verses 6–15.

7 Sûrah 75 [*Al-Qiyâmah*]: verses 1–10, 20–25.

By the Same Author:

IN FRENCH:

Revolution in the Hour of *Islam* [*La Révolution à l'heure de l'islam*], 1980

Toward a Dialog with our Westernized Élite [*Pour un dialogue avec l'élite occidentalisée*], 1980

IN ARABIC:

Islam between the Appeal and the State, 1971

Tomorrow *Islam!* 1972

Islam—or the Flood: An Open Letter to the King of Morocco, 1974

The Prophetic Method, 1982 (4 editions)

Islam and the Challenge of Marxism-Leninism, 1989 (2 editions)

Exemplary Men, 1989 (first in the series *Al-Ihssân*)

Introductions to the Method, 1989 (2 editions)

Islam and the Challenge of Secular Nationalism, 1989 (2 editions)

Historical and Doctrinal Survey, 1990

Muslim Reasoning between the Sovereignty of Revelation and the Domination of Secular Rationalism, 1994 (2 editions)

A Dialog with Honorable Democrats, 1994

Spiritual Letters:

- Spiritual Gems, 1992
- Letter of Reminder, 1995
- Letter to Students and to All Muslims, 1995
- Spiritual Poems, 1996

On the Economy, 1995

Guide to Believing Women, 1996 (2 editions)

Shûra and Democracy, 1996

Dialog of the Past and the Future, 1997

Dialog with an Amazighit Friend, 1997

Spirituality [*Al-Ihssân*], 1998

Memorandum: To Whom It May Concern, 2000

Justice: Islamists and Power, 2000

N.B. All of these works have been published in closed circulation, since the author (and his thoughts) as well as the Justice and Spirituality association *Al-'Adl wal-Ihssân* are subjected to strict surveillance. The author has been confined to his domicile since December of 1989.

About the cover:

Rohana Filippi is an Italian artist who has lived and worked in Europe, the United States, and South America. Ms. Filippi has developed her own artistic style, combining the beauty of the Arabic script with a technique that uses watercolor and wax. Her art is devoted to the expression of "Allah's presence everywhere." She finds inspiration in the Holy Qur'an as well as in her inner guidance. Ms. Filippi currently lives in New York, where she is working on new projects with the Islamic Community.

"Feelings open the door of the imagination then the rest follows . . . that's how this book-cover came about," says Rohana Filippi. She explains: "A world precipitously sinking in a desert landscape is suddenly and mercifully rescued by Allah's word. The Qur'anic quotation is permeated by Allah's Power creating a two-way movement: from up to down, and from down to up. The light blue script and the little flags evoke a sense of peace and relief as well as victory. Both concepts perfectly match the title of the book."